FREEDOM IN THE MOUNTAINS
FREIHEIT
LIFE ON THE WILD SIDE

Freedom in the Mountains: Life on the Wild Side is published under
Catharsis, a sectionalized division under Di Angelo Publications, Inc.

Catharsis is an imprint of Di Angelo Publications.
Copyright 2024.
All rights reserved.
Printed in the United States of America.

Di Angelo Publications
Los Angeles, California

Library of Congress
Freedom in the Mountains: Life on the Wild Side
ISBN: 978-1-955690-96-6
Paperback

Words: Thomas Huber
Cover Design: Savina Mayeur
Interior Design: Kimberly James
Translator: Paul Lydtin
Editors: Matt Samet, Willy Rowberry

Downloadable via www.dapbooks.shop and other e-book retailers.

No part of this publication may be reproduced, distributed, or transmitted in any form or by any means without the prior written permission of the publisher, except in the case of brief quotations embodied in critical reviews and certain other noncommercial uses permitted by copyright law. For permission requests, contact info@diangelopublications.com.

For educational, business, and bulk orders, contact distribution@diangelopublications.com.

1. Biography & Autobiography --- Adventurers & Explorers
2. Sports & Recreation --- Mountaineering
3. Sports & Recreation --- Extreme Sports

FREEDOM IN THE MOUNTAINS
FREIHEIT
LIFE ON THE WILD SIDE

THOMAS HUBER

CONTENTS

Foreword   11

The Invisible Line   13

My Little World   17
Childhood
How My Father Discovered the Mountains
Bringing the Mountains to Palling
Sturm und Drang
The "No Fall" Zone

Rock -n- Roll   49
Coming of Age
From Climber to Adventurer
Military Service
Free at Last
Silence

My New Home   77
Berchtesgaden
The Shadows Grow Longer
Dark Days

The Wall   85
Light at the End of the Tunnel
Another World
A Life for the Mountains
Stone Monkey

Starting a Family — 109
Marion
Elias

The Ogre — 115
The Myth of the Man-Eater
Back Home

The Millennium — 123
Shiva's Line
The Spirits That Called to My Brother
Golden Gate

My Way — 139
The Decision
What You Do to Sleep Well
Brothers
A New Horizon
Grounding

Patagonia — 177
Somewhere-Nowhere
Exit

The Movies and the Arts — 205
At the Limit
Scene 7
Scene 8
Life Doesn't Stick to Your Plans
Dean and His Art
The Red Carpet
Silence at Last

Expeditions through Golden Granite — 235
The Pink Crocodile
Eternal Flame-The Legacy of Our Idols

Through Valleys and Up Mountains — 249
Up from Below and Back Again
In the Vacuum of Time
The Abyss
Back to Life

Finally on Top
The Wave

Latok 1 — 285
The North Face
Cerro Kishtwar
Courage and Success
Home-Dahoam

The Line of My Heart — 319
Choktoi Again and Again
Grasping for Freedom
A Stone Creates Ripples

Toward Freedom — 335
Why We Do What We Do

Brothers and Sisters — 352

The Complex World of the Huberbuam — 355

Appendix-Climbing Grades — 359

For my sisters and brothers

FOREWORD

by John Long

Freiheit: Freedom in the Mountains, runs down the life and storied career of Germany's Thomas Huber, one of history's most accomplished climbers. The magic here is not so much in the derring-do descriptions of free climbing El Capitan in Yosemite Valley, say, or scaling mountains of ice in the Karakoram. Rather in the inside story, the internal DNA of Huber himself, with no holds barred. In these pages lies a legendary life people will still talk about in five hundred years, with the many rock faces and mountains Thomas has climbed towering as monuments to one of the greatest figures in modern adventure sports.

INTRODUCTION

The Invisible Line

July 16, 2019

Once again, I sit in front of this wall and am drawn to an invisible line that I have climbed umpteen times in my mind. This wall will demand everything I have been allowed to learn in my mountaineering life. There is a deadly, incalculably deep bergschrund at the base of the wall where a massive hanging glacier overlaps this simple-looking snow flank leading to the entrance. The rule here is that there are no rules. If you take the easiest route to the wall, any moment could literally be your last—an avalanche could thunder down the snow slopes. This area must be circumnavigated via a complicated rock pillar. After two hundred meters of steep climbing, you rap off left and traverse above the avalanche area into the snow slopes below. From here, you can access the north face proper, moving through a vertical tube of ice right into the center of the wall to the "heart," a bivouac niche—our first camp on the wall. From there, my climbing partners and I head up left into the central, less steep ice field, perhaps the easiest but most dangerous section.

Everything that wants to come down from the mountain—stones, avalanches, and spindrift—must inevitably pass by here. This section can only be climbed at night when it is cold. From the end of this steep snowfield, a vertical granite wall rises over 800 meters. The natural, climbable line moves steeply upward to the right over a system of ramps reaching the summit gully. Here, at 6,700 meters, we find a last chance to bivy. Now we can climb a razor-sharp ridge or use an icy dihedral to reach the summit at over 7,000 meters. This is the final exam, the climax of the wall, and will demand everything we've got.

What a line—unspeakably beautiful, totally inaccessible! Latok I's North Face towers 2,000 meters above Pakistan's Choktoi Glacier, presenting an imposing wall of rock, ice, and snow. I have already invested a lot in this wall. I'm here for the fourth time because I believe in the perfect moment: this seemingly impossible line will become feasible when the team and the mountain unite. Others say I'm here because I'm a weirdo, out of touch with reality, a surrealist. When I look at the wall from their point of view, I can relate. When I tie in here, I put everything on the line: my life, my future, the here and now with my loved ones and my friends.

At the same time, I am aware that the world continues to turn with or without our climb; we will change nothing, absolutely nothing, by climbing Latok I. And yet it will change everything—not for the world, but for me because I dared to follow what I believe in. And if I want to tell the whole story, what I really believe in, why my life is the way it is, and maybe also justify why I am here, on the Choktoi, I need to start from the beginning.

CHAPTER ONE

My Little World

Childhood

1966: I looked out into the world with curious eyes, unaware that I was a little overweight. As my parents later assured me, there were more beautiful children than me. But I was doing just fine because I felt loved. According to family tradition, I was named Thomas, just like my father and his father before him. I was already walking at ten months, spoke soon after, and straight from the get-go, I could not wait long for most things.

As an infant, I once had a very restless night. My mother, being concerned, came to my bedside. At that moment, she noticed an unusually bright light outside. Our stables were ablaze! The fire department in our village of Palling, Germany, at the foot of the Alps, came and tried to prevent the worst. With our neighbors' help, at least all the animals were saved, but the stables burned to the ground—the cause never to be determined. The fire department also saved our house. Within a year, everything was rebuilt, and my parents switched to fattening bulls. Dairy farming meant much work. My father preferred spending time in the mountains over toiling on the farm.

During this time, another Huber announced himself. My brother, Alexander, was born shortly before New Year's Eve, 1968, a beautiful boy if you can trust the photographs from back then. All these significant events have entirely disappeared from my mind; my first conscious memory is that the new farm had a completely concrete yard area, which was later perfect for driving go-karts. Meanwhile, our father was completing a banking apprenticeship, our mother was single-handedly managing our farm, and we were playing outdoors. We had no idea how vital the mountains were to our father. He was gone almost every weekend, off on some vertical adventure.

When I was four, our father had a climbing accident. He took a 100-foot fall on the north face of the Bischofsmütze in the Dachstein massive, sustained a deep flesh wound on his shin where the rope had wrapped around his leg, and ended up in the hospital. When we visited our father at his bedside, he explained what had happened. That was when I vowed never to go into the mountains—and I didn't want my father to do so again, either. Mountains became synonymous with everything deadly and dangerous! They were going to take my father away from me!

While he did not let this little incident get in the way of his passion for climbing, he did keep his mountain adventures more discreet after that. A hiking vacation in the Dolomites confirmed my aversion to the mountains. How pointless it was to struggle laboriously up a mountain, and I vociferously resisted any future mountain activities.

Apart from this, my early childhood was basically a fairytale. There were boisterous pranks conjured up by my friends at the village kindergarten, which was run by a cranky nun from the local convent who gave us a good hiding whenever she thought fit. And there were our first attempts at skiing on the Pallinger Berg—a 330-foot-tall, 6-mile-long rampart bordering town to the west whose bed was formed by the last ice age—as well as the countless visits to our grandmothers. Although our grandfathers were around, our grandparents' houses were strictly called by their matriarchal names: "the Pallinger Oma" and "the Tyrlbrunner Oma."

The two granny houses were very different in kind, just like the two villages: Against the rural, wildly romantic town of Tyrlbrunn, which consisted of five farms and one church, Palling was a modern, large village. It had a church, a cemetery, one school, a monastery, a restaurant, a butcher, a baker, a grocery store, a pharmacy, a country doctor, and even a dentist—everything you needed to live a good life. To the east, the farmers' fields extend into the gently rolling foothills of the Alps; to the west, the village is bordered by the forested Pallinger Berg, which stretches from north to south.

Pallinger Grandma lived in a small, separate house next to our farm and always had snacks for us kids. She told stories of the old days; Grandpa, on the other hand, talked about the war. He had been on the front lines as a medic in World War I and II. He did speak of comradeship but, above all, of the senselessness of war.

In Tyrlbrunn, we lived only in the present. It was a big, beautiful, old farm; outside in front of the house stood a huge oak tree, and behind the stables was a large garden with sweet fruit and berries to pick. Even today, I can still smell the house—a blend of the odor of stables and fresh home cooking. When we spent the night at Tyrlbrunn, we'd be fully involved in the farm life. At dawn, we were awakened by the rooster; in the kitchen, the wood crackled in the stove, the big iron hotplate held the milk pot, and grandma made hot chocolate using milk from the stables, on which a fine skin would sometimes form due to the milk's freshness. Even though she often told me it was healthy and made me strong, I was horrified by that slobbery, sweet mass floating on my favorite drink. So, I always got my chocolate milk with no skin, using it to wash down a jam sandwich. Grandpa would drink freshly brewed coffee with plenty of milk and three tablespoons of sugar while smoking his pipe. I was allowed to try

Grandpa's brew once, and that's probably why, to this day, I like my coffee black.

It would then be off to the barn to feed the cows, milk them, and herd them out to pasture. Afterward, we would enter the henhouse to gather eggs.

Grandma was usually busy in the kitchen, baking bread, making jam, and preparing my favorite dish in the world: homemade beef soup with steamed noodles, chives, and so much pepper that my eyes watered. There would be a big iron pot on the stove with a wooden lid and linen wrapped around it, and only Grandma knew when they were ready—her special yeast dumplings for dessert. They were white and fluffy on top and had a sweet crust on the bottom, the so-called "printsch." When they were ready, we would pair the dumplings with homemade apple compote. Yes, Grandma was the best, and Tyrlbrunn was our best time.

Shortly after our grandfather from Pallingen died at the age of 82, there was a German/American military maneuver in our village, and I was allowed to ride in the tank. My father told me how, decades earlier, my grandfather had climbed onto an American tank when the Americans liberated the town from the Nazis.

The war's end began to loom in the winter of 1944/45. The Allied bombers flew more and more frequently over Palling heading toward Salzburg, Austria. At the sound of the wailing sirens, the villagers climbed into the potato cellar and waited anxiously for the all-clear. Often at night, the sky to the east was brightly lit after an air raid, and little Thomas, my father, knew that this time brought only death.

Little Thomas was glad that his father did not have to return to the French front after being wounded and that the war was finally over.

The Americans took village after village, and when this moment was approaching Palling, the farmer from Riedlhof, my grandfather, dared to go up the Pallinger Berg with a white bed sheet to welcome the approaching American tank column and to signal that Palling would surrender peacefully. As the tanks rolled off the Pallinger Berg, little Thomas stood in the village square with his mother and the other townsfolk. On top of the first tank sat his father, an American soldier holding a gun at his back. The village was ghostly silent, and everyone looked at the Riedl farmer. Little Thomas was never to forget this moment: on the one hand, he was so proud of his father, and on the other, he felt paralyzing fear while his dad was at the soldiers' mercy.

When my father told this story, I felt how proud he was of his father and how much he admired his courage.

I also loved my father, and there could not have been a better dad for me. But I couldn't cope with the fear that one day my father wouldn't come back from those dangerous mountains. However, as I grew up, I began to be curious about why he went to the mountains; I wanted to know why one would voluntarily expose oneself to mortal danger. This is when he began to tell me stories from his mountaineering life. First came the ones about his harmless, beautiful climbing experiences. But as I listened ever more eagerly, he unpacked his even crazier adventures, from winter ascents with cold bivouac nights, to steep climbs with his friends in the local Wilder Kaiser and Berchtesgaden Alps, to ascents of big walls like Les Droites North Face and the Walker Pillar in Chamonix, and the Matterhorn's North Face.

Each adventure was a story, and he told them with so much excitement and passion that I realized there was much more to this heroic mountaineering life than "just mountaineering."

My father took me to his mountains for the first time because I wanted to go. I suddenly experienced a new world that had nothing to do with the world I'd experienced before. My father let me climb on small rocks, explaining how to link the footholds and handholds in sequences. He told me about the beauty and freedom that can only be found in the mountains, and from that moment on, I understood him.

THOMAS HUBER

How My Father Discovered the Mountains

When my father, Thomas, was a little boy, often on a beautiful day after school, he would walk along a dirt road to a small hill just a mile or two from his village, sit in a meadow, and gaze up at the mountains. He embraced the mountains surrounding him with curiosity, and he soon knew all the ridges, summits, and rugged faces without knowing any of the official names. This vista became his own, a world of adventures. In his mind, he had already climbed all these mountains several times before his uncle heard about his longing and told him the mountains' names: Dachstein, Watzmann, Untersberg, and Wilder Kaiser. The same uncle took him into the mountains for his first proper hike, with my father wearing sneakers and his Sunday best; they marched up the peak of the Reiteralpe to the Wartsteinhütte refuge and, the following day, embarked upon summitting the Häuselhorn, a craggy 7,500-foot summit.

Usually, there is a mellow path winding its way up toward the top, but little Thomas was everywhere but on the path. Like a playful chamois, he climbed on all the rocks or jumped from stone to stone; even his uncle's words of warning could not curb his enthusiasm. It was the best day of his life so far, and things would only get better from now on!

A unique feature of the Pallinger Berg is a seventy-foot-high quarry made of Nagelfluh, a conglomerate found in the Alps. Here, Thomas would seek out doable lines, climbing in his sneakers to link short sequences up small rock steps with connecting ledge systems. This was the best schooling and preparation for his newfound alpine passion. His uncle, perhaps the only person who understood what was happening, gifted him a book titled *Das Klettern im Fels* (*Climbing on Rock*) by the "Kaiser-Papst" Franz Nieberl. On weekends, 13-year-old Thomas started skipping Sunday mass, secretly cycling into the Chiemgau Mountains and climbing the peaks of the Hochfelln, the Rauschberg, the Hochgern, and even the steep Hörndlwand.

Hörndlwand: this name alone would get him excited. The summit can be easily hiked via the south side, but the north side is defined by a steep, 600-foot rock face. Gazing up at this wall, he spotted climbers for the first time. He watched their every move and started hunting for other climbable routes.

On the left edge of the north face, he finally discovered a weakness that might offer a feasible climb. Here, a deep chimney—the Red Witches' Chimney—leads to a sharp ridge, which could then be followed straight to the summit. From then on, he could not shake the idea of trying this possible climb. When he finally cycled home, his parents were, as usual, unhappy with his absence. But he was not going to let anyone stop him. He continued to practice his climbing skills in the quarry, experimenting with low-cut shoes with rubber soles offered superior friction to his sneakers.

One day, when Thomas finally felt strong enough, he cycled into the mountains and climbed back up to the start of his route on the Hörndlwand. He braced himself confidently against the tight walls of the chimney, shinnying upward until he reached a chockstone that halted his progress. Turning around now would have been cowardly; therefore, there was only one possible option, and that was up. At least that's how the sport had been depicted in *Das Klettern im Fels*: climbing mountains meant facing dangers with courage and mastering any problem that arose with skill. He was determined to become a real mountaineer. So Thomas mustered all his strength to pull his body weight over the overhang, hoping to find more straightforward climbing above. But instead, the climbing became even more complex, and only now did the realization settle in that following his heroic dictum here would indeed be a big mistake. Thomas's legs began to tremble, the dreaded "sewing-machine leg" taking over and spreading upward until his whole body was quivering with fear and effort. He could see no way up or down; his situation was hopeless. Only one thing was sure in his mind: he would need to go down—either by falling or downclimbing.

He managed to stay alive, but the details of how he has never been able to recall. Humbled, he cycled back to Palling with an experience that would leave an impression. But to give up the idea of mountaineering now would have meant embracing his future as a farmer, praying in church on Sundays wearing fine clothes and a hat. This was not his world! Music and playing the violin offered some escape from the reality imposed by his parents. But not enough. Thomas could not erase the mountains from his life.

After his terrifying experience on the Hörndlwand, my father veered out onto the easier ridges of the Berchtesgaden Alps. At the summit of the Watzmann Südspitze, he hurled his Sunday hat into the abyss of the east face. This was his ritual of liberation from his family constraints, his rebellion as he defined his identity. Mountains and music would offer the medium. Standing on a silent summit by himself, he would play a Beethoven violin concerto in his head; when he picked up his violin back home, the music transported him to this place he longed for. Only when he found this world for himself could he finally accept his family obligations as a farmer's son.

At age 16, Thomas joined the Trostberg Alpine Club and climbed his first actual route as a roped team with Walter Kellermann from Teisendorf; the pair climbed a V+/VI- (5.8), the *Direct West Face* on the Kleiner Watzmann. He climbed without fear, moving smoothly as if he had never done anything else. The ice was finally broken; he now knew what he could do, and his self-confidence grew exponentially.

One sunny weekend, he and his new climbing buddy Franz Dürrschmied rode their 200cc Zündapps mopeds all the way to Berchtesgaden, to the Scharitzkehlalm alpine hut and restaurant in the Endstal valley. Their backpacks were fully loaded with climbing gear, and they were ready for action in this paradise for climbers, where the hut sat amidst lush green meadow with 1,600-foot walls rising directly above. On the top left, the

Kehlstein. From here, the jagged Mannlgrat ridge stretches to the summit of the Hoher Göll. Below are the often-compact rock faces of the Endstal, a valley enshrined by a massive rock face and that resembles a giant rock cauldron. The walls grow spectacularly out of the scree; from all sides, they are dense, initially overhanging, and of the best rock quality imaginable. The more significant smaller crags stand out clearly with crack systems. It's an Eldorado of rock made for great adventures for generations to come.

Not knowing about climbing harnesses, the two boys tied themselves directly into the rope and headed up into the rock amphitheater. Franz belayed with the rope running over his shoulder, while Thomas quickly mastered the first crux section of their prospective climb. Then one of the holds snapped, and Thomas suddenly fell, hurtling through the air for ten-plus feet. Franz caught the fall using his shoulder belay, leaving Thomas surprisingly unshaken by the first fall in his climbing career. All he could think was that if he'd had a rope and a climbing partner back on the Hörndlwand, he would become an actual climber so much sooner. The rope now made him feel that the dangers in a vertical wall were controllable and that he could push the limit as far as possible.

The fall had left one of their two ropes with sheath damage, but turning back now was out of the question. At dusk, they reached the end of the difficulties, where most climbers would end their adventure with a handshake and a *"Berg Heil."* But not them, because according to alpine tradition, every climb needed to end on a true summit. They climbed the last 1,600 feet up easier terrain, and by the time they had their first 5.9 under their belt, it was pitch-black. Proud and ecstatic, but navigating without headlamps, they slowly walked down to the valley floor before heading back home on their Zündapps, tired and fulfilled. The light was still on at home, and Thomas found his parents sitting upright in bed, praying by candlelight. Having expected the worst, they were wrung out and bedraggled.

At the next meeting of the Alpine Club, the rope attendant loudly lectured Franz and Thomas about their irresponsible handling of club property, demanding that they return and replace the damaged rope immediately. This was followed by Steff Rausch, an experienced mountaineer, standing up passionately for the aforementioned antics of the alpine clubs' younger members. He declared that one should be ashamed only of *the Alpine Club's* behavior. It was as quiet as a church; no one dared inveigh against Rausch's passionate defense of the spirit of adventure. In Thomas's mind, this moment marked his private knighting into the world of mountaineering.

Soon after, the castle wall in Stein a der Traun became the new meeting point for the enthusiastic climbing youth of the Trostberg Alpine Club. Made of Nagelfluh, the wall sported crimps and pockets on rock that was of much higher quality than Thomas's former training ground, the Pallinger quarry. The walls offered perfect traverses, great for improving one's finger strength and footwork.

But above all, the climbers would hatch their plans for the upcoming weekend here. Meanwhile, Thomas had finished school. He took on his share of responsibility on the family farm and attended the agricultural vocational school once a week.

At the week's end, he and his climbing partners headed into the mountains to climb. He had become used to his mother's countless simulated heart attacks, which by now were part of the weekly farewell ceremony. Afterward, he entered his private realm in Berchtesgaden on the Mühlsturzhorns, the Göll and the Untersberg, the Gesäuse, the Dachstein, and the Wilder Kaiser. He usually took the lead when the going got tough, and was known to his peers as a smooth and solid climber, making him a sought-after partner for vertical adventures. If he was benighted while climbing a wall, he bivouacked. If the weather turned sour, he found an escape route. He extended his mountaineering radius to the Central Alps and discovered his love for mixed terrain, climbing on ice and rock. He mastered all the routes of the north face of the Großglockner and the north faces of the Königsspitze, and even the infamous Ortler.

Alpinism soon became his new passion, because these mountains were lonelier, higher, and more expansive than those of the Northern Alps. From Thomas's point of view, they offered greater potential for adventure. Because the most logical lines on the Alpine faces had already been climbed, he saw the newer first ascents, on which climbers aided a *direttissima* up the blankest section of rock using bolt ladders, pitons, and etriers, as illogical and uninspiring. Thomas wanted to move, climb free, and—even better—climb big faces on mixed terrain.

At age 22, Thomas met a girl from the neighboring village of Tyrlbrunn. She also came from a farming family with the surname Huber, although there was no family relation. She was happy to see something other than her parents' farm, and he liked to pick her up on his motorcycle and whisk her away to the mountains for the weekend. Most of the time, Maria would stay at the hut or hike up an easy trail to a summit while Thomas climbed a challenging route with a mate. Maria must have been impressed, because they were soon out and about together every weekend.

One weekend, with the two of them staying at the Griesneralm hotel in the Wilder Kaiser, Thomas was stood up by his climbing partner. He looked up at the peak of the Predigtstuhl, studying its steep north face and formulating a new plan. This was his strength: he could handle if not make the best of any situation. He showed Maria the north face and said that everything looked far scarier than it was, and that the climb would offer a great introduction to alpine rock climbing. Thomas was so passionately enthusiastic that Maria could hardly say no—or maybe their love and his confidence were greater than the fear inspired by this towering piece of rock.

Maria got served everything a first alpine climb can throw at a person: beautiful moments for sure, but also situations in which there was no turning back; mastering your fear using your strength; unconditionally trusting your partner; the feeling of exposure above a bottomless abyss; the mountain jitters that come with over-gripping the handholds. Reaching the summit with Thomas let her forget everything in a heartbeat. The experience triggered intense happiness.

After this little escape, Thomas was very proud of his girlfriend. He now had one more climbing partner, and even though Maria was always afraid when she tied in, she realized that the experiences gained were more than worth it. It was soon clear that they belonged together and wanted to spend their lives together. And although they could both imagine leaving their everyday farming life behind and starting a new life in the mountains, with Thomas earning his living as a mountain guide, they still took over the Riedlhof, his parents' farm in Palling, out of respect for the family.

In 1965, Thomas married his Maria, and they managed the farm with its chickens and cows; pretty much exactly one year later, I was born as their first child, followed two years later by my brother and after another four years later by my sister, Karina.

I started school at age 6, and I was not exactly what you might call a model student, daydreaming myself into the mountains and beyond. Therefore, it was no surprise that my teachers treated me to the somewhat barbaric and often painful side of their pedagogic measures, doing things like rapping my knuckles with a ruler when they caught me drifting off in class. For me, this only furthered the liberating pull of the mountains.

When I was 12, I was allowed to participate in a ski-touring week in the Ötztal Alps, summiting my first 3,000-meter (~10,000-foot) peaks. Alexander was not allowed to come along. From our mother's point of view, at 10 years old, he was still too young for such exploits. After the summits of Similaun, Fineilspitze, Wildspitze, and Hinterer Schwärze, I was ecstatic, and my father promised that we would tackle the 4,000-meter (13,000-foot) peaks together in the years to come.

Although the above sounds perfect, everything in life comes at a price. There was a nagging doubt, eating away at the little mountaineer within me. Whereas Alexander was an intelligent kid, I struggled in school. I was a bit too rebellious, too cheeky. I tried to be studious, but nothing seemed to stick, and my homework was always returned to me covered in red ink. Nevertheless, my parents wanted me to attend high school because getting my higher qualifications meant keeping all future options open. I studied like a madman because my father had promised to take me rock climbing if I got in. And I did pass my entrance exams—by the skin of my teeth.

My year group was second to none; I made some good friends from the get-go, and was nicknamed "Toffi" the first week of school because I often stashed a box of toffee under my desk to get me through class. (I was to keep this name throughout my school years.) I also had some awesome girls in my year, but one did stand out: Mara. Shoulder-length brown hair, dark eyes, and such a sweet smile that I was madly in love with her from the moment I set my sights on her. Mara wasn't the best academically either, so we were a match made in heaven. I used to see her early in the morning, standing hidden in the schoolyard with other students before school, sneaking a cigarette.

I tried smoking, too, because I wanted to be part of the gang. Soon we were meeting between lessons, slipping through the fence and smoking together. In the fall, we visited the Bavarian Forest on a field trip. Like Mara, I had cigarettes and a small bottle of rum I'd nicked from home. On the final evening, I was with a couple of boys at the girls' house, puffing away on the balcony, and Mara took one sip too many.

When our teachers stopped by to check on us, we were unable to hide our shenanigans. It was clear that we were tipsy.

After this rum-induced fiasco, my father fought to keep me from being expelled. After the incident, my alter ego Toffi became far more known around school than my actual person. I differed from my classmates—I was just a bit wilder and more unpredictable. Some teachers found it impossible to place me in their precise-cut molds. I brimmed with energy that needed venting in physical activity. I was lucky enough to discover rock 'n' roll in these formative days, singing and playing the guitar in our school band. The band, named Move On, played German classics like "Skandal im Sperrbezirk" by the Spider Murphy Gang or "Alles klar auf der Andrea Doria" by Panik-Udo. I barely passed my exams. Unfortunately, Mara failed and had to leave school, a sad event as I had never really told her how much she meant to me.

Summer holidays would finally bring freedom. My father kept his promises, and we climbed the south face of the Untersberg, a third-class scramble. On the summit of the Berchtesgadener Hochthron, I was overjoyed, and on the descent, all we talked about was climbing. At home, I proudly wrote the first lines in my climbing diary: "Untersberg-Südwand, difficulty III+, hot weather, with Dad my first climb."

We climbed the Fleischbank's north ridge in the Wilder Kaiser a few weeks later. I sketched out a very cool plan in my head: "As I'm 12 now, and I'm already following the upper third grade (5.4) of difficulty, then at 13, I ought to be leading the third grade (5.4), and then at 14 the fourth grade (5.6), at 15 the fifth (5.8), and as a logical consequence at 16 the [in those days) ultimate sixth grade (5.9). Then I should be able to climb almost everything because only a few Alps routes are graded VI+." However, what I didn't know was that this little plus, far from representing half a climbing grade, was an open-ended rating that represented the ungradable, tough climbing at the cutting edge.

In those days, Alexander was not involved in planning our mountain adventures; he was still too little. But he was as passionate about the mountains as I was.

We would both study the alpine literature around our house, and Alexander soon knew all the Alps' 4,000-meter peaks, including their specific heights. Together we memorized the pages of the book *Im Extreme Fels* by Walter Pause, which featured iconic routes like the *Hasse Brandler* on the Große Zinne, the *Cassin* and the *Schweizer Führe* on the Westliche

Zinne, and above all, the *Carlesso Sandri* on Torre Trieste. These climbs looked extreme and were given the highest grade, 6+ (5.10-).

The following year, my father, Alexander, and I stood on our first four-thousand-meter peak, the Allalinhorn. My brother, only 11 then, was beaming!

Our father must have been immensely moved, seeing the two of us sitting side by side, gazing into the distance with our children's curiosity. For him, these wild, glaciated mountains symbolized freedom that could rarely be found elsewhere, and he sensed at that moment that we were kindred spirits. Every day on that trip we took it up a notch, the mountains becoming a bit higher every time. At the end of our trip, we summited the Dufourspitze (15,203 feet). I was overjoyed at what the three of us had accomplished in only a week.

After these intense adventures, we were brutally catapulted back into school. Daydreaming, I could still feel the wind across my face and see myself hiking side by side with my brother, navigating around crevasses, breaking trail through knee-deep snow, and sitting on the hut terrace in the afternoon, taking in the vista from the Matterhorn clear to Mont Blanc.

In the meantime, we had given up the family farm, leased out the stables, and began managing the woodlands ourselves. My father was working a full-time bank job and had built a modern building next to the old farmhouse: our new home. Each of us three children now had their own room. The house also offered a large living room, a dining room, a kitchen, and one unique feature: an entrance hall open to the upper floor with a wood spiral staircase leading from the cellar to the second floor. Aspiring mountaineers at heart, we quickly saw its potential for excellent climbing opportunities. In our minds, we were already climbing overhanging walls and knew precisely which routes we would be climbing for real in no time.

THOMAS HUBER

Bringing the Mountains to Palling

The quarry where our father had first started climbing, free-soloing its walls, lies on the outskirts of Palling. Although the 240-foot bell tower of our village church was visible far out into the countryside, the quarry from which its ashlars were cut was of poor rock quality. It was conglomerate, compressed river pebbles, and what was left after the church was built was mostly a crumbly pile of sand. But a crag is a crag, so we climbed our father's climbs on this friable rock.

Perhaps the best training opportunities were offered just five miles from Palling at the historic castle of Stein an der Traun, built by the robber baron Heinz von Stein. In this idyllic place, in an open forest under old chestnut trees, an ancient castle wall—the Steiner Castelwall—about thirteen feet high and twenty-five feet long, provided the training ground my father had used as part of the Youth of the Trostberg Alpine Club. He explained the route options: a IV (5.4), a V (5.7), and the one on the far-left edge could easily be a VI (5.10a). Our father belayed us with a rope, and we climbed up to the fifth grade in difficulty.

We discovered another climbing opportunity on our apple tree in the back garden: a slightly crooked, thick main trunk that branched off at six feet into three large forks, forming the crown.

The tree yielded countless apples yearly, a finely tart Boskop that was good for making juice. The tree was an ornament for our garden, our family tree, but it represented far more to us. It was the gateway to our fantasy world of mountain adventures, and we named each branch after a well-known route from classic Alpine literature. So there was the *Swiss Roof* on the north face of the Westliche Zinne (Cima Ovest); and we couldn't miss the *Carlesso* at Torre Trieste. We aid-climbed these routes using our father's alpine ladders. Later we tried to master them by free climbing, practicing rope management, building hanging belays, and rappelling, and even reenacting historic alpine dramas, such as Toni

Kurz's tragedy on the Eiger's north face in 1936. We wanted to be ready with the techniques to help us survive an emergency, and found never-ending possibilities in our tree. In hindsight, this allowed us to develop the crazy creativity that later helped us envision many of our first ascents.

Sturm und Drang

On November 18, 1982, I turned 16, and celebrating with friends, I reminisced that the past year had gone quite well. I might not have passed school with flying colors, but I had passed, and my nickname, Toffi, had begun to fade from popularity. At the Trostberg Alpine Club, I met Fritz Mussner, who was two years my senior and who, like me, was passionate about climbing. Finally, we solved a big problem—Alexander and I had had to share our father as a partner for our alpine endeavors, but now we had a fourth. We all went to the Wilder Kaiser; I climbed the Southeast Face on the Fleischbank with Fritzi, and Alexander and our father climbed the Christaturmkante.

Everyone was happy with the new situation, although I did wish that my alpine journal sported a few more entries. And yet we made immense progress because climbing no longer took place only on the rarely accessible alpine walls. By now, the limbs on our apple tree were well worn, our parents allowed us to cycle to the castle wall in Stein on our own, and we inhaled the climbing magazine *Der Bergsteiger* and the catalog for SportScheck, German's biggest sporting-goods store. This was another world, and deep in our hearts, we knew it was our world.

In the meantime, the old six-leveled UIAA grade table had become outdated, and climbers like Sepp Gschwendtner, Wolfgang Güllich, and Kurt Albert were mastering the ninth degree of difficulty (5.12+/5.13-) in the Altmühltal and the Frankenjura. They specifically trained their fingers and did endless sets of pull-ups to reach this level of climbing. We studied their training methods, added wooden dowels and crimps to the walls of our boiler room, built our first pull-up bar, and then got after it. Our goal was 100 pull-ups a day, in as few intervals as possible. This boosted our endurance. We would also campus and brachiate along the bottom of our family home's spiral staircase until our fingers exploded.

A single photograph had triggered our overenthusiastic behavior. Blue shorts, shirtless, tanned mountains of muscle, snow-white hands from all the chalk, long, dark hair—the image was of Wolfgang Güllich, hanging by a hand jam in the *Alien* roof crack in Yosemite Valley. This photograph proved that the impossible was defined only by your own weakness, and that Wolfgang Güllich had long since overcome the impossible through training and sheer strength. Güllich's peregrinations with Kurt Albert, a giant with wild hair, a daring mustache, bulging muscles, and usually wearing a torn, unwashed T-shirt, represented the vertical dirtbag rebellion more than anything. Together they formed the most potent climbing team of the time. Kurt, the visionary and adventurer; Wolfgang, the intellectual athlete. And so it followed that Alexander and I wanted to be just like them.

Come spring, I was off climbing with Dad in the Wilder Kaiser on the Karlspitze East Face, and all that training on the tree, the castle wall, and the spiral staircase had had an effect. My alpine journal reads: "Wilder Kaiser, Karlspitze East Face, *Göttner*. My first redpoint graded VI [5.10a] with Dad." Redpointing was a then new term that meant leading a pitch without falls, using the gear only to protect yourself if you did fall, not to rest on or for progress. This climbing style was developed and propagated by our idols Kurt and Wolfgang. Kurt started to mark the routes, which they climbed "free and without falling," with a red dot at the base. Thus, redpointing was born. Funnily enough, this style of climbing envisioned in the Franconian Jura (aka the Frankenjura) is still the globally recognized gold standard for free climbing.

School was becoming less and less relevant, and my performance in some subjects reflected my lack of focus, except for PE. On the other hand, my "studies" at the Steiner Burgmauer were advancing in leaps and bounds. I could climb the VI traverse several times in a row and discovered a new traverse in the back part of the castle wall. There I bumped into a climber with long hair, a trimmed goatee, and bulging biceps who reminded me of Güllich. He grinned at me and asked my name.

"I am Thomas from the Riedl farm in Palling," I uttered.

"Ah, I know your father; he was a great climber back then and still is. I am Gottfried Wallner from Altenmarkt, and I climb a lot with the youth team in Traunstein. What's this traverse you've got here, then?"

I explained the intricate combination of hand holds and footholds on the fifteen-foot traverse, which ended at a very thin fissure—a finger crack that jetted up to reach a window ledge above. It was far from easy, but it was possible. My goal was to connect the two sections, linking the crimpy traverse into the finger crack.

Gottfried was visibly impressed by my climbing skills, even though I didn't manage to send that day.

But Gottfried didn't send either and said we should come back together another day. He wrote down my telephone number and pointed out that I'd need better climbing shoes if I wanted to solve my little problem.

I was buzzing on my bike ride home. The meeting with Gottfried, the Traunstein youth team, the climbing shoes, the joint climbing session, Gottfried's wild mane of hair, his bulging biceps—I blurted out every detail when I got back home, and above all, I wanted to know from my father who and what this Traunstein youth team was. He laughed and said, "The team simply has the best climbers from our region!" They had established many of the toughest modern routes on the north side of the Reiteralm, he said, and had also been on expeditions to South America and the Himalayas. Electrified by this encounter, I hoped that Gottfried would call soon and join me on my traverse-crack combination. But before that, I needed good climbing shoes.

Two days later, Gottfried rang me. He wanted to know if I had time on the weekend to join him in the Wilder Kaiser. He wanted to climb the

Rebitsch Cracks on the Fleischbank pillar. I was speechless. My father had to smile and tell me about his adventure on this storied route.

The *Rebitsch Cracks,* in the Wilder Kaiser Massif, was one of the cutting-edge free climbs of its time, Dad said. In 1946, Hias Rebitsch and Sepp Spiegl were the first to find a climbable route through the steep Fleischbank pillar. Hias had to use a few pitons on the lower slabs to get over an imposing blank section. But in the upper dihedral, he showcased his mastery and climbed it almost without protection. The sheer boldness of this lead has halted many subsequent experienced rock climbers dead in their tracks.

And, of all things, Gottfried wanted to climb this VI (5.10a) route with me! My father reacted calmly and only said that with Wallner by my side, I could climb anything, but I had to promise him that I would only second—not lead—the upper crux pitches. Excited, I dialed Gottfried back and agreed.

Early the following day, Gottfried's Opel Kadett was parked in our driveway. "Since we'll soon be tied in together, I'll be Godl to you; that's what all my friends call me," he said. I told Godl everything I knew from my father about the *Rebitsch Cracks* and that I could only follow the crux. He just laughed, let my torrent of words wash over him, and said we would be fine.

Godl let me lead the first pitch, which I dispatched quickly. After that, he took over, and we made fast progress alternating leads.

Suddenly, I found myself standing on a small ledge on lead and looking up. A shoulder-width crack with a slight overhang at the end rose steeply away from me. Thirty-odd feet above me on the right wall, I eyed a rusty, old piton—perhaps the belay anchor for the crux pitch my father had told me about.

Hias Rebitsch's masterpiece, the crux, is where many climbers have thrown in the towel. I hesitated, because I'd promised my father I wouldn't lead this pitch. But it did not look that complicated—*Why not give it a try?*

I smeared both feet on the right wall of the corner system while laybacking the crack with both arms—a classic limbs-in-opposition crack technique I had repeatedly practiced on a wooden beam at our house. Soon, feeling great as I shinnied up the crack, I found myself twenty feet higher, reaching the small roof. The last piece of protection was already too far away, and downclimbing was not really an option on this physical climbing.

I stayed calm and kept climbing smoothly, just like my father had shown me. A little later, I yelled to Godl: "I'm saaaaaafeeeeee, juuuhuuiiihuuiiii!"

That might still be the best "Off belay" I have uttered in my alpine career.

And it was accompanied by a triumphant cry of victory. Godl followed, and as he climbed past me, he just winked and muttered, "Well done, Thomas!" At the top of the Fleischbank pillar, he held out his hand for a compulsory "Berg Heil," and said I should join the youth team in Traunstein—"Whereby there are not many, Thomas, who will be able to keep up with you—respect!"

I turned red and was lost for words. The Traunstein youth team would turn my life around almost immediately. There, no one knew me as Toffi; I was just Thomas, and I was allowed to join Godl in the evening at the climbers' favorite watering hole, the Festung, a dark bar in Traunstein. We drank beer, smoked, made plans, told funny and heroic stories from our climbing escapades, and listened to The Doors, Led Zeppelin, Jimi Hendrix, Motörhead, and Black Sabbath. Janis Joplin's lyrics from "Me and Bobby McGee" summed up the vibe in that smoky speakeasy: "Freedom's just another word for nothing left to lose."

I felt that rock 'n' roll pulse through my veins; I was a climber with every fiber of my being, and I could orient my life in a singular direction: to live that freedom—as a climber in the mountains. I found this freedom in solving climbing problems, whether on the Steiner castle wall, at the local Karlstein crag near Bad Reichenhall where the Traunsteiners trained, or on an alpine wall. At least, this was my romantic teenage idea of freedom.

Summer holidays were finally here. I kicked my school bag into the corner, exchanging it for my climbing backpack. Godl and I were heading for the Dolomites. We climbed the north face of the Große Zinne, the Punta Fiames, and the Cima Scotoni's south face as a grand finale. We lived in the hikers' parking lot, looking up at the peak's broad south face. Gazing up at the Milky Way, all I could think of was tying in and setting off on the next lead.

The *Lacedelli* would undoubtedly be the most challenging route on our introductory trip through the Dolomites. As always, I could not stop badgering Godl with questions, exclusively about climbing and our planned route for tomorrow. Finally, Godl barked, "Your questions are getting on my nerves, and tell me, is there anything else in your brain besides climbing? Women, for example?"

I didn't know what to say, because I had zero experience with women. I had been in love many times but had never been lucky enough to have that love reciprocated. So, I just muttered a silent "Goodnight."

The next day everything was forgotten, and we climbed into my private universe, where only rock and the mountain jackdaws existed.

Toward the end of summer vacation, the time had finally come for Alexander and me to step our game up. It took all our powers of persuasion to convince our mother that the two of us, aged 16 and 14, would be fine going on a climbing trip into the Wilder Kaiser for several days alone. Our father set clear-cut rules and wrote down route recommendations—it was only these routes that we were explicitly allowed to climb. Most of the suggestions were V (5.7 or so) moderates. The most difficult on the list, the *Göttner* on the Karlspitze, I had already climbed twice. Alexander was only allowed to second, and we had to call home every evening via the hut's landline. We accepted the many rules and conditions, because we knew there was no way around them if we wanted to be independent climbers. Our father handed over full responsibility to me for the coming days. I dealt with this new role quite calmly, because I felt like I'd become a proper "little" climber and competent mountaineer over the past year.

Somewhat reluctantly, our mother drives us out to Elmau. As we say goodbye, all we hear is, "In God's name, everything will be fine, and 'Buam'"—the German suffix for "boys who are brothers"—"please be careful, don't overdo it, and, Thomas, you're in charge now!"

"Yes, Mama, everything will be fine, and we'll take good care of each other."

One last goodbye kiss and a hug from our mother, and a little later we are both finally left alone. We each lug a heavy backpack; we climb to the Gaudeamushütte. In front of us is the Wilder Kaiser—and the freedom to decide where to go! I have long forgotten Father's handwritten note, which I have stowed in my pants pocket. At the hut, the proprietor, Hansjörg Hochfilzer, is expecting us. Our father informed has him by phone that we will stay for four days, and which routes we are allowed to climb—so much for our newfound freedom!

The next day, we wake to blue skies and start hiking up to the saddle of the Elmauer Tor; I point out everything that I have already climbed: *Rittlerkante* and the *Lucke-Strobl-Riss* on the Bauernpredigtstuhl and the *Göttner* on the Karlspitze-Ostwand, which we will indeed also get to sample in the upcoming days.

Alexander is thrilled and says, being here now, why not attempt the Karlspitze? He doesn't have to tell me twice, and we are soon standing below the *Göttner*.

It is an emotional moment when Alexander and I tie in together for the first time. Now we are connected on the mountain as a ropeteam, our first time as autonomous climbing brothers. I climb the now-familiar pitches, and Alexander follows them passionately; we are back in the cirque around noon. It is still much too early for us to lounge with the hikers at the hut. Alexander is like a small, curious puppy; I only have to glance at him to know what he wants. As we tie in again, this time below the *Old West Face* of the Bauernpredigtstuhl, he asks, "You or me?"

Alexander wants to show me that he can do it too—lead, be an actual climber, and take responsibility. I know that he can do so, having led before on the Steiner Burgmauer and followed perfectly this morning on the *Göttner;* I know that he can crimp down hard, and above all, that his climbing technique is excellent. If ever a section has stymied him, it's only because of his lack of reach; nothing else could get in his way. However, having him lead on this route also means breaking our father's rules on the first day.

I can feel how much he is inspired by the sharp end as he tries to execute perfectly. He pulls out all the stops, trying to show that that he, Alexander, is the best alpine partner I can imagine and that our brotherly bond will take our climbing partnership places. After the fourth pitch, however, there is no longer any sign of this euphoria. Alexander's forearms are rock-hard and almost twice the size of when he started.

"Thomas, I don't have any strength left; I'm totally pumped out," he says, sounding broken.

"That's completely normal," I say, trying to motivate him. "You've done an amazing job. Come on; we can do the rest!"

I take over the lead for the final pitcher, and at the top of the Bauernpredigtstuhl, we shake hands and end this perfect climbing day with a "Berg Heil."

"Alexander, you climbed great," I praise my brother, and his slightly flushed cheeks show me that he is well proud of himself, too. I experienced a similar moment on the Fleischbank with Godl four months earlier. Without having to say another word, we now know that we are made for each other when it comes to climbing.

"We did the *Göttner,* and Alexander was always well-behaved at the belay"—that's all we say during our evening phone call to our father because, on the one hand, we don't want to lie to him, and on the other hand, we don't want to risk being picked up the next day for disobeying his rules.

"Please take it down a notch, and don't climb any more difficult routes!" are his final words. Due to the weather, we follow his request the next day and climb the mellow *New South Face* of the Hochgrubachspitze in the fog.

In the meantime, we have also gained the sympathy of the hut's proprietor, impressed by the routes we've climbed; he is taken by the fact that we, as brothers, move so independently and responsibly in the mountains. On the last day of our Kaiser excursion, it is thus no surprise that he offers a little prize. We had our eyes set on the *Lucke-Strobl-Riss* crack on the Bauernpredigtstuhl, classically rated VI-A0 (5.8 AO) but with an all-free rating of VI+ (5.10/511), at the time basically the ceiling of difficulty on the grading scale, as climbers were still debating the reality of VII and VIII rock climbs, grades only slowly beginning to filter into the Alps from the Frankenjura. "If you climb the *Lucke-Strobl-Riss* without pulling on any gear, then I'll give you a prize," he spurs us on. That alone is motivation enough for us to give it our all on our last day in the Wilder Kaiser.

Alexander puts on an amazing show, and suddenly we are back on the summit of the Bauernspitz, as the Bauernpredigtstuhl is also called. And Hansjörg Hochfilzer stands by his promise: Alexander gets a liter of lemonade and I, as the older one, a liter of the most excellent shandy.

Shortly thereafter, school retook hold of our lives. But our weekly excursions either to Karlstein or to some alpine route served to recharge our batteries.

One week before my seventeenth birthday, I was given a climbing farewell at the old Traunsteiner hut, and I was ceremoniously accepted on to the Traunstein youth team. The next day I was so hungover and in such a bad mood that I vowed never to drink alcohol again, a resolution that I broke just one week later.

The following year was characterized by a certain lack of concern over social norms or where life would take me, just living in the moment. The psychedelic rock music of The Doors accompanied this feeling of being alive and free. I wanted to live this rock 'n' roll, this concrete freedom, and experience this inner revolution. To be a nonconformist, although I conformed the most myself. I wore black leather pants with a studded belt, a white shirt, and a red-and-white necklace, just like Jim Morrison. "Break on through to the other side"—the other reality was my world! I wanted to delve deep because I was all too often misunderstood and labeled an introverted weirdo by my contemporaries, who seemed firmly rooted in the here and now.

With Godl and Fritz, I climbed the tough *Directe Americaine* on the Dru's West Face in Chamonix, and toward the end of our summer holiday, we brothers wanted nothing more than to leave a mark of our own. To climb where nobody had ever been before, making an actual first ascent.

The No Fall Zone

On the last day of our vacation, our mother drives us to the village of Reit in the morning. Several times during the drive, we promise her to be careful and to climb only easy routes. Hypocritically, we give our word with straight faces. Our project may be more straightforward than expected—we will see. In any case, we know exactly what we want. We want to experience a whole new territory. Using a slide projector, we projected an image of the Wagendrischlhorn's south face onto the white wall of our bedroom, studying each rock feature. It was a jigsaw puzzle of cracks, slabs, and water grooves forming a dream line, our new territory.

An hour after sunrise, Alexander and I are standing below the south face of the Wagendrischlhorn (Reiteralpe), the nervousness of the night having long since disappeared. We look up at the slabs. Our prospective line takes shape; yes, it should work, and that calms us, even if Alexander's only comment is "Steep!"

Alexander climbs up a section of relatively easy stemming, to where the walls close down and the rock becomes more compact. Here, he leaves the lead climbing to me because of my experience. I sort out the rack, hang it off my harness, prepare myself, recheck everything, take a deep breath, and then set off into the unknown.

Nearly thirty feet above the belay, I place a piton and traverse left on good holds toward the blank void. Although the difficulties do not exceed the sixth degree (5.10), my movements are more restrained than usual; I climb with greater concentration and more precisely. I cannot permit myself sloppiness or a mistake.

I place a nut, which I must now trust 100 percent, and creep up the holdless slab to the left; after ten shaky feet at the limit of my sole rubber's friction, I finally latch a good grip at the base of a deep, beautiful water runnel. It's hard to rate the technical difficulty of this slabby crux; all I know is that falling would have been uncomfortable. The following two pitches up wide runnels and clean slabs are exciting but less challenging. So far, everything has gone well; the path into the unknown coincides precisely with the line we've been aiming for.

But from here on up, the climbing seems to get even more severe than it was on the second pitch. Two parallel, shallow water grooves run for 100 feet through a steep, compact wall up to a small ledge. This will be the key, not only in terms of difficulty but also danger. This double water gully hardly seems protectable; the feature is far too shallow for that. My heart skips a beat, so we pause to take a break on a band of rock that crosses the wall. It's a beautiful place: green grass cushions to sit on, sun, and blue sky—complete isolation in a wild mountain landscape. But I can't enjoy it; I have a sinking feeling. There's only one thing on my mind now: the next 100 feet of rock.

Alexander nibbles on a granola bar, looks up, and says, "Hey, Thomas, that's a nice face; I'm looking forward to climbing that pitch!" He knows I'm in charge of our ropeteam today, and he can enjoy what's coming above us with a nice belay from above.

"Phew, Alexander, from the looks of it, it's going to be pretty wild; I'm a bit nervous right now!" I reply.

"Oh, Thomas, don't shit yourself; you'll manage. Besides, I'll belay you well so you can do it!"

I sort rack on my harness. I won't need much: Nos. 3 and 3.5 Friends and three small Knifeblade pitons. - It's way too little gear for a ropelength that looks this difficult—it's undoubtedly a VII (5.10+/11-)—but no other protection appears to fit, so I don't need to drag it along. It would just be unnecessary ballast.

So now I'm here, exactly where I wanted to be and doing exactly what I've always dreamed of doing. Uncharted territory, untouched rock, nothing but uncertainty in front of me. I take another deep breath and realize I must give everything in the next half hour. The only thing that counts now and will dominate my world is getting to the small ledge 100 feet above.

The first thirty feet are more accessible than expected. I sink a Friend with two lobes engaged in the back of the water groove; it provides only minimal security but at least calms the nerves. So far, the climbing is not so difficult that I can't downclimb to the belay if I get into trouble, though I don't intend to use this option. Above, the wall steepens into a bowl, and then the groove disappears in a smooth, slabby wall. Yet the rock is featured, with shallow pockets and indentations throughout. And if I'm lucky, there may even be a hidden crack that will take a Knifeblade.

I try not to picture any worst-case scenarios. I take another deep breath and dry my hands with chalk. Then, after another meaningless request to my brother to watch me, I set off. I forget everything around me, register neither sun nor blue sky; I no longer think about the tempting, grassy belay ledge below. Everything in me concentrates on the quality of my next moves. And they become increasingly shaky, my body vibrates slightly, and I can no longer place my feet as precisely as I want on the friction smears. I smear off small, obscure holds on the runnel walls, moving up this way through the next twenty feet, continuously at my limit. Finally, I reach a stance on sloping footholds, but it's not relaxing at all, and the best I can do here is clear my head and understand the situation I've found myself in: The questionable belay lies far below me; under no circumstances will it now hold a fall. I must not fly; I would thunder down next to Alexander on the ledge and strip us both from the wall.

I discover a seam behind a tuft of grass and try to jam in a Knifeblade with two careful hammer blows. Then, "Zziiiinnng," the piton flies out of the wall in a high arc. I scold, curse, and even beg God to help me find protection, but nothing works. The rock is too compact: there's no Knifeblade, no Friend, no nut placement—nothing. The way down is cut off, and it's enough to make you cry. I'm stuck on a one-way street with an arrow pointing upward, and a flashing red sign that reads, "No falling!" The only safeguard is myself, my fingers, my feet, my mind. I can't make a mistake now, or that's it for both Alexander and me.

"Kiss my ass, you have to know, but you can do it too!" I tell myself. I start climbing without thinking, making a succession of fast, dynamic moves on crimps and water pockets. I am a mere spectator of what I am doing, and only when I feel an enormous grip in my hands do I snap back to reality. Slowly I dare to look down—what a crazy way to get here—and choke the last remnants of my despair from my body.

Everything else on the climb is pure pleasure. At the top, we pat each other on the back and congratulate ourselves on the first ascent of our route through uncharted territory. We have turned the uncertainty of this line into a certainty that can be put into words: eight pitches on the best rock, a difficult grade VII, with physically and psychologically highly demanding slab climbing. We also have a name for it: *Rauhnachtstanz*.

We abseil down and hike back into the valley. Now we're bubbling over with energy, climbing through those slabs repeatedly in our minds and rejoicing like two rascals who've just pulled off a successful prank.

CHAPTER TWO

Rock -n- Roll

Coming of Age

Eighteen at last! Finally, that magic piece of paper in my pocket, a driver's license! And, finally, the ability to hop into the car and go to any crag, just me and my brother. This mobile independence meant my absolute freedom, as it did for Alexander. Arco, Dolomites, South of France—here we come!

But we still needed money to maintain and put gas in the car. Hence, we remained dependent on our parents' goodwill. For trips to school and Karlstein, we were lent our mother's car, a small, red Italian sedan that was far from a testosterone-charged muscle car. I wouldn't be impressing any girls with this thin sheet metal on four wheels, but it still did what we brothers wanted: getting us to the crag at every possible free moment. At school, too, things had changed for the better. I dropped annoying subjects like Latin, and by electing PE as one of my higher subjects, I could compensate for my academic weaknesses. Little by little, with the addition of each dent and scratch, the red Italian car slowly became our own.

When summer holidays rolled around, we packed the little car to the brim, including the entire contents of our house's larder, a tent, sleeping bags, ropes, and climbing gear. As we drove up into the mountains, Alexander sat next to me studying the guidebook for the Dolomites. We wanted to climb the classics: the Drei Zinnen (Tre Cime di Lavaredo), the Tofana, the Sella Towers, and maybe even something on the infamous Marmolada. Simultaneously, Alexander helped navigate, using the map to find the quickest and most cost-effective route to the Auronzo hut at the foot of the Drei Zinnen. First, the Brenner crossed only on country roads, then turned into the Pustertal and, at Toblach, veered off into the Italian South Tyrol. We passed the toll station to the Auronzo hut late at night. We couldn't afford the then 50 Marks for a one-way trip. We had only about 300 Marks with us for gas, food, and two weeks of climbing.

We pulled into the Auronzo hut's parking lot in the pitch black of night. No stars were visible. The clouds hung threateningly low and swallowed up the towers of the Zinnen. We pitched our tent in the meadow next to the car and settled in, after packing our backpacks in record time for the next day. However, lightning, thunder, sleet, and snow soon beset us—a typical Alps cold front raging in. We dove back into our sleeping bags and braced against the wind. After a few hours, we abandoned our now-tattered tent and huddled in our car for the rest of the night.

For now, we could only dream of climbing the pinnacles, so we looked for an inexpensive place to sleep in the valley to wait out the weather. Maybe it wasn't legal, but it was dry. On wooden planks, we lay in the attic of an abandoned ski-lift station just outside Cortina. It was pretty darn cold, whilst outside rain came down by the bucketload. Up on the peaks, it was all coming down as snow.

We hunkered down in our sleeping bags for three long days and learned the Dolomite guidebook almost by heart. When the cold front finally passed, leaving behind a cloudless sky and snow-covered mountains, full of the enthusiasm of youth we flew up the Gelbe Kante on the Kleine Zinne. On the following day, we climbed through the still highly iced up

Comici on the north face of the Grosse Zinne, and then traveled on to the Tofana, where we scampered up the roofs of the exposed pillar, ticking *Fata Morgana* and the *Messner* on the Second Sella Tower as a side note.

Yes, finally, we were getting after it and climbing every day. In the evening, we would drive our little Italian car over the passes toward the next objective, park on the roadside, and cook spaghetti with tomato sauce on our gas cooker or heat tinned egg ravioli. We listened to The Doors, Led Zeppelin, and Danzig on our tape recorder and slept in the car on the folded-back front seats because our tent was no longer serviceable. We were living and traveling according to the romantic ideal of the climber that we'd conjured in our minds: uncomplicated, free, and, above all, honest to ourselves.

At dusk, we topped our final big climb, up the world-renowned limestone massif of the Marmolada, which tops out at nearly 11,000 feet. Outside the Falier hut, we gazed up in awe at this giant gray face. "Thomas, do you see that fish in the middle of that prominent slab? That's exactly where *The Way Through the Fish* must go."—"Yeah, man, we should climb that route someday, but we need to improve our skill set beforehand, Alexander. If you want to believe our guidebook, it's the most difficult line in the Dolomites!"—"That's it, brother, but if we've got what it takes in the future, count me in as your partner, Thomas!"—"Right on, Alexander!" I retorted, winking at him with a grin.

The Way Through the Fish, on the Marmolada's impossibly broad, 2,600-foot-tall south face, was first climbed in 1981 by the Slovakian climber Igor Koller and Indřich Šustr, who was only 17 at the time, without the use of pitons, marking an irrefutable milestone in climbing history. "Look, Thomas, there's a ropeteam climbing below the 'fish' on the right! Ahhh, that looks super exposed"—"According to the climbing guidebook, there's no route there. Brother, I believe that must be somebody making a first ascent!"—"That's nuts; they are nuts!" We declared them crazy, although we would have liked nothing better than to be in their place, climbing into the unknown. Luckily, we did understand that this wall was of a completely different magnitude from climbs we'd done, and that we didn't "yet" have what it takes.

Just left of the *Fish*, there was a modern, new route, partly protected by expansion bolts, which would not be too out there and difficult—*Via Fortuna* (VIII-, or 5.11d)—with one minor flaw. For some inexplicable reason, the route ended about 100 feet below the big band running across the middle of the face, and the guidebook recommended rappelling the route instead of continuing upward.

This was motivation enough to get us out of our sleeping bags at dawn. The team pushing for their first ascent was still climbing just to the right of the *Fish* while we climbed some of the most beautiful slabs we had ever touched. This did get a bit spicy, and the difficulties challenged us. But all went well, and we reached the last belay of *Via Fortuna* in the evening. One hundred feet above us, dubious, fragile, slightly overhanging rock blocked passage to the large band.

"Ahhh, the first ascensionists wanted to leave a route with only the best rock, and the good rock ends here!"

"Yes, that's true, but it's a shame because, in my opinion, a route should always end on top and not just stop in the middle of a face!"

"Annoyingly, if we had a few pitons, we could easily climb the last few meters, but without, it's going to be rather dangerous!"

"Yes, too bad!"

As we were getting ready to rappel, we heard voices from above, and three climbers peered down at us from the large ledge. "Do you want to come up? Do you need a hand?" one of them asked.

"Hey, Alexander, why not? Why don't we bivy up there, and tomorrow we can summit?"

"Let's do it, Thomas. Every route should end at a proper summit!"

In our rudimentary school English, we answered the three climbers: "Is it possible to lower a rope, because the route ends here?"

A little later, a rope snaked down to us, and we toproped up to the rim, climbing through the broken stone.

"Thank you very much. We are brothers and are from Bavaria."

"I am Igor, Igor Koller, and we just climbed a new route right of the *Fish!*"

Alexander and I were gobsmacked. We were standing in front of the legend of the Marmolada, a small man with a short, trimmed beard, wild eyes, and bruised hands, the first climber to ascend *The Way Through the Fish,* perhaps the craziest, most modern route in the Dolomites. We were soon deeply immersed in their adventurous stories; they told us about the *Fish* and their newly climbed route, and Igor assured us that we, too, could do the *Fish*. And that, to his current knowledge, their masterpiece had only ever been repeated by the two Italians Heinz Mariacher and Luisa Iovane.

The seed that Igor sowed in us began to grow from the outset. We both instinctively knew from then on where our journey would lead. The three climbers shared their last food, cheese, and bacon from Slovakia; as long as we exchanged stories, they shared their sleeping bags. We took turns singing songs late into the night. They busted out a Slovak mountaineering song, and we countered with a Bavarian tune. But our repertoire ran dry at some point, and the Slovaks wanted their sleeping bags back because they needed to rest. Alexander and I sat on a backpack and listened to the three men's snoring chorus while we experienced our first shiver bivy. It was the most grueling and longest night of my then-young life.

In the first morning light, we continued to climb. We said goodbye to the Slovaks and promised to contact them when we had climbed the *Fish*. The weather was too good to go home right away. Hence another route, again on the south face of the Marmolada, the *Ezio Polo,* a cracking chimney visible from the valley floor. To prepare, we treated ourselves to a pizza in Cortina, and then drove back up to the parking lot below the south face, packed our backpacks, and set our alarm for five o'clock.

We fell asleep immediately in our car seats because it was so snug and warm. So snug that I stayed in bed despite the 5:00 a.m. wake-up call. I blinked briefly at my brother, but he didn't move an inch—just another half hour.

That half hour turned into two hours, and when we both woke up startled at 7:00 a.m., it was already far too late for the *Ezio Polo*. "What a bummer, Alexander, we blew it."—"Yes, we overslept."—"I think the best thing is to go home right now!"—"We've done our fair share of climbing, Thomas, haven't we?" Alexander said with a wink, and I could only agree with him. I was exhausted from the last two weeks of climbing. On the drive home, we both confessed that neither of us had really overslept—like me, Alexander had only pretended to be in a deep sleep because he didn't want to climb anymore either!

It had been an insane two weeks, and we had the rest of the vacation in Karlstein to hone our skills. It was there that I climbed my first VIII+ (5.12), *Hypofax*, whose crux is a perfect dynamic move to latch a small crimp. Maybe I was lucky to have stuck the hold, but it was time to break through the next grade barrier. My math, which I had done as a 13-year-old, had been right after all. At 13, the third grade . . . and now, at 18, the eighth grade!

From Climber to Adventurer

I was 19 years old. Over Christmas vacation, the Traunstein youth team went on a trip to the South of France, and when my friend and fellow youth-team member Hannes Weininger asked me and Alexander if we would like to join him and his brother for two weeks in Buoux, I was game. Next to Verdon, Buoux was undoubtedly the most famous sport-climbing area in Europe. Here you found some of the world's earliest and most famous 8a+ to 8b+ routes—*Chouca, La Rose et le Vampire, Le Minimum,* and so on—and you were sure to meet all the living legends of the international climbing scene. I could not say no, and as soon as Alexander found out, he started pestering my parents for permission to join until they gave in—but not before enacting their usual ritual of loading all the responsibility for my little brother upon my shoulders.

Shortly after Christmas Eve, we set off. Traveling in the backseat of the Weiningerbuams' car (in German, the suffix -*buam* means "boys who are brothers"), we, the Huberbuam, set off on our second big trip abroad without any parents, leaving behind wintry Bavaria. Somewhere in France, we pulled into a parking lot and slept in our sleeping bags under the open sky. The following day we motored on, crossing the hills of Provence, with a short stop in a boulangerie to grab a coffee for me, a hot chocolate for Alexander, and some croissants. By noon we had arrived in Apt, a small town just outside Buoux. The town itself, at the time perhaps the most famous place in the sport-climbing world, was just a collection of small farms with a kilometer-long rock band above.

Free camping, what we loved and were used to, was strictly forbidden. So we checked into the climbers' campground in the middle of Apt. Alexander and I were left open-mouthed. They were all there, the stars we'd known only from catalogs and magazines. There were the Le Menestrel Brothers, the "housekeepers of Buoux"; the Parisian Jean-Baptiste Tribout, who looked like a rockabilly; Isabelle Patissier, who was even prettier in real life; the redheaded Beat Kammerlander from Austria; the two English legends Jerry Moffatt and Ben Moon, the latter sporting dreadlocks which must have weighed a kilogram; the Bavarian Sepp Gschwendtner, unmistakable with his large sideburns; and the tall, gangly, spider-like Müller Wolfi from Munich. And now Alexander and I in tow with the Weiningerbuam.

We pitched our tent silently and full of awe, but I could not help but gawk. Yes, Isabelle was the vertical princess in town. Then, from the back corner of the campsite, two more climbers came into view, back where Ben and Jerry were frantically pantomiming the beta—reenacting the sequences—on a route as if being puppeteered from above. One of the other two climbers was tall, and the other broad; one had wild, tousled hair, the other black, straight hair; and both wore very short shorts and torn T-shirts. And then we recognized them. They were my absolute superstars, my idols, the Albert Einstein lookalike Kurt Albert and the vertical athlete Wolfgang Güllich.

Curious, Alexander and I strolled into the middle of the campground, earning a friendly *"Servus"* from Wolfgang and Kurt. We answered in kind, but to be honest were too starstruck to carry on much of a conversation.

Instead, we just stood there like two good schoolboys, listening to their Franconian-accented discussion of some extremely difficult route. When talking beta, it can sometimes resemble a wild, full-body dance. In the anticipated movements, the muscles strain, the veins bulge, and often the fingers squeeze an imaginary hold way above your head. Alexander and I were particularly impressed by Wolfgang's athletic elegance as he pantomimed a strenuous crux sequence.

Over the next two weeks, we climbed until our fingers oozed blood, watched our heroes, and marveled at their varied climbing styles. Except for Wolfi the miller, who slithered over the vertical realm like a snake, the Germans were more powerfully athletic, while the French danced up the rock balletically. And then, when an Isabelle tied in, everyone got quiet—and time passed too quickly. We also passed many a fun evening in the bars of Apt, sharing great conversation, especially with the Bavarians Sepp Gschwendtner and Wolfi Müller, who already had some wild first ascents in the Wilder Kaiser under his belt and owned his own little company called Gentic, which sold climbing gear.

Sepp, a bit older than us, had already sent a few IXs/Xx (5.13s). We raved about our limestone home crag of Karlstein and about our VIIIs (5.12s), but also about an overhanging wall on which there was not yet a single route and which looked so impossible to us that it was sure to offer the next level of difficulty. "Yes, boys, I'll just have to drop in on you one day!" Sepp said.

We brought home an incredible amount of motivation from the South of France—we wanted to climb as well as the rock gods we'd seen in action. We built our first home wall out of wood in our cellar, screwed on wooden crimps and slopers, and got after it daily. When we finally returned to Karlstein in spring, we exceeded the previous year's physical limits. I climbed my first route graded IX (5.12+/13-). It was short, about thirty-five feet, slightly overhanging, and protected with only two bolts—I called it *Jenseits von Eden* (*Beyond Eden*) and thought it was the best thing ever, offering brutally tricky moves. This ascent we celebrated immediately at the Kugelbachbauer, the alpine inn next to our crag. It was my masterpiece so far, the first of many to come.

If the weather turned sour in the northern Alps, we went to Arco on the south side of the range for the weekend to climb and enjoy the Italian flair, and were soon regulars at the Caffè Centrale, where we could marvel at all the famous climbers' pictures hanging off the walls. One climber stood out clearly. He was constantly photographed in a perfect pose, and from what you could read, he damn well climbed at the highest level: Stefan Glowacz, who would become the serial winner of the Rock Masters climbing competition held in Arco starting in 1987. We didn't know that our paths would cross more than once.

Alexander and I climbed whenever possible, sometimes in Karlstein and sometimes in Arco; in between, I was still preparing for my high school diploma. In spring, we started a new route on the north side of the Reiteralm, one of the major massifs near Berchtesgaden, a wall 1,000 feet tall and more than a mile wide. Alexander climbed the first pitch into uncharted territory, and from today's point of view, it still is quite a serious lead, one requiring advanced nut-craft. The second pitch also offered long runouts. I put a Cliffhanger hook in a hole and climbed past it, using it as protection. Our motivation was always to use as few pitons as possible.

After the two pitches, it started to rain, and we rappelled to the ground.

We were happy with the day, and it was only when we got home that we heard there'd been a catastrophe of international proportions. There had been a reactor fire at Chernobyl, a nuclear power plant in the Soviet Union, and the radioactive clouds had drifted across Europe, reaching Germany. Radioactive rain came down all over our home region. We were speechless, and hoped this rain would not have severe health consequences; we thus called our project *Gone with the Wind*.

Come early summer, Gschwendtner raced his Porsche out to Karlstein, wanting to inspect the wall we'd raved about in France. He was ecstatic, and bolted a route along a fine crack line. "Hey, boys, I must say, this is one of the best routes I've seen in a long time. I've only seen cracks like this in America." he said. He climbed it, graded it X- (5.13), and called it *Cannabis*. Since then, this wall area in Karlstein became known as the Drugwall, and all the other first ascents would likewise take their names from mind-expanding drugs. Many more climbs were added over the years, with some even reaching the eleventh degree of difficulty—upper-end 5.14. The names range from *Marijuana, Sweet Smoke, Speed, Magic Mushroom, Stoned Monkeys, Heroin, Cocaine, Mescalito,* and *Red Bull,* to endogenous drugs like *Endomorphin* and *Adrenalin*. Everything can be sampled with ease at the Drugwall!

Karlstein now became a special place where we spent most of our time. This is also why the Kugelbachbauer alpine inn became so crucial for us. It had always been a tradition to go there after a session for a beer or a banana-flavored buttermilk. Soon the proprietor, Haidi, a loving, warmhearted woman in her late 30s with short brown hair, knew us by name. She had a soft spot for famished climbers and usually gave us cake leftover from the afternoon for free. Haidi was our friend and something of our "climbing mom," and she had an educational influence on us over the years. She always said what she didn't like, and if we ever visited her with a "new" girlfriend, keen to impress the young lady with our climbing prowess, Haidi was sure to reprimand us: "You can forget her." Or: "You don't deserve her!" We knew the girl was right for us if Haidi thought as much.

Our circle of friends started to grow, and, slowly, climbers from Berchtesgaden, which had been very isolated until then, dared to come to our Karlstein crag, which had become known for its intricate and high-quality routes. Alexander and I had already been alpine climbing in Berchtesgaden once or twice, up on the Hoher Göll, the highest peak in the Göll Massif, on the border between Germany and Austria, and on the Untersberg, a half-mile-long limestone escarpment with many classic and modern multi-pitch climbs. But the climbing scene there remained underground and peculiar, if not downright insular: the locals were not interested in outsiders nor in ideas from the outside. "Sewn into the cauldron"—that's how we understood them.

We should have gotten that climbing was developing in a cosmos of its own in this small local scene. At the beginning of the 1980s, six years earlier, the Klaus Brothers had climbed perhaps the first IX (5.12+/13-) in the region, *Pumping Iron,* on a small rock in the middle of Berchtesgaden. The group surrounding the Klaus Brothers bouldered a lot and pushed their skills into a range where, indeed, not a single person from Traunstein could have kept up; one of them, with the mysterious name Moon, soon put up a short, benchmark X- (5.13) with *Assiniboine*. Somehow, everything had a whiff of myth or magic up in this cauldron. Only two of the locals had any contact with us from the "outside." One could be smelled from afar, because of the sweet-smelling smoke he spread with his pipe wherever he went; Klausner Rudi, ten years older than us, an athlete with biceps-like calves, could easily do two pull-ups with one arm. The other, Stocker Peter, was our age; he was tough, athletic, and equipped with fingers of steel.

Slowly we got it—Berchtesgadeners and Traunsteiners could be friends—and soon I was invited to join them on the "inside." Rudi lived in a dark, little room on the shady side of the 8,900-foot peak of the

Watzmann, but it nonetheless had its special flair and was almost like a bandits' den full of treasures. Rudi was a sculptor, and there were sculptures everywhere, some realistic and some imbued with mystical Indian symbolism. In addition, Rudi had on display mysterious, demonic wooden masks, resting between special stones and roots from the mountains, and decorated with eagle feathers. Blues riffs by John Lee Hooker sounded from his stereo, underlining my feeling of diving into a completely new, remarkable world.

One day, as Rudi pulled on his pipe, brewing coffee to go with a plate of butter cookies, we talked as usual about climbing. Then he launched into an explanation of the Kramperlloafn, which I had mistakenly called "wooden masks." They are used in the Buttnmandllaufen, a wild tradition around St. Nicholas in which unmarried boys dressed up in straw or fur, and wearing cowbells and the demonic-looking masks, parade through the Berchtesgaden valley.

In the evening, he took me out to his favorite watering hole, the Kuckucksnest. It was a music bar, like our local die Festung in Traunstein, but completely different. Pictures of Native American chiefs hung on the walls, a large buffalo skull was mounted over the bar, and everything was peculiar and alien to us "outsiders." There were also some more climbers from Berchtesgaden, including Peter. They all talked a little slower than we did, and their dialect was rounder and smoother. They always greeted each other with a unique handshake, as if they were about to start arm wrestling.

"Yes, haaaaaweediieeehhre!" was all you got at first.

They were headstrong, maybe even anarchic, and their pub reflected that. Above the door was a red star, the symbol of the pub, which embodied its owner, Bodo, 100 percent. Wild blue eyes, long black hair, and a full beard with tailored black-and-red leather pants—a mountain Jim Morrison. "And you're from out there?"—"Yes, from Palling!"—"Aha, and what would you like?"—"A beer."—"It's nice that you've got the guts to join us; sometimes, we do need some fresh blood from outside!" Bodo said, winking at me and asking if I had a specific music request. "Yes, a blues song by John Lee Hooker!" When Bodo played a song, Rudi's pipe started steaming like a locomotive, and he just said, "Hey, Thomas, the blues are such a good thing. It doesn't get any better than that, does it?" I nodded because then and there, he was right. He sure was right.

I finally graduated from school and was quite pleased with my performance. But I was far more excited that I finally had more time to climb. In August 1986, Alexander and I went on another big climbing trip with our now-rusting Italian automobile, initially to the Dolomites, to the Marmolada, where we had finished our last trip. But not to the *Ezio Polo*, which was now too easy for us at a rating of VI (5.10); no, we went to the *Modern Times*, the top route of Heinz Mariacher. We climbed back up to the Falierhütte and, this time, paid for our bunks. Sipping a glass of beer, we stood on the terrace in the evening light and looked up at the slab of the "fish." It was incredible, and although our innermost calling was to climb this route, we still had too much respect to tackle the *Fish*, an IX- (5.12c), right away. *Modern Times*, graded VII+ (5.11), posed less of a challenge.

It went perfectly, and *Modern Times* taught us a valuable lesson. We now knew without a doubt that we did not have to be afraid of the big names. We did a little tour of the Alps, bagging the first redpoint ascent of the *Blue Lagoon* (IX-/5.12c) at the Wendenstöcke and testing our skills with similarly graded *Amarcord* and *Möwe Jonathan*, and then returned to the Marmolada full of psyche. Because actually, only one route spoke to us: *The Way Through the Fish*.

"Look, Alexander, tomorrow we'll sleep at the top of the Fish!" I said, talking about the niche-like feature the route is named for—"Yes, but this time with a sleeping bag; I don't need another night like last time."

We'd done everything right. The small alpine tour had given us much-needed confidence. We cruised the first part of the *Fish*, onsighting all the cruxes often far above our last piece. Just below the "fish," I briefly slowed down, tinkering for an eternity to set up a belay—two shallow holes, several clustered pitons, and a small prayer that this wonky set-up would withstand a lead fall. But Alexander climbed solidly—which is just as well, because while breaking down the anchor I realized it was merely sturdy enough to hold my body weight. We finally reach the Fish. What a crazy place this 20-foot long, 5-foot wide ledge is, capped by a small overhang in the middle of this crazy wall. Above us, the wall steepened, and it is from here that Heinz Mariacher described the wildest climbing on hooks, inadequate belays, and long runouts. But all that would have to wait until the next day. We bivvied in our sleeping bags, feeling like lords of our royal palace, 2,000 feet above the Falierhütte.

We started early in the morning. Now we would have to show off all our skills! But we were surprised by the holds on offer and the quality of the protection, and around midday, we reached the big band and, with it, the end of the main difficulties. We hugged each other and cheered with joy. We now knew that no wall would ever be too difficult for us. We were born for adventure, born to climb, and meant to succeed as brothers.

After we wrote a letter to Igor Koller about our successful ascent of the *Fish*, he returned a picture of us together, bivouacking. On the back, it read: "I promised that you would make it!"

Military Service

Shortly before my twentieth birthday, I was drafted, part of German's then-compulsory military service, which ran from 1957 through 2011. With my long hair shaved off, it was off to the Bundeswehr, Bad Reichenhall, and the 4th Mountain Company, where, fortunately, mountaineering and climbing were encouraged. Although I was drafted in prime physical shape, this period also saw me facing my first severe health crisis. It started with slight discomfort in my spine, but the military training aggravated my back day by day. After a week, I could no longer straighten my left leg and limped when marching. My instructor shouted at me: "Hunter Huber, please walk straight. If you climb the way you walk, you'll never get up anything!"

If he only knew, this douchebag, I thought as I went to see the staff doctor. After I underwent a few examinations, a massive, herniated disc in the lumbar region was diagnosed, and I was first sent to the barracks infirmary. The doctors and nurses tried to help my condition with warm baths and massages, but it worsened by the day. By now, my left leg was numb, and because of the pain, I could no longer sit upright. Finally, I was transferred to the military hospital in Munich, to the psychiatric ward—there was no neurological ward, but as my case had something to do with my nerves, that's the deal I got. I was in a room with nine young soldiers, all trying to be discharged from the Bundeswehr because of alleged mental ailments. They were a wild somewhat weird bunch. It was always entertaining, but the time there seemed endless.

After two months, there was still no improvement in my condition. The ward doctor told me flatly: "Hunter Huber, we're going to operate on your disc in two days; prepare yourself mentally for the procedure." I swallowed hard, knowing that this military hospital had no specialists in spinal surgery, and replied, "I still have to think about whether I want it, because the most important thing for me is that I recover 100 percent and can go mountaineering and climbing again."—"Hunter Huber, I can promise you one thing, you can forget mountaineering—be happy if you can march in a straight line. And this is an order. We will operate on you! But don't worry: even though we've hardly done this operation before, we know what we're doing here and will do a good job!"

I was at a loss for words. I promptly called my father and told him the whole story. The following day, the ward doctor did not come to my bedside during rounds, and the next day I was transferred to a private health clinic in Bad Griesbach. I don't know what levers my father set in motion, but it worked. I stayed there for almost two months while the physiotherapists tried in vain to improve my condition. Finally, I was transferred to the Bundeswehr University Hospital in Ulm and operated on by experienced surgeons.

Things started to get better, slowly but steadily. I learned to walk normally again, and the feeling in my back and legs gradually returned.

Although it was a long time before I could do my first pull-ups and easy climbs, day by day I could feel myself shedding the shackles that had held me for the past three-quarters of a year. My hair was also getting longer again, although I remained a soldier on paper. However, the Bundeswehr had lost all interest in my person, and to be honest, I was not too keen on military service anymore either. I wanted to prove to everyone, but especially to myself, that what the senior physician at the Military Bundeswehr Hospital in Munich and various other experts had told me was absolute bullshit.

After a monthlong convalescence phase with many physio and strength-stabilization exercises, I made my first attempts at climbing, on easy routes in Karlstein. Initially, I felt very rusty; I only toproped, as I didn't want to risk a fall. Not yet. But what you've learned, you don't unlearn, and fortunately, it all came back quickly. After the first moves in the Vs, I immediately climbed a VI, then a VII, and soon after, the VIIIs were no longer posing a serious problem. My enthusiasm for my newly gained freedom of movement acted like a duster on my joints. My body still knew exactly how to position itself, and my herniated disc was history come autumn.

In the meantime, Alexander had graduated from high school with straight As and was doing community service—and was now climbing in a different league. He dispatched the then most difficult route in Karlstein, *Cannabis,* the 5.13 on the Drugwall. As happy as I was for his success, it also gnawed at me because I was ambitious and motivated to climb hard. In the most positive sense, my brother was, at that moment, my biggest competitor. After all, we were a climbing team, so I wanted to climb as hard as he did.

Eventually, the Bundeswehr sent me a letter informing me that I'd been classified as unfit for service, and I was discharged. I solemnly bolted an awesome arete in Karlstein, and a little later, I sent the route, *Albatros,* an awesome IX+ (5.13a/b). It felt too good to be true: the handshake of my brother, the pint of beer at Haidis, and the entry in the Karlstein book, where all the new routes were listed. I had felt like a climber again *and* I'd learned some valuable lessons: I had learned to fight and to never give up on myself, and I'd learned that even seemingly insurmountable hurdles can be overcome by enthusiasm and the power of the mind.

Free at Last

School, the Bundeswehr, and all these tiresome obligations were now things of the past, and now I was responsible for my own life—the time of my emancipation had finally arrived. I was still living at home, enjoying the benefits of a full fridge, but I already had different ideas. With a mohawk haircut and later with dreadlocks, I wanted to set myself apart from my parents in a provocative way. I began earning pocket money as a waiter at Nanu, a hip pub in Traunstein. My long-term goal was to work as a high school teacher, integrating climbing into school sports programs. There was no official climbing instructor for public schools in those days, so I began training as a certified mountain guide, enrolled in a PE program at the Technical University of Munich, and began to build my foundation for a financially secure yet climbing-filled life.

Along with Alexander, Rudi Klausner from Berchtesgaden had become one of my closest friends. We both were in awe of nature and of life, and could spend hours conversing about climbing training and performance optimization.

Rudi was savvy, incredibly creative, and smart about improving his performance. With his individualized Klausner training plans, we brothers improved our climbing performance quickly; we were now climbing in the lower tenth grade and, with some good results in national competitions, had made it onto Germany's national climbing team.

In addition, we had our first sponsor, Wolfi Müller, whom we knew from our time in Buoux. Thanks to his then hottest and coolest climbing-clothing company, Gentic, we were now seen at the crag wearing white, sporting ibexes and Japanese lettering—and were even paid a little pocket money. Kitted out thusly, we clipped the chains on *Vom Winde Verweht* (IX, or 5.13a/b) on the Reiteralm's north side and dispatched our first 8a's (5.13b's) in the Verdon Gorge. Nevertheless, we still had to acknowledge without any envy that in terms of climbing style and ability, we were still miles behind the French stars like the angelic Isabelle Patissier and the golden-locked Patrick Edlinger.

In late summer of 1988, I made the big move to Munich, into a two-room apartment in the Sendling district. Although it was a dark apartment—the high rise opposite blocked the sun—it had a unique flair. When both Alexander and I had signaled that we wanted to study in Munich, our father had bought this old apartment, which we lovingly renovated. Its 500 square feet comprised a small entry hall, a small bathroom, two rooms, and a kitchen. And because it was an old building, we had high ceilings—ten feet tall.

It didn't take long for me to remodel my four walls to have a space to sleep, study, relax, work out—and *climb*. Six feet off the ground, I built a false ceiling over half the room. Up there was my sleeping level, and below that I framed in an overhanging home wall that folded down from above—a simple, unique design which allowed for a completely revolutionary training method. Rudi had the simple but ingenious idea of systematically integrating the finger-strength exercises from a hangboard or pull-up bar into climbing movements. I put his concept into practice by symmetrically fixing four rows of holds, each including crimps, pinches, sidepulls, slopers, and two-finger pockets. Below these rows of handholds, I bolted on small, symmetrically arranged rows of footholds. The world's first system wall was ready, creating a training tool that would be copied globally and, shall we say, "revised" by intellectual-property pirates.

Alexander moved to Munich a year later, took up residency in the spare room, and began to pursue a physics degree. The Leipartstraße metamorphosed from a student flat to our very own training temple. During the day, we went to uni, and at night, *we trained,* the hard music of Monster Magnet, Motörhead, and Nirvana roaring out of the speakers in my room. Everything was coated with chalk, and the air was saturated with the smell of sweat. We were "on fire," hungry for training, and banged out Rudi's protocol on the system wall like fiends.

On the weekend, we drove back home. A quick hello and, typical for most spoiled, post-pubescent wannabes, we dropped off the laundry at Mom's because Mom still did everything for us. Then, that same evening, we'd head to Nanu, where I'd kept a part-time job tending bar, while Alexander had also found work pulling pints. This went on until one in the morning. Afterward, we went to the Blue Velvet, a great rock'n'roll club out in the sticks, where they played our kind of music. This went on until about 4:00 a.m. Then we would all get out to Karlstein in the late morning, where we climbed on our projects. Every aspect of our life was geared toward performance.

Our most memorable adventure during those days was perhaps climbing the route *Scaramouche* on the west pillar of the Hoher Göll, the high point of the Göli massif in Austria. The route climbed a gray, blank 650-foot slab with far-out-there climbing, including moves on monodoigts (one-finger pockets), frictionless slabs, and desperate dynos to crimps. We placed all the bolts on lead while hanging from fragile body-weight placements. And we did take some desperate whippers—one 50-foot flight left Alexander limping off the mountain with a sprained ankle. And yet, weeks later, we each climbed all the pitches free on lead. A dream line that deserved to be graded X (5.12+/5.13-). At that time, we were unaware that we'd established one of the most difficult alpine routes ever, and even today, a repeat counts for something. The *Scaramouche* became synonymous with adventure climbing. While all the bolt-spoiled climbers avoided it, there was certainly nothing *'plaisir,'* as the Swiss would put it, about our route.

We finally traded in our run-down Italian car for trusted, sturdy Swedish steel. We embellished our new vehicle, a sky-blue Volvo station wagon, with a diabolic black buffalo head painted on the hood and adorned the rear-view mirror with eagle feathers. Motorhead's "Rock 'n' Roll" would blare from the speakers when we brothers left university and steered our wagon east out of Munich toward the limestone cliffs of Schleier Wasserfall. Life was perfect in many ways. As Motorhead's Lemmy Kilmister, my godfather of rock 'n' roll, put it, ". . . cause I'm in love with rock 'n' roll, satisfies my soul . . ." Never failing to add, "And don't forget to rock 'n' roll!" to all his words of wisdom.

And he was right, there. There is much more to rock 'n' roll than the pure, raw music. It is an unconditional philosophy of life, wild, rebellious, anarchic, not letting anyone take away your right to freedom, going for your goals no holds barred, using your maximum power and all your energy. If you were to describe it in musical language, all the knobs would be on top, with the volume turned up to 10. No half measures, nothing half-baked, full throttle at any given moment, and no accountability for one's actions, not even to one's parents.

Of course, our parents still supported us almost 100 percent, but only on one condition: that we study! We fulfilled this condition without protest, except for our days off to go climbing. While Alexander disappeared into a world of mathematical and physical formulas that was alien to me, I did gymnastics, swam, and ran laps on the track; played soccer, basketball, and handball; and studied training theory, biomechanics, and pedagogy. These were contrasting academic pursuits, contrasting personalities, but an identical goal: to get a job that left plenty of time for climbing. Like our shiny blue Volvo, the future looked bright. We passed each semester's

FREIHEIT

exams while simultaneously pushing our climbing grades and even dabbling in competitive climbing.

Perhaps the most noteworthy competition was the German Climbing Championship in Munich. Alexander and I had got our training down to a T and were ready to go, maybe even for the podium. Expectations were high from the national coach and my private coach, Rudi. Alexander and I started late in the rotation because the best always came at the end, and by chance, it was my turn directly before my brother. Fully focused, I stood before the wall, tied in, chalked my hands, and placed my foot. I lifted off with the second foot, and exactly then, my first foot popped, and I was back where I had started. *Off you go, untie, and please leave the stage. Next, please.* I couldn't believe it. Embarrassed, I walked off the stage, trying to hold my head high. Alexander was already on his way out. Sadly, he made the same error as I had—and that no other competitor did—and we finished last.

It seemed that the world of competition was not for us. Nevertheless, we were rewarded with a great time outdoors; on Karlstein, at the Reiteralpe, in the Dolomites, and throughout the South of France and Spain. We pushed each other and were usually the first to repeat each other's projects. Being brothers that shared precisely the same passion, we were always compared to each other. Alexander was the "Little Huber" because he was shorter, while I was the "Big Huber." Or Alexander was the "Smart Huber" because he was bright while I was the "Pretty Huber," not because I was any better looking but because they couldn't think of anything else to say about me.

But then there was the all-important matchup: Who was the better climber? All the humorous comparisons were easy to brush aside, but this comparison went right to my ego. Superficially, we were equally strong: Alexander tended to be better on athletic, overhanging routes due to his shorter levers, while I was stronger on slightly overhanging, crimpy face climbs. Most often, however, it came down to the day's performance.

If you listed the routes we ticked that year as a basis for comparison, my brother came out on top. In climbing and life in general, the more structured individual thus always focused exclusively on one project at a time. On the other hand, I was often too playful in my approach and creative in my implementation, letting myself get too excited by multiple projects at once.

This was also the case come autumn of 1991. I checked out this route, then that route, then I tried another new project while Alexander concentrated all his energy on sixty-five feet of rock at the Schlangenfels cliff in Karlstein. When the temperatures finally dropped, offering the necessary friction, he climbed his first route in the lower eleventh grade: *Shogun*, a 5.14b. That got me started, and I was suddenly motivated to be disciplined and more focused. I also wanted to break into this next level of climbing. This inner competition pushed us brothers to strive for the next hardest thing.

After a subsequent winter of hard training on our system wall, I repeated *Shogun* surprisingly quickly. My redpoint burn was crazy. I campused through the right-handed slopers, the crux of the entire route, and only when I was clutching the finishing jugs did the realization kick in that I had done it. Everything had felt so easy, filling me with an inner understanding that this climb had by no means been at my limit.

Alexander, who belayed me on my surprise send, was grinning from ear to ear. "Nice one, Thomas, that was fast!"—"Ahhhh, Alexander, that was unbelievable. Suddenly, I was hanging off the jugs. I cannot remember getting there!"

All he had to say: "I can only tell you that it looked too easy, as if you were climbing 5.12!" It was an experience I would have time and time again: with proper preparation and rehearsal, if you do something at your limit, it can feel easy, while a lower-graded route that looks easy on paper can feel desperate.

At the time, our lives still felt inspired by our success on *Shogun:* full of surprises and always in the fast lane. I was a qualified mountain and ski guide: I had a loving girlfriend; my brother and sister, Karina, who climbed with us sporadically; an awesome climbing community; and the Kugelbachbauer.

We always had a plan, a line, and a project, especially in Karlstein. After a successful ascent, the route was toasted with the clinking of beer steins at the Haidi vom Kugelbachbauer and then christened with an appropriate name: *Wotan Wahnwitz, Easy Rider, Sexplosion, Sex on the Rocks, No Woman No Cry, Violent Femmes, Halber Mensch, Skyline,* or *Hypergalactic Donnergurgler.* We spent much of our time tirelessly hunting for new projects. Bolt, clean, work, send, and off to the next. From the outside, we surely looked restless, sprinting from one project to the next. Alexander found a fantastic line on the Göll west face, while I spotted something on the Feuerhorn north face, ten pitches, ultra-beautiful—it looked impossible.

I had discovered this line years ago, before my time in the Bundeswehr, when 5.12 had been my upper limit. Back then, Alexander and I were already addicted to first ascents. We climbed *Utopia* and *Dave Lost* on the north side of the Reiteralm. Once those were done, we were back on the hunt until I spotted this line with slabs, cracks, and blank sections on the Feuerhorn. It was love at first sight, and from that moment on, I lived in fear that someone might snatch this line away from me. Even though I was out of my depth on this wall, I immediately placed a first bolt. After that, I calmed down because it was now my project, reserved for me as if marked by a dog urinating on a fire hydrant.

It took me a few years to equip the climb, but in the end, I'd created a piece of art consisting of ten fantastic pitches just waiting for a free ascent. (I bolted this route in sport-climbing style, installing the bolts on rappel; however, on alpine walls and in big-mountain terrain like the Himalayas, we've always had a strict ethic of climbing ground-up, to preserve the adventure.) My masterpiece, taking my skills as a sport climber and projecting them onto an alpine face, seemed to be X+ (5.14a) or even harder. The difficulty stems from the sum of so much intricate climbing, until you reach a breather 650 feet above the ground. Then the next 10 feet put you to the test: everything that has come before feels like a warm-up. After this crux, the climbing is still hard but manageable. Although the crux moves are unforgiving in their compressed nature, they also embody all that is best about climbing.

You must lock off tiny underclings, perfect incut crimps, and gastons, making big moves between the grips. The only downside is the minuscule, sometimes slippery footholds. Hanging onto two handholds, you need to forget the fatigue from all the extreme climbing below and wait for your inner voice to order you to "go": now everything has to fall into place; you only have enough in the tank for one proper burn.

Silence

I trained all summer with one goal: my route up on the Feuerhorn. I was mostly alone on the wall, working the moves on a static rope. Alexander sent his route in Berchtesgaden and said it was the most challenging thing he had ever done: 8c+ or 9a. This put it up there with *Hubble* by Ben Moon and Güllich's *Action Directe*. He named his masterpiece *Om*. Of course, there was some discussion about whether a Huberbuam could perform such feats in the first place. But nobody could prove the opposite if nobody repeated it. And since Berchtesgaden is not on the climbing world's map, *Om* slumbered on unrepeated for quite some time.

Of course, I wanted to follow suit, maybe not with a high-end sport climb but with an alpine route in the upper tenth degree of difficulty. The conditions were good, the cool temperatures offered excellent friction, and Roman, a good friend from Ruhpolding, held my ropes for my first redpoint attempt. I immediately sent all nine pitches to the rest point before the crux. "Then go get it—get it over with before winter kicks in," I quietly said, chalking my hands and blowing the excess powder off my fingers.

I slid into the complex series of moves, which I had rehearsed for days. With seemingly limitless power, I locked off the undercling, did a slight crossover, sorted the fingers into the incut slot, fully crimped, and pulled far right to an incut sidepull, and then brought my feet over onto the tiniest of dimples—all to get my body into the launch position for the most complex move. Now I spanned far left into a shallow dish, which fit just my index and middle finger, and locked off. "Ahhhhh, Thomas, pull, don't let go!" Roman's voice drifted up from the hanging belay below. At that moment, my foot popped, and I fell, hitting the end of the rope fifteen feet below the crux.

"Fu . . . I was so close!" I was happy and surprised that I had gotten this far, but disappointed simultaneously. "Man, all I had to do was grab the good hold. I could see the jug in front of me."

"Take a break and try again!" Roman recommended.

"For sure, I'll try. I won't give up!" But a slight melancholy was already audible in my voice.

With such a feeling surging in your gut, performance seldom follows. But there was something I was missing at that moment: This repeated popping of my foot, only inches from latching the exit jugs, was a turning point. If I had sent there and then, I would have given this route a proper name, celebrated a successful climbing year together with Alexander and our friends, and probably our rock 'n' roll would have continued—studying in Munich, training, partying, and training again. We would have cheered each other on and, after a successful climb, would have philosophized, slightly intoxicated by beer, about what name to give this new, hyper-vertical work of art. What wild times those would have been.

But everything turned out differently. Winter came too early, and the Feuerhorn route remained unclimbed. This bullshit situation weighed heavily on me, perhaps also because our mental calculus of achievement, which was fed by 8b and 8c rock climbs, was massively out of balance.

Thus, this fall on the Feuerhorn was not just fifteen feet onto the rope, but a plunge into a dark void of sadness. I suddenly questioned everything: this rock 'n' roll lifestyle, my studies, my goals, my career prospects. To top it off, my girlfriend dumped me for another guy, and soon I was drowning in tears.

It was almost unbearable, and I returned to the solitude of my chilly north face of the Feuerhorn after a long, dreary winter in Munich. I climbed alone, on a fixed rope, living as a hermit in this vertical arena, rehearsing the moves daily, inhaling the silence, the wind, and the whistling of the birds. This gave me the peace of mind I had hoped for because, letting me leave everything that annoyed me in the valley below.

But this state only lasted as long as I was in training mode. When I planned my first ascent, the stress returned because I wanted to prove to myself and the world that I had not forgotten how to climb. On the approach, I already knew that I needed to be in a better headspace. What good are massive biceps if your mind is shit? As Wolfgang Güllich put it, "The most crucial muscle in climbing is the brain."

How right he was. Most of the time, I'd launch into the crux lead feeling like I was unlikely to reach the top, and with such an attitude, I may as well have stayed at the belay. But how do you explain that to your partner, who was motivated beyond belief: "Today, Thomas, it's going down; I've got a gut feeling!" Of course, I couldn't say anything negative and didn't want to look like a person riddled with doubt. So I'd bury my anxiety and hop into the passenger seat.

On try after try, things would go smoothly until the tenth pitch, where again history repeated itself: At that damned smear, my foot would pop, and seconds later, I would be hanging in my harness, screaming, raging at my inability. I couldn't wrap my head around having failed yet again just inches from the finish line. Soon the anger vanished, to be replaced by resignation.

Permanent failure had caused severe disorientation, which led me to quit university. I moved into a flatshare in Traunstein and took work as a mountain guide, and typically leading my clients up the East Face of the Watzmann. Soon after, I got a nine-to-five at an experiential-education facility close to Berchtesgaden; their base was an old, stately home in a beautiful location with a view of the Göll, Watzmann, and Hochkalter. But during a liquidation case, this property was to be sold.

I almost didn't dare give voice to the notion buzzing around my head about living and working here, in this place, which could be turned into a conference hotel, offering guests one-of-a-kind mountain adventures. These activities could support me in better mastering my inner hullabaloo because nature is the best teacher anyway.

That's it. It would be perfect.

CHAPTER THREE

My New Home

Berchtesgaden

I told this story to my father, who in the meantime had finally parted ways with the rigid banking business. He'd begun tinkering with real estate on his own, buying old properties, renovating them, and then selling them off for a profit. He was finally free, self-employed, and loving it. He was not only enthusiastic about the property, but also about my vision. It didn't take long before this property was ours, and I knew that I'd finally found my place in this world. Now I could shape my future in the mountains, just as I had dreamed of as a child.

I moved to Berchtesgaden for good, and with Mic, a good friend and fellow mountain guide, I was soon immersed in planning out our new project in this uniquely beautiful space.

In the meantime, I trained a lot with Rudi on my new home climbing wall, was a daily regular at the Kuckucksnest, was invited by the *Ganghofern* to join in the wildly archaic custom of the Buttnmandllauf (with the "demonic" masks), and slowly found my way into the Berchtesgaden climbing scene. And yet some stubborn Berchtesgadeners kept telling me that I would always remain an "outsider," because only those born and raised in the valley were real locals! I could live with that. My thoughts were freer than ever, and what I could not have imagined months ago, I went for today: I returned to my personal drama on the Feuerhorn, but this time with a completely different energy and mental attitude. Alexander belayed me on the first attempt. I got back to that darn spot, and this time my left foot didn't slip; it held, stuck to the tiny foothold now black with shoe rubber, and the next move suddenly felt very easy. Finally, those few inches were no longer missing. I held the exit jug. I shouted out my joy, and the Feuerhorn, the mountains, Alexander, and the alpine swifts rejoiced with me and returned my shouts as an echo.

I named the climb *The End of Silence* because it was truly the end of my inner vertical loneliness and silence, and graded the individual pitches from VII+ (5.11-) to X+ (5.14a). However, as a multipitch route, I dared to dish out an XI- (5.14b), given the cumulative fatigue and the fact that the crux came on pitch nine. For me, it was the most difficult thing I had climbed. This subsequent assessment of an overall rating was based on my experiences with *Shogun, Mercy Street,* and *Princess and the Hero,* all routes at the upper end of the scale.

At the same time, Beat Kammerlander established the multipitch *Silbergeier* in the Rätikon and Stefan Glowacz climbed his multipitch *Des Kaisers neue Kleider* in the Wilder Kaiser, and they also rated their routes X+ (5.14a) without giving an overall rating. *Klettern* magazine presented our three routes as the "Alpine Trilogy," with my route being the most difficult, at least numerically, because of the suggestion of an overall rating. This was provocative, especially for Glowacz. After the tragic fatal car accident that took Wolfgang Güllich's life in 1992, Glowacz was undisputedly the most famous rock climber in Germany. And now we—the simple Huberbuam—were sharing the proverbial red carpet, myself with *The End of Silence,* and Alexander with *Gambit* and *Om.* Our climbs caused much debate within the climbing world, and I was accused, for reasons of marketing and showmanship, of using the overall rating to artificially inflate the grade of my route. Alexander was likewise criticized for grading his climbs with the holy 9a (5.14d) label without ever having repeated any established 9a's first.

Glowacz did not like this at all, and he immediately set his bearings for the Feuerhorn. Up on the crux pitch, he found a shallow pocket a few feet left of my crux and thus an easier solution; making quick work of my route, he publicly downgraded *The End of Silence* to X- (5.13c), not without adding: "If you stick your neck out the window, don't be surprised if you are hit by oncoming wind." That really cut deep, and I was simply lost for words. It wasn't until years later, when the Alpine Trilogy had become a coveted feat and must-do for many a well-known climber, that *The End of Silence* was upgraded to X+ (5.14a), despite Glowacz's solution.

The Shadows Grow Longer

For weeks now, I was once again bedridden in hospital. This time in Innsbruck, with a beautiful view of the calmly flowing Inn and the silhouette of the Martinswand in the background. I had first damaged my knee while snowboarding, and then completely ruined it during a bad landing with a paraglider. The cruciate ligaments, the meniscus, and the capsule were no longer in their original condition. Lucky for me, there was a specialist here in Innsbruck, Dr. Golser. He spent hours crafting a functioning knee out of this mess, but before I could walk on two healthy legs again, let alone get cranking on rock, I would have to be very patient.

Alexander, on the other hand, was on a sending train. He treated himself to a semester off after his undergraduate degree, first visiting the Catalonian mountain village of Siurana and establishing the now-infamous *La Rambla,* perhaps the craziest, steepest, and most difficult route in Spain at the time.

He then flew out to Yosemite Valley, practiced granite climbing for his upcoming Latok II expedition, and ticked off, as a side note, the first complete redpoint ascent of the *Salathé Wall* (VI 5.13b) on El Capitan. Heinz

Zak took some pictures and set new standards in climbing photography, especially with his pics of Alexander climbing in golden light on the Salathé Headwall. Alexander was suddenly everywhere, on the covers of all the international climbing mags, either with the *Salathé* or *La Rambla*.

One of these climbing magazines was propped up on my bedside table at the hospital. There was a time when I would have reprimanded myself, "What the fuck are you doing? Why can't you go the same way he did? We'd be out as a team, climbing together, fighting for the same goals, and celebrating at the top of El Cap with a can of Bud!" It would have been awesome. But this time, self-pity failed to materialize. Instead, I was deeply content for my brother's success. It seemed like I was growing up.

After Alexander's trip, he came to Innsbruck and told me about this Yosemite about which we'd both dreamed as teenagers. He let me know that I also could send the *Salathé* with ease. Alexander then left for his expedition, his words having kindled my inner fire to get myself walking again and to get myself back in shape—and able to climb El Cap, maybe even the next year.

When I was back in Berchtesgaden and had finally recovered from my injury, Alexander returned from Pakistan, his team's attempt on Latok II having been unsuccessful. He'd been through a lot, but maybe he would try again, after his degree and with me on board.

Dark Days

It was winter of 1996, and we celebrated with a boisterous climbing party in a small hut high up in the Zillertal Valley in the Austrian Tyrol. Everyone had a story at the ready, and there was much philosophizing, debating, flirting, drinking, and singing. Just the way it ought to be: drawing a slightly inebriated line below a successful year of climbing. Then came a message that slammed into us like a cold front: Wolfi Müller, not only our sponsor but also our best friend, had had a serious ice-climbing accident. He'd sustained an open skull fracture, and mountain rescue and a helicopter evac had been called in—the full bloody program. Wolfi had just undergone surgery in Innsbruck, but his life was still very much in danger. According to the doctors, it was uncertain whether he would survive the night. This killed our enthusiasm, and we just sat there staring silently at our half-empty mugs of beer and waiting for seemingly endless hours, praying for good news. Wolfi survived the accident and got through the surgery, but Gentic, his company, went bust. And with it I lost my only sponsor.

Then came the fire. One of our father's properties burned to the ground overnight, leaving him a total financial loss. Even though he was entitled to compensation, the insurance company saw a chance to shirk their obligations, and teamed up with the bank to undermine our father's business. Payments were stopped for the time being, provoking a construction stop on all his jobsites. Within just a few weeks, our father's business collapsed like a house of cards. We had lost everything—only Berchtesgaden stayed in our name . . . for now.

In the meantime, our parents had migrated to the foot of the Watzmann, and it was hard to get our heads around the fact that all this was really happening. Our father approached each day with renewed hope of finding a way to save the house in Berchtesgaden. He was a fighter, never wanting to give up, and I tried to follow his lead. I worked in the mountains, took guests up the Watzmann, and climbed as much as I could. In addition, I tried to improve my financial situation by garnering additional sponsors, but I usually only received a polite refusal.

Usually they needed "only one of the Huber Brothers, and we would prefer the better one." This was too much. I'd rather do an honest day's work, so I started as a landscape gardener at a garden construction company and tried to get by. But the shadows in this paradisiacal valley were getting longer, and I knew that something needed to change if I was to have a future.

The following year I went all in, cleared out my bank account, bought a plane ticket to San Francisco, and used the leftover money to get by in Yosemite Valley, attempting to climb the *Salathé*. First, because I really wanted to experience the unique exposure on the headwall, just like Alexander had. And second because I wanted to just be there—to stroll along Merced River; lie down in El Cap Meadows with a beer and a bag of chips in front of the world's largest movie screen, El Capitan; live as a hippie at the climbers' campground of Camp 4; touch the holds or maybe even climb *Midnight Lightning,* the most famous boulder problem in the world; hear and see the thundering, giant waterfalls; and smell those beautiful pine forests.

I had been through all this in my mind umpteen times since reading the German climber Reinhard Karl's book on Yosemite. It was an intense and nerve-wracking time, and in the end, I spent two months in the Valley (plus all my money), all whilst not having completed the *Salathé*.

I had probably dreamed this dream for too long, and it became more and more presumptuous every day, to the point where it was no longer feasible for me. My ambition numbed my sense of reality, and I failed to realize that main goal of redpointing the 3,200-foot wall in a one-day push, following the original line exclusively, lay outside my reach—at least at that time. Alexander had done better: he was more of the modest type, more pragmatic, and had found a detour for the most difficult passage on the nineteenth pitch via the Monster Offwidth, a wide and grueling crack that went at 5.11+ instead of 5.13. Above all, he took his time. He sent the wall over a relaxed three days.

"Free *Salathé*" was still a brilliant adventure on my behalf, but just not perfect, because this "free" always needed an explanation: "Free, yes, but only redpoint, starting from the last 'No-hands rest,' and not in one day either, because on the first day I fell at the very top of the headwall and could only finish climbing it the following day." Explanations I wish I'd never had to put into words.

At home, stagnation had set in, perhaps because of our ongoing financial predicament. I pruned fruit trees, mowed lawns, planted flowers, and guided guests up the Watzman on my days off from gardening. Alexander finished his degree, and Karina was able to continue her sports studies with state funding. We had come to terms with our new situation as best we could and practiced minimalism wherever and whenever we were able. Even though it is said that money does not make people happy, in our situation money did indeed become synonymous with happiness.

Only the mountains were able to put my mind at ease. Up there, we were allowed to experience a freedom that money simply could not buy, a freedom which could only be purchased via our own inherent climbing skills. Summiting a peak with my dad, I let him know: "Hey, Dad, look, they've taken everything from us, and we'll probably lose Berchtesgaden, too, but no one can take away our beautiful living room!"

"That's right, my son!" he replied and smiled.

CHAPTER FOUR

The Wall

Light at the End of the Tunnel

We printed countless folders outlining our expedition. On the cover sheet, an artistic drawing of a mountain, boasting the words "Latok II: The Wall." A mountain of dreams in Pakistan, 7,108 meters in height and with a crazy, El Cap–sized wall rising from a base of rock, ice, and snow at 6,000 meters. The face was vertical, monolithic, unique in its form, and perhaps one of the highest big walls on Earth. Alexander had already attempted it in 1995. Back then, however, he had had to switch to the left (southwest) ridge due to rockfall in the approach couloir. He got up to about 6,500 meters with his team and had to abort because of the weather. But he knew then and there that he would return.

"Thomas, when you stand in front of it, you'll see: there's no other wall like it!" he'd told me.

Of course, I couldn't say no and was full of enthusiasm from the get-go.

The organizational effort was enormous and dragged on for months. Understandably, we wanted to get everything perfect in advance, to fine-tune our tactics and increase our chances of success.

To avoid rockfall in the couloir, we wanted to start earlier in the year, when the temperatures were still low. In addition, we had a powerful and functional team. This included: the "Wasserer," real name Franz Fendt, a tall Berchtesgadener, headstrong, athletic, and totally fearless in the vertical realm; Michael Grassl, also known as "Gschlosei," "Michal," and "Michi," also a Berchtesgadener, and the first ascensionist of the most difficult routes back home; the Munich lad "Schlesi," Christian Schlesener, perhaps the wildest, most unpredictable of them all, a man who had no limits; Toni Gutsch, also from Munich and, in contrast to Schlesi, a calm, appeasing person who was a world-class expert on high-alpine terrain; and the team doctor, Bernd Geffken. On paper, a harmonious, promising team. But this "alpha community" did come with great potential for conflict, which we could not yet evaluate accordingly at this early stage in our expedition.

Together with Alexander, I went to ISPO, the international trade fair for sporting goods and sports fashion in Munich, to solicit sponsors for our upcoming expedition. My brother had already found a new partner in Berghaus after the insolvency of Gentic, and I decided to knock on The North Face's door because for sure we needed their top-quality A5 portaledges. As I searched for the right contact person at the booth entrance, a proper cowboy approached me—or was he a surfer? In any case, he looked cool, with his blond hair, tanned skin, surfer shirt, and baggy pants.

"Hi, *ick bin Conrad Anker, man nennt mick auch Conny, ick sprecke ein bisscken Deutsch*," he said with a broad grin, eyeing me with his piercing blue eyes.

When I heard his name, I knew who he was: not a cowboy, not a surfer, but America's mountaineering icon par excellence, one of the best big-wallers and alpinists around. He worked for The North Face.

"What can I do for you?" asked Conrad.

I briefly introduced myself and told him about my mountaineering biography in fast-forward. Finally, I added my experiences from the previous year on the *Salathé*.

"Hey, I almost live on my parents' ranch in the Valley!"

I congratulated him on his good fortune that El Cap was virtually his local crag. We climbers are all wired the same way, after all: A climber's real home is defined by his favorite mountain or crag. For me this is in Berchtesgaden; for Conny it is Yosemite. We laughed a lot, hit it off right away, and drank a beer together at the booth.

Then I casually pulled our expedition folder out of my backpack. "Hey, Conny, that's actually why I'm here. Alexander and I are going on an expedition to a wall with friends, and we need your portaledges to do it!"

He flipped through our file and was visibly impressed. "That looks like a lot of fun!" he said, adding that he thought it would be best if we came back to the Valley before the expedition to train and climb a tough wall together. "Let's climb there. We'll send a super wall and bivy up high. I'd be happy to show you everything you need for your objective. Up there on Latok, you don't have to climb 5.14, but you have to know big-walling techniques—otherwise you will not make it!" He held out his hand to me, and I shook it laughing! In the end, he even promised three new portaledges and held out the prospect of a future collaboration with The North Face.

A month before our expedition, I was over in the Valley with Conny climbing *Gulf Stream*, a hair-raising "New Wave A4 Aid Climb" on El Cap that he had made the first ascent of previously.

We got on, and Conny sent me straight up the A4 pitch. The climbing was right on the edge!

"You'll get the hang of it; it's a rodeo," he said with a grin, giving me my first lesson: "Listen, I'm going to tell you how to lead. This is a so-called 'expando' flake. Now you have to widen this five-meter-crack. To do this, you first drive a Knifeblade down at the bottom, then place a wider piton—a Lost Arrow—then a wider one again, and finally an even larger one above. After that you can place micro-cams in the flake and climb up them!"

Crazy stuff that I'd never been done before, but I trusted Conny and did exactly what he said. And sure enough, with each blow of the hammer and each piton, the tight-fitting flake expanded a touch more.

"Hey, Conny—and when it cracks like that?!" I looked down questioningly.

"Yes, if the flake might plate off with you attached, then you should stop!"

Bloody hell, there was nothing like this on our Alps limestone. Back home, nothing expanded, and if it cracked, then everything immediately exploded off the mountain in a fusillade of loose rock.

"And now, Thomas, work upwards using our cams, but take them all out again after, so 'back-clean,' because when I take the first piton out at the bottom, the flake will clamp down like a muscle and crush the cams!"

"Okay, thanks, Conny!" *Makes sense,* I thought.

During that vertical camping trip with Conny, I learned everything there was to know about big-walling—all the technique and tactics, like pitching and breaking down a portaledge, general life in the vertical realm, how to organize, how to cook, and how to take a dump in a paper bag, and then stow it in a "shit-tube"—a long PVC tube with a screw-on lid—all while someone brushes their teeth next to you.

Hauling, cleaning, hooking, Copper heading, and calmly planning your next move on some marginal bodyweight placement—this was big-walling at its best. It was a crazy adventure, and it was a lot of fun learning from this blond cowboy. Instinctively, I knew that Conny was not only a grand teacher but someone who would increase our chances at Latok II exponentially. That's why I got Alexander on the phone. He could also see Conny taking our team to the next level.

"Hey, Conny, would you like to go to Pakistan with us in three weeks, to Latok?" I asked after hanging up with Alexander.

The blond Californian just smiled and said, "Yeah, let's have some fun!"

FREIHEIT

Another World

Almost naked, we lie in a sweltering room at the Paradise Inn. The fan half-heartedly shovels cooler air down onto our sweat-drenched bodies. Sleep is hardly to be thought of. The night is almost over. While back home the rooster crows with the break of dawn, here, in Rawalpindi, Pakistan, the call to prayer from the mosque sounds loud and shrill instead: *"Allahu akbar! Ashhadu allah ilaha illallah . . ."* First we hear only one muezzin; soon after, many muezzins mix together in a cacophony, as if the prayer callers were holding an early-morning competition.

Alexander, Toni, I, and Jan Mersch—also from Germany, and who wants to try the Ogre with the Austrian Jochen Haase, and who has joined us for the preparations and the approach to basecamp—have already been in Rawalpindi for a week. There are still no agencies that offer an all-round package for expeditions. We do everything ourselves: visit the officials; go to the briefings; purchase all the food such as rice, lentils, potatoes, noodles, and chocolate; and buy toilet paper, cooking pots, cutlery, kerosene stoves, fuel, and tents.

We then pack everything into garbage cans as fifty-five-pound packages each, simply because that's how much a local Balti porter will carry. For this he gets a daily rate, which is the equivalent of about ten Deutschmarks—around $5 per day. It is stressful, sweaty, and dusty in Rawalpindi, but also exciting to get to know this new culture from the inside. I pretty quickly understand that anything is possible, if Allah intends to provide it. *"Inshallah"*—God willing.

A week later, we pick up the rest of our crew from the airport. But someone is missing: Schlesi. Michal immediately has a story ready that we can hardly believe: "We had a farewell party in Schlesi's sports store, Bergbaron, and shortly before we left for the airport, Schlesi vanished off the face of the earth. We left without him, checked in our luggage, and then suddenly he was standing in front of us, visibly haggard from the night, but in a victory pose, and just said, "All is good— do you have everything?" We had almost everything—except his ticket. He himself didn't have it either, and no ticket, no flight. He was pretty relaxed about it, and just said he'd find it and come after us!"

Typical for Schlesi: unpredictable, and perhaps a bit too wild for this world.

The next thirty hours are also too wild for us. With a fully loaded bus, worn tires, and a stoically silent driver, we embarked upon the Karakoram Highway, which might more aptly be named the "Highway to Hell." Nonstop, without a single break, a journey of about 500 miles carried us from Islamabad to Skardu, winding through narrow valleys, along deep gorges, and past the snow- and ice-covered Nanga Parbat, always following the mighty Indus River. In parts, this highway is not even recognizable as a road, often just cut into the rock or cleared out of vast scree fields, framed by steep rock faces and tottering boulders that just need a little push to send us off for a swim in the Indus raging far below. Every now and then we see a rusty, dented bus lodged between the boulders on the riverbank. None of us really wants to know the story of how it reached its final resting place.

In this barren, rocky landscape, almost cheesy green oases pop up on occasion, near streams with human habitation. Along the roadsides are small stores and restaurants where you can get everything you need for your journey: fruit, vegetables, coke, tobacco, the local chapati flatbread, tea, and—if need be—machine guns. The latter does take some getting used to, but in this corner of the world there are a handful of rebellious tribes, and firearm sales is a lucrative business.

Our guide, however, reassures us that we're definitely likelier to have an accident on the Karakoram Highway than to be caught in a Taliban roadblock. When we do get around to asking how long the drive might take, we get an answer of, "*Inshallah*, tomorrow, *Alhamdulillah*."

Aha, I see—depending on how it suits Allah best, he'll let us either crash or arrive safely. Perhaps because of this devotion to God, the entirety of the journey is entrusted to only this one driver, who never leaves the steering wheel, driving all day and all night, and adding another twelve hours for good measure. Without stopping once. We are at the driver's mercy, but because God wills it, we do survive this journey from hell and find ourselves sitting in the well-kept rose garden of the K2 Motel in Skardu above the calmly flowing Indus River, sipping on cool cans of Coke.

The highlight of our adventurous voyage is the final stretch, the gravel road to Askole, a village only reachable by SUV. I take photos at the most spectacular spots and thus have a good excuse to get out of the car. "And now a smile please," which is difficult to tickle out of the meanwhile pale, fear-stricken Caucasian faces. Only the Pakistanis are laughing, showing off their snow-white teeth and sun-tanned faces, steering their vehicles along the precipice with amazing precision. The thundering Braldu River below, which would swallow anything and anybody in a heartbeat, adds an ominous soundtrack.

"Look at the road, not the camera!" I shout at our driver.

He responds with a nonchalant, "Inshallah—no problem, sir, I am a good driver!"

What an adventure! I feel totally at home!

Askole, a green oasis amidst this brown, lunar landscape, is the last inhabited settlement before the granite towers and snow-covered giants of the Karakoram rise into the sky. About 1,000 people live here in simple huts, providing for themselves from what the land offers. In addition, they earn a little money by carrying loads. And because every expedition must pass through this place, the people here are not doing all too bad in their simple abodes. Most of the men are employed as porters, while the women and children work in the fields. In many ways, the world is still okay in Askole. It's not so much farther down-valley where the women also do the field work, but rarely get any support from their husbands. The men there mostly sit around in the bazaar, debating vigorously whilst sipping tea. These are cultural differences that we cannot understand, and when we try to talk to the Balti about whether this is fair, they reply with a smile and a, "This is normal like this."

But how they like to laugh, these Balti. They are a happy, very hospitable people, and here in Askole we can't drink as much tea as we have invitations to come sip. There are far too many. And always the same procedure: We sit in the best parlor, and the master of the house serves us hard-boiled eggs, tea, Coca-Cola, and cookies. He himself stands silently by our side and watches us eat. When asked how his children and wife are doing, he replies, "Wife happy, working in the field, and children in school—all good!" That's what Askole is like.

A few days later, with 100 porters, 10 chickens, and a goat in tow, we leave the last green wheat fields of Askole behind us. A new sight pops up around every corner, fueling our sense of discovery and adventure. The mountains get higher and steeper, while below roars the icy Braldu; behind the next ridge loom the first granite towers, which look like caramel slivers on a scoop of vanilla ice cream. Then the path divides: on the right, the more traveled route runs into the Baltoro, along the Braldu to the world-famous Baltoro Gacier and Concordia, from where one can see all of the Karakoram's 8,000-meter peaks: Gasherbrum I and II, Broad Peak, and the king of the range—K2. These are the mountains everybody comes to see; thus, the path is well worn.

We follow the left path into the valley of the Biafo Glacier, which is relatively empty since there are none of the magical views of the 8,000-meter peaks. And yet it also has its superlatives. It is home to one of the widest and longest glaciers on earth. This tongue of ice stretches almost 30 miles up to Snowlake, the glacial plateau, and on the other side as the so-called Hispar Glacier down to the village of Hushe. In addition, impressive mountains frame this river of ice, some of them unclimbed 6,000- and 7,000-meter peaks. Our destination, Snowlake, is almost at the top: above it rise the 7,000-meter peaks of the Latok Group. In three days' time, we will see them with our own eyes.

We are impressed by the way our porters, with 55 pounds strapped to their backs and wearing plastic sandals, scamper over the initially heavily crevassed glacier, whilst we teeter across the ice with our modern boots, not looking our sharpest. Again and again, we get a "Sir, do you need help?" from the Balti and a "Be careful, here—little bit dangerous." We stifle our laughter, and instead thank the Balti politely for their care.

At the end of the day, we set up camp on the edge of the glacier by a small patch of grass.

The Balti light a fire, boil salty tea with rancid butter, and eat their bread, freshly baked over the open fire. We, on the other hand, are treated by our cooks Ismail and Quasim to a freshly slaughtered chicken complete with curry and rice. After the meal, the big consultation with our expedition doctor, Bernd Geffken, takes place, and the porters, so lively during the day, finally reveal their aches and pains. From headaches to deeply chapped, purulent abscesses, and from diarrhea to toothache, everything is on offer. Our medicine box contains the remedy for almost every case, and if we don't have it, then we offer a placebo multivitamin capsule—faith really does move mountains, and in the end everyone is happy. Afterward, the Balti cuddle up close, partly wrapped in blankets, whilst we slip into our sleeping bags and zip up our tents.

Early in the morning of the third day, we leave the Biafo Glacier and climb through green meadows to a ridgeline. The day couldn't be more beautiful: not too hot, not too cold, with the wind still and the mountains etched against a deep-blue sky stretching as far as the eye can see. As we stand on the ridge, all I can mumble is, "Are you crazy—it's beautiful!" This sight is utterly overwhelming and so surprising; nothing compares— the others are lost for words. Below us is the massive Biafo Glacier, and stretching out before us is the boulder-covered Uzun-Brakk Glacier, leading up toward the valley of the Latok Group. To do this place justice, I would have to use every possible metaphorical superlative, and even then, I would fail. Suffice it to say, this landscape is a paradise for extreme alpine climbing.

At 7,285 meters (23,901 feet) high, the Ogre is the highest mountain. Broad and mighty, it towers above all others, crowned by a striking orange-colored summit tower, and with the pyramid-like Ogre III (6,950 meters/22,802 feet) superimposed in front of it. To the right of it, the Latoks line up: first Latok II (7,108 meters/23,320 feet), then Latok I (7,145 meters/23,442 feet), and on the very outside Latok III (6,946 meters/22,789 feet).

In the middle of this colossal vista rises a monumental granite tower: the Ogre's Thumb, certainly 800 meters high but nearly invisible against the majestic mountain backdrop.

Except for Ogre III, each of the major peaks has been climbed, mostly via its "easiest" route, which is nevertheless still extreme. Perhaps the most hair-raising story from this mountain region is the first ascent of the Ogre. This fortress of rock, ice, and snow is recognized as one of the most difficult mountains in the world, and was first climbed by Chris Bonington and Doug Scott in 1977 via its West Ridge. On the descent, Scott broke both legs whilst rappelling at 7,000 meters, and farther down Bonington suffered multiple fractured ribs. This was the beginning of one of the most dramatic stories in alpine history, which the two climbers survived only thanks to their climbing partners, Mo Anthoine and Clive Rowland, who had stayed behind in their last camp on the mountain. Since then, 20 other expeditions had attempted this mountain, mostly via the prominent south pillar, but none succeeded in climbing the "Man-Eater" again. In comparison, Latok II is a sleeping beauty.

The mood in our group has been electrified—Conny puts his hands together in a namaste, I take a picture of this magical moment, and the Balti shout, "*Khuda hafiz*": "May God be our protector." After this short break, our porters shoulder their loads again, and our little band of brothers winds its way across the scree-covered glacier. At the end, we pass a steeply ascending graveled incline, and then we suddenly find ourselves in paradise, having just emerged from lifeless high-alpine terrain into a meadow covered with flowers of all colors, surrounded by the noble white of the glacier. A stream meanders through the greenery and flows into a small lake. A few large boulders that would be good for climbing and a pack of ibexes grazing on mountain herbs far up the steep slopes further highlight this idyllic setting. Directly in front of us stands Latok II—"The Wall," as we have named our project. It's incredibly beautiful and more a sculpture than a mountain; a work of art, symmetrical, carved into stone by Mother Nature.

Another handshake, and each porter receives his wage, plus a good bonus. The Balti thank us with a rhythmic song, and with an "Alhamdulillah, we will pray for your success," they say their goodbyes.

A week later, we have acclimatized to the altitude of basecamp (5,000 meters), and the weather is perfect for now. Ismail and Quasim cook for us with a lot of humor, always taking turns, always fixing something tasty. One day we have rice with dal, the other chapati with dal, plus chicken and a freshly slaughtered goat—meat while supplies last. We have cheese, sausage, and chocolate in abundance, plus *Playboy* magazines so that we don't completely confuse the peaks around us with the female anatomy. The team is strong; everyone is focused on climbing this amazing wall. But what Alexander could not have foreseen in Berchtesgaden was that our team had a certain explosive component.

Initially, everyone is still very relaxed, but when it comes to the opening planning phase—how we'll approach the mountain and with which tactics—the first loud discussions kick off. Each of us climbers know a better way and wants to advance his agenda, things like who climbs with whom, how far can we push the line, and who will do the work of carrying the gear through the couloir. At this point, it would take an expedition leader in the authoritarian style of Karl Herrligkoffer to bring structure to this anarchical uprising. But even though Alexander is the expedition leader on paper, everyone rejects this antiquated expedition style. We must make a democratic decision. That's why we argue—because we are all stubborn and unwilling to compromise.

Everyone is looking for his or her personal ideal line: I see a direct line, while Alexander envisions a less hazardous path to the left. Perhaps the greatest potential for conflict, however, is offered by the American way of climbing, represented by Conny and his immense big-wall and expedition experience. Franz and Michal, in particular, are unwilling to adapt to American ethics—leaving camps in place and so on—or to break with their roots in traditional Bavarian mountaineering.

Then, in the middle of it all, Schlesi appears from behind the gravel mounds and approaches us with his arms stretched high and the words, "Hey, guys, it's easy. Now I'm here, tomorrow I'm heading for the mountain. Who's going with me?" Inspired, Toni whips the group to get ourselves together and to find a solution, so that we can finally get started! The charged atmosphere only dissipates when we split into two self-sufficient expedition teams: Michal, Franz, and Schlesi, who want to try a line on the right side of the wall; and Toni, Conny, Alexander, and trying the line up the middle.

The situation remains tense. Of all people, Bernd, our expedition doctor, gets altitude sick, while Michal gets painful pelvic inflammation after spending an uncomfortable night in the snow cave at high camp, having slid off his sleeping pad. Both have to leave the expedition early, and again we discuss how to continue on the mountain. In the end it remains the same: Toni, Conny, and us brothers will tackle the central line, whilst Schlesi and Franz do their own thing.

Down in the huge entry couloir, we are all still together. Although we can climb everything more or less without a rope, we are extremely mentally challenged. It's dangerous, maybe even too dangerous, and we mostly just close our eyes and scamper on up. This snow gully acts as a funnel for everything coming off the mountain. Above it, after all, is a huge rock face over 3,000 feet high. And when the rounds the corner, around noon, then a lot comes down from up there. Conny is also visibly tense: "Hey, boys, we are dancing with the fat lady of fate in the ballroom of death," he says. Survival has become a gamble. We can only minimize the risk by climbing through the snow gully at night and in the early-morning hours.

For tactical reasons, we set up what we consider a safe camp halfway up the wall, under a rock overhang on the right edge of the couloir. We haul, fix, and bivouac, and after a week we have everything in place. Alexander and Toni start climbing exactly at 6,000 meters, at the base of an ingenious crack system that runs with slight interruptions through the middle of the wall. A hundred meters to our right, where the wall is shorter but steeper, Schlesi and Franz are also climbing. They manage for 200 meters before the cracks fade out in the compact granite, the next section looking possible only via extensive bolting. But that's not their style, so they rappel. Our rock features are more defined, and we manage at least 350 meters in the first few days, fix our ropes, and then descend to basecamp.

Afterward, bad weather follows. It snows on us all the way to basecamp; climbing is out of the question. Jan and Jochen reach 6,400 meters on the south pillar of the Ogre, and then have to abort their push when the snowstorm moves in. In the end, they are glad to be back at the bottom. Their adventure is over, and they decide to return home.

This time around, forecasting the weather and finding a good, weeklong window for a summit attempt is the crux. Satellite phones don't exist yet, so our forecast is based on our own observations, on an altimeter that helps us measure the air pressure, and on our personal gut feelings. Our plan of action is thus to wait for the weather, and then go full throttle on our next "go."

Schlesi and Franz also have a plan, but a secret one. They don't want to tell us how they want to climb Latok II. Even though the mood is not quite as heated as at the beginning, these discussions do leave their mark.

After the snow, the sun finally comes out again, and we are back on the wall. Toni and Alexander climb ahead, while Conny and I haul two portaledges, gas, food, and sleeping bags up to about 6,500 meters. At the only small band of snow, we set up our hanging bivy with 1,640 feet of void below us, plummeting to the 60-degree snowfield in the couloir. We tighten down the fixed ropes and work our way up from this camp. On the second day, Alexander and Toni take a break and spend the whole day lounging in the ledge, melting snow and enjoying the view, while Conny and I work our way up pitch by pitch over cracks, slabs, and overhangs. Toward evening, we fix our day's work and slowly float back down to camp.

"We had a great day today, four new pitches, difficult but doable, and tomorrow it's your turn again!" I euphorically tell Alexander and Toni.

"Clean, Thomas!" Toni says, pleased.

"I can even imagine, if we make it two more pitches, then we can get through to the summit!" I continue.

"That sounds great!" Alexander replies.

Suddenly Conny intervenes: "I am here to lead!", signaling that he has climbed too little today and absolutely wants to lead another pitch tomorrow.

I'm left speechless, but Alexander reacts calmly and shows his true greatness: "If you want to do it unconditionally, then go ahead and make sure you do it well!"

Conny is satisfied and climbs the following day with Toni—or rather, Toni belays Conny while he leads.

Alexander, who gets to experience his second day of rest in our luxury abode at 6,500 meters, plans to push to the summit the following day: we want to start at 1:00 a.m., jumar the fixed ropes, and then tackle the first pitches in the initial morning light. Alexander climbs ahead. It's a sound strategy.

When Toni and Conny return from their high point, Conny only says that it was great, but that he can't climb tomorrow because he's too tired.

"Tomorrow, you don't need to climb, Conny—Alexander will lead, get us to the summit. You just have to follow on the jumars," I explain to him.

One can vividly imagine the ensuing discussion.

With incredibly stable, high-pressure weather, Alexander hangs out in the ledge on day three as well, the only difference being that we don't have much to say to each other this time. We launch the next morning at 1:00 a.m., ascend the fixed ropes to our previous high point, and at first light Alexander is fighting the cold on steep mixed terrain at 7,000 meters. Toni belays, and I cheer on my brother.

An hour later, we are standing at the top of the peak. Everything is different than expected. There's no exposed, rocky spur at 7,108 meters, but rather a summit plateau almost as big as half a soccer field. It's crazy how beautiful it is here, and indescribable what one feels in such a moment. With absolutely no wind, it even feels warm in the sun. We calmly suck in the thin air and take in the vista—from K2, to Broad Peak, to Masherbrum, to Nanga Parbat. But none of these mountains is as crazy as this Latok II and all the other peaks of the Latok Group. And the longer I look at the Ogres and Latoks, the more they become a part of me.

As beautiful and intense as this moment might be, emotionally the climb has been a big challenge, and maybe that's why we aren't as jubilant as one might expect. We take photos, shake hands, and rappel back to our portaledge. The next day, we continue to Camp I in the couloir under the rock overhang. Toward evening, the fat lady shows us what she's made of, sending room-sized boulders through the gully—only ten meters from us. It seems utterly surreal. Almost in slow motion, the giant boulders tumble into the void, leaving deep craters in the steep snow. A minute later, it's all over. It smells of sulfur in this ballroom of death—this really is hell in paradise.

At night, another fist-sized stone smashes through our tent. Alexander reflexively pulls his feet up, and the rock tears his sleeping bag apart. We are shocked and have had enough. *Pack up and get down!* Our luck is exhausted.

When we get off the mountain, Franz and Schlesi are just coming toward us. They want to climb farther left in the couloir and then reach the summit via the northwest ridge. We tell them about the rockfall, but they continue undaunted. They reach the top within thirty hours, and twelve hours later are back at basecamp.

In the end, though we all feel satisfied, this adventure has left its mark. I now know that I wouldn't want to take part in such a major expedition again. The dust of the adventure is still visible on my trousers when we return to Berchtesgaden. Sporting thick, full beards, our eyes are aflame as we tell our mates in the Kuckucksnest about this heroic, weird expedition over a fresh pint of beer: rambling on about the wall, about Ismail and Quasim, about the rockfall, and about the fact that we only sent because we lucked out with the weather.

A Life for the Mountains

"Latok II: The Wall" brought Alexander and me together on stage for the very first time. The premiere took place in Munich at the beer hall of the Salvator-Keller on Nockherberg, of all places on those same boards where Alexander and I had embarrassed ourselves at the German Climbing Championships years before. But this time, we were successful. The astonished audience applauded, and almost every day thereafter we set up our screen in a different town, adjusted the projectors, and introduced ourselves with a hearty Bavarian "Servus, we are the Huberbuam! We are mountaineers." With each slideshow, our presentation got a little better. We quickly learned how to work the audience.

Eventually, we told our story from the bottom of our heart, so that we ourselves got sweaty palms and were once again hanging from the steep southwest face of Latok II in the rarified air above 6,000 meters.

In fact, by reliving this adventure, I gradually realized that this wall was much more to me than just another big wall in the Karakoram. "The

Wall" literally became the crossroads of my life. Gazing down from the summit, it seemed like I had been an apprentice for thirty years—since birth—training hard with Alexander to learn how to climb and become mountaineers. We pushed each other to ever new and higher difficulties, and started to look beyond our studies to carve out a professional future for ourselves, all of it culminating in finding this unclimbed wall.

I accepted the challenge, cleared the last of my savings from my bank account, and went practically "all-in" with a lot of courage, skill, fighting spirit, and will—but above all with Alexander by my side. Latok II was our masterpiece. When we'd stood on the summit on July 16, 1997, I was overjoyed, but I did not yet realize what we'd accomplished. It was only on the stage, when I stood in front of the projected image of our summit forcing me to reflect, that I saw this new vertical horizon spanning before me, this steep life ahead in which there were only mountains. We had both decided to follow our passion and had signed our work contract with the mountains.

Stone Monkey

"Never on the right side."

That's what my brother and I heard the aid climbers proclaim. They were implying that there were no free-climbable lines to the right of the *Nose* of El Capitan, on the overhanging and largely crackless right side of the wall. But to us—Alexander Huber and me—the proclamation was an invitation, and we found ourselves pitching our tents back in Yosemite Valley come autumn 1998.

A gangly, middle-aged man welcomed us back to Camp 4, the climbers' campground and beating heart of the Yosemite climbing scene, amidst big boulders and towering pine trees.

"How is it going boys? You're back again—I remember you from last time."

With long, straight hair worn in a ponytail and his nose crowned by

Lennon-esque spectacles, this climber had a camera dangling from his shoulder.

"Hi, I'm Dean Fidelman, but my friends call me Winky."

"I'm Thomas, and that's my brother, Alex. Fancy a beer? It's certainly not as good as the beer you get in Berchtesgaden, where we're from, but beer is still beer."

He gratefully accepted our invitation, and we cracked our brewskis.

"Cheers, brothers," he said. "You're lucky to have each other. I never had a brother till I found climbing. Then I came to Yosemite, and the climbers became my brothers and sisters. We were the Stonemasters, and let me tell you: It was a crazy time! Our life was centered around 'To-tock-ah-no-lah,' the 'Rock Chief.' That's what the Awahnechee called their 'native stone,' El Capitan."

We nearly choked on our beers. We were in direct proximity to a flesh-and-blood "Stonemaster." Being that we were well-versed in Yosemite's climbing history, the thought alone turned us somewhat reverent.

The Yosemite climbing revolution started with the Golden Age in the late 1950s and 1960s, a time defined by Warren Harding and Royal Robbins battling it out in the vertical arena. Come the 1970s, the baton was passed to a young and wild generation, a climbing—hippie subculture whose acolytes sported long hair, dark tans, and athletic bodies seemingly made for this vertical playground. The saying "sex, drugs, and rock 'n' roll," probably stems directly from the dirt of Camp 4, because the Stonemasters—a group of climbers who'd come together in Southern California, out at Stoney Point, Tahquitz, and Joshua Tree—were crazy birds, dropouts, and unforgettable characters. Among others, there was: "The Bird," Jim Bridwell, their unchallenged leader, followed closely by Ron Kauk and John Bachar, by far the best free climbers of this band of brothers. And you couldn't forget John Long, Lynn Hill, and John "Yabo" Yablonski, whose crazy antics and cutting-edge free climbs were slowly being caught on camera.

They were united by the search for a new form of climbing, a spiritual interaction with rock—seldom sober, but always free, athletic, crazy, and never in adherence to societal conventions. These were the climbers who gave us *Midnight Lightning,* the infamous boulder problem situated on the centerpiece Columbia Boulder in Camp 4, and the horizontal roof crack of *Separate Reality.* It really was another dimension, if not a new vertical art form. These two symbols, formed from the granite, became symbols of freedom—and of an understanding that impossibility is a barrier you define. If you managed to connect to the rock via movement, it was indeed possible to break through the impossible and into another realm.

Meanwhile, a small airplane that crashed into Lower Merced Lake in the High Sierra brought sudden wealth to the Stonemasters. They scouted out the wreckage and hauled the cargo—immense quantities of Colombian marijuana—from the wilderness. Then they sold the aviation-fuel-soaked weed in San Francisco. Most used their newfound money to purchase land and build houses. But with this financial security, the community also seemed to lose its foundation. They weren't really dirtbags anymore, and the community dispersed. Apart from Bird: he stayed in the Valley, invested his money in psychoactive substances, and opened some of the hardest aid climbs on El Cap, sometimes while tripping on LSD.

When this golden era of free climbing, pushed by the Stonemasters, petered out, technical aid started to play a more central role. Bird was one of the chief protagonists and made his mark with such routes as *Wyoming Sheep Ranch, Heavy Metal, Tinker Toys,* and *Plastic Surgery Disaster.* All are graded with A5, the hardest aid grade out there: it's high-stakes, technical climbing, with strings of body-weight-only placements and the ultimate consequence if you fall: possible death. This genre has something heroic to it, but only for those that take a shine to such antics. Only years later, in 1993, did a female member of the Stonemasters, Lynn Hill, kick off a new era by redpointing the *Nose,* then doing it in a day in 1994. But what does a new era really mean? Her brilliant performance merely reawakened the free-climbing revolution from its slumber. Only this this time around, El Cap took center stage.

Did this 3,000-foot big wall offer more? The US boys Todd Skinner and Paul Piana went on the hunt, searching out a free-climbable line along the crack systems of the *Salathé Wall*, but it was Alexander who managed the first clean redpoint ascent of the *Salathé*, leading all the pitches himself. He became famous overnight—aided also by Heinz Zak's epic photographs of him climbing the headwall. Of course, this was not really every American's cup of tea, seeing a Bavarian lad writing climbing history on their holy shrine of El Capitan. This is also why some hardliners, incumbent within the hardcore aid scene of the day, felt it necessary to downplay Alexander's achievement: "The 'Left of the *Nose*' is a slab littered with cracks, and thus free climbing here is of course far more feasible. But right of 'the *Nose*' is the habitat of 'Hard Aid,' and anybody trying to free-climb here is doomed to fail!"

Winky started grinning and opined casually: "I reckon I know what you've got planned . . ." Later, he let us know that he'd immediately felt a strong connection to us, both because of our focus and curiosity, but also because we had left an impression on him as being rebels lusting for freedom. From the moment we wholeheartedly showed our respect for the Stonemasters and praised their sense of community, as the epicenter of their climbing, he'd known without a doubt that we would continue along their trajectory.

We had to laugh, as Winky seemed to know us as better than we did ourselves. And we decided to take him under our fold: "The free right side"—that was why we were here.

In the end, all he had to say was that our plan would be an eye-opener to many. From the meadows below El Cap, we inspected the rock right of the *Nose* using a telescope, and finally found rock features along the classic *North America Wall* that might allow for free climbing. Just a heartbeat later, we were high up El Cap, embarked on an adventure second to none.

Tied in, Alexander and I, for a defined period, once again became a partnership for life. Just like on Latok, we slept in our portaledge, but this time with the difference that we weren't on the wall solely by ourselves—the nights high up on El Cap had a more than unique dynamism to them. More than ten teams were spreadeagled across the face, all in their own portaledges fitted with rainflies, the colorful tents illuminated by headlamps. Far to our right on *Plastic Surgery Disaster*, Peter Zabrok ("Pass the Pitons Pete") was having his own little private party in his hanging belay, bombarding the "Right Side" with his ghetto-blaster playing "Highway to Hell." It did not take long for another's voice to cut through the darkness: "OHHHHHJJJJEEEEAAAHHH, we love to rock 'n' roll, livin' easy, lovin' free! AAA-CCCC-DDD-CCC!"

Answered immediately from high up left: "Shut up, you asshole. I wanna sleep!" Retorted then to our bottom right with, "Huuuuuuuuuuuiiiiiiaaaa, you fucker. Shut up! EIeieieieieihhhhhh!" This back and forth lasted at least half an hour. It was heaven on earth.

Whilst Alexander and I were drinking our nightcap in form of a beer, lights from the ledges surrounding us slowly turned off. Silence came over the wall. The only thing still blinking was the gigantic sea of stars above. Slowly, the moon creeped into our vista. Suddenly, we heard a whooshing noise, which was getting closer and louder at an alarming pace, and then a human body came rocketing past. Seconds later, a parachute opened with a loud bang, immediately replaced by an eerie silence. Only a "Jiiiiiiiiiuhuuuuui" could be perceived in the distance, which let us conclude that all had gone well, and that someone had had a lot of fun.

I muttered, "Hey, Alexander, that must be a nuts feeling, to jump off El Cap like that! I think I'd also be up for that."

"Yes, Thomas, go to sleep now! Let's get up this thing, which will be enough for now!"

El Capitan is not only a holy place for us climbers but revered by BASE jumpers the world over. Maybe this wall even offers the best jump Mother

Nature has on offer. Some people even go so far as to proclaim that God himself must have designed El Capitan with BASE jumpers in mind, because the exit point high up on the summit is crowned by a "diving board" sculpted out of granite and extending over the abyss. But as with so many things, this sport is strictly prohibited within the boundaries of the national park, and BASE jumpers are hounded by rangers as if they were serious criminals. That's why most of them prefer jumping at night.

Daytime, on the other hand, belongs to us climbers, questing for the correct path. Alexander and I swung back and forth on the "Right Side," checking out the moves and bouldering through sequences, until we finally managed to suss out what we'd been searching for. Eventually, we would name this 3,000-foot granite line *El Niño*. This climb runs along the *North America Wall*, with alternative pitches, offering free climbing up to 5.13+. Our ascent silenced quite a few of the aforementioned traditionalists. After that, because we were so inspired by climbing on El Cap, we followed up with a one-day redpoint of *Freerider*, which would turn into one of the classic freeable routes on El Capitan. Winky and many others were psyched about our successes, but for many others, we were a tick too focused and goal-oriented, which is why they pigeonholed us as "typically German." They just could not wrap their heads around two Bavarians having raised the bar on El Cap twice in a row. But at the end of the day, that was their problem. It was important for us that we had something to celebrate—because we had broken into a totally new dimension.

These weeks in Yosemite also saw us implement the *monkey call*. It was "Uhhhhh, uhhhhh" or "UHHHAAAHHHAAAHHH," which is how the Stone Monkeys—a new tribe of irreverent free and wall climbers in the vein of the Stonemasters—liked to communicate. It was the ultimate way of letting others know where one was to be found. Or it could be used as a discrete warning, letting other dirtbags, who might have outstayed their welcome of the Valley's maximum ten days, know that a ranger was on the prowl checking permits.

A designated table in the back left-hand corner of the somewhat sterile Mountain Lodge Cafeteria close to Camp 4 became our basecamp. Early in the morning, Chongo Chuck, the spiritual leader of the Stone Monkeys—a name we liked much better than "dirtbags"—might be found here. As a homeless person, he had for years been living in the boulder fields behind Camp 4. He was more philosopher than climber, a genius-level slackliner, and the author of a scientific theory, which he would later self-publish in his book *The Homeless Interpretation of Quantum Mechanics*. Then there was the Bulgarian Ivo Nivov, an illegal resident of the United States of America and Yosemite Valley for quite some years, a real brother in spirit, who with his mantra, "'The Monkeys are raging," was down for any vertical adventure. There was also the "Wall pirate," Ammon McNeely, anarchical to his core; the charismatic Dean Potter; the artist Renan Ozturk; and Micah Dash, Ben van der Klooster, Cedar Wright, the Brit Leo Houlding, and many more hardcore climbers from across the globe.

Most important to this community was a rebellious, freedom-loving attitude, and it did indeed mean the world to us to be real Stone Monkeys. Of course, all of us were somehow athletic and cool. And it goes without saying that our table was visited by beautiful girls at times. In some way, it did really feel like we were building on the foundational philosophical principles of the Stonemasters: "Sex, Drugs, and Rock'n'Roll." Alexander and I replaced the drugs with the liquid Bavarian variant. But Rock'n'Roll saturated every fibre of our bodies: "Uhhhhh, uhhhhh!"

CHAPTER FIVE
Starting a Family

Marion

After returning from Yosemite Valley, we immediately began planning our second major expedition to Pakistan the following summer, 1999. Ismail and Quasim would be on board again, setting up the same basecamp at the foot of Latok II, as we aimed for the coveted second ascent of the Ogre, the mountain on which so many have failed. But no mountain seemed too difficult to us at the time, and we were sure that if the weather cooperated, we would get up it. And only for one reason: If not us, then who else? The team would be Alexander and me, joined by Jan Mersch, who two years earlier had been unsuccessful on the Ogre. We were hoping his inside knowledge of the mountain would come in handy. Toni Gutsch, who had had helped us be successful in the past, was also on board.

Even though Alexander and I had now dedicated our lives to the mountains, I still worked part-time waiting tables in the Kuckucksnest, simply because I enjoyed it and because the bar was my local watering hole. One day in early summer 1998, Bodo, the pub's proprietor, asked me to show somebody the ropes. With a twinkle in his eye, he let me know:

"Thomas, you know her already. She's the one with the braided pigtails and braces. She's a real beauty! You would be a match made in heaven!"

Her name was Marion, and luck was on our side: there were almost no guests in the "nest," and we had time to get to know each other, introducing our own, personal worlds. Mine was steep and exposed, hers artistic and philosophical. But though we were so different on paper, there was a mutual understanding. We laughed a lot, and the time until closing flew by; because we had so much more to tell each other, we didn't end that night when we locked up the pub.

A very intense relationship developed from that first shift together.

It only took a few weeks for our passion and love to kickstart a new chapter in our lives. It was one that demanded responsibility and called into question many of our previous life choices—we were about to become parents. For both of us, this came as a real shock. Marion was going to be a mother, although she was still in the middle of her architecture degree. And I would be a father, even though I had just gained my financial freedom. Neither of us could imagine giving up our freedom right now, starting a family, and pushing a toddler through Berchtesgaden in nine months' time. Our backs were against the wall, and yet there was only one right thing to do, even if it meant sacrifices—we instinctively knew that nothing in life happens by accident. Slowly but steadily, the idea of fatherhood and starting a family with Marion became a distinct reality. It was a totally new experience, my greatest adventure to date, which I would only be able to master together with Marion. Much like climbing: we only grow by attempting the seemingly impossible.

Elias

Two months before we left for Pakistan, a major event took place: in April 1999, our son, Elias, was born. With his reddish hair, he was the most beautiful child Marion and I could have imagined. All doubts as to whether I, the vertical rebel, could bear this responsibility were blown away in an instant. Being a father and having a family with Marion was from now on the most natural thing in the world. And, if I'm honest, it was the best thing that had ever happened to me.

With my income from the lectures and sponsorship money, Marion and I had set ourselves up humbly but cozily in a building site next to my parents' Berchtesgaden home. Our front door was made up of wooden planks nailed together. Behind this was a bathroom, a kitchen, a bedroom, and even a small nursery for Elias. In my fatherly euphoria, I bolted a route in the Endstal right after he was born: *Little Red Star*, graded X (5.13d/14a).

Two weeks before I left for Pakistan, we hosted an excessive baby shower in the shell of our stately home. Elias lay in a wicker laundry basket, which we'd attached to a climbing rope and suspended in the middle of the terrace, offering the best view of the Watzmann. What a picture, and above all what a great moment—us and all our friends celebrating our new lives as parents.

Later that evening—Elias was already fast asleep in his bassinet—the mood quickly became more jubilant. We celebrated our redhead with songs by Kyuss, Fu Manchu, and Monster Magnet, and I philosophized about music with Manni, a good friend. During the evening, we found out that we shared the same taste in music down to a T. Euphoric, we decided to form a band as soon as I got back from the Ogre, cranking out bass-laden stoner rock that went straight for your guts. We turned up the volume as "Rodeo" by Kyuss boomed from the speakers.

Just then, I realized what a brilliant life I was leading. Apart from our building site being on hold, I had everything a man could dream of: Elias; Marion; my career as a climber and alpinist, which was my vocation; and maybe soon my own rock band. I was ecstatic, buzzing with joy, and gave it my all throughout the night—just how everybody ought to celebrate new life . . .

As beautiful as the celebration was, the next morning knew no mercy. The pogo dancing of the previous night had taken its toll. I woke up heavily hungover and with a painful, thickly swollen left knee I could barely put my full weight on. In this condition, I could probably say goodbye to going on an expedition in a few weeks. But even though I knew that I was fully to blame—he who climbs high also falls far—I was in no way willing to accept my miserable, self-induced situation.

Dr. Golser from Innsbruck, who had already patched up my knee once before, examined the damage and once again diagnosed a torn cruciate ligament. I almost didn't dare tell him how it had happened, but when I did, he just laughed and said that something like this can and has happened to the most dedicated mountain athletes. Besides, he gave me hope that if I could get the swelling down, I might even be able fly to Pakistan. From a medical point of view, mountaineering with a stabilization brace would even be good preparation for an operation, because afterward, the knee would be free of inflammation and the muscles would be trained—ideal conditioning for a quick and successful rehab.

CHAPTER SIX
The Ogre

The Myth of the Man-Eater

Back in Islamabad, the sweltering, early-July heat hit us full-on. The airline had scattered our expedition luggage all over the world, and, without our gear, we were going nowhere—waiting it out in our air-conditioned hotel, hoping that the airline would find our bags. In those days, Islamabad was not exactly the best place to expect your lost luggage to turn up. India and Pakistan had revived their long-standing conflict, with troops facing off in the mountains of Kashmir at the now-infamous Line of Control. According to various daily newspapers, both powers threatened to launch nuclear weapons. When we finally received our luggage ten days later, we fled from nuclear Armageddon into the mountains, grateful not to hear any more of this nuclear saber-rattling as we traveled the Karakoram Highway to Skardu. And, without a satellite phone, we were cut off from the outside world in the mountains above Askole.

At the base of Latok II, we found everything just as we had left it two years earlier. On our way to basecamp, we were accompanied by the constant dull rumble of artillery fire from the frontlines, only twenty-five miles away. In hindsight, I'm not sure why we didn't sack the expedition then and there, amidst an escalating conflict between two nuclear powers. At the time, however, we could ignore this hot war because we only had eyes for the Ogre. And, we reasoned, if the war spiraled out of control, we could make our way home by going over the mountains and across China.

"Very nice to be here!" Our cooks, Ismail and Quasim were right about that. Still, the war was just audible in our peaceful little paradise at the base of Latok II and its towering west face, each deep, dark *boom-boom-boom* an instance where humans were being killed, a fact that was hard to overlook. The Ogre's Thumb, the meadow, the stream, the lake, and our tents further painted an idyllic picture. Our objective, the Ogre, dominated our surroundings, and we were keen to get started. Even my knee gave me no trouble walking and climbing, so we started our approach sooner rather than later.

We made rapid progress over the next few days, profiting from Jan's knowledge of the peak. He knew every detail, the best places to camp, and the safest route up the incredibly steep south pillar. After only two weeks, our preparations were complete—we'd fixed ropes to a portaledge camp at 6,000 meters, from where we'd launch up the pillar. Now all we needed was a stable weather window, a minimum of six days because that is how much time we figured we'd need to get from basecamp to the summit and back again. Rock 'n' roll, as they say! But the weather wasn't playing ball. And without today's digital weather models that can be accessed daily via satellite phone, a long-term forecast was challenging to make. Our only measurable variable was the barometric pressure, which we could gauge via our portable Thommen altimeter. If the altitude rose, the pressure was falling and the weather would likely worsen; but if the altimeter dropped, the pressure was increasing and the weather would likely improve. However, our high-precision gauge kept going up and down, plus the cloud patterns needed to be clearer, and never indicated a rising, dominant high-pressure influence.

Just going for it, all while praying for the best, was a strategy not suited to this mountain. So once again, the waiting game started, and we were mostly tied to basecamp. With too much time on our hands, we had time to think. My heart was filled with a longing for Elias, Marion, and home. These moments were painful because I didn't know how my little family was doing; I would have given anything to make a short phone call to hear Marion's voice and Elias' babbling, letting them know that we were okay. But there was no telephone—only the silence of basecamp.

Because of the remoteness, we had already thought about another form of communicating with our loved ones back home. Thus, every day at 6:00 p.m., one minute belonged to my family alone: at that time, I would meditate in the direction of home, while in Germany, at their 2:00 p.m., they would think of me. We were building a mental bridge over space and time that could overcome technological barriers. Later at night, the moon would function as the parabolic mirror bringing our thoughts together. (The moon is the same in Pakistan and Bavaria.)

We were getting tired of waiting at basecamp. We had already made one desperate attempt, but after some debate at high camp, we decided to bail, eying a dark bank of clouds on the horizon. Back at basecamp, the clouds dissipated, and the next few days blessed us with the best possible weather. The team's mood was at rock bottom. No one said a word, but everyone believed we had pulled out too early and thus blown it for good. However, when it started to rain early on the morning of what would have been our summit day, our lousy mood got washed away. Everyone celebrated this bad weather because, in the end, it was proof that we had indeed made the right decision.

Still, our situation was becoming more and more unbearable; the Ogre loomed higher and higher, while our little paradise was starting to feel like our little prison in the mountains. Every day, I sat for hours on the moraine using binoculars, scanning the scree-covered glacier for porters, who would bring fresh food and, above all, news from home. After a tough five weeks at basecamp, I finally spotted movement on the glacier. A short time later, they were there: two men from Askole who supplied us with fresh vegetables, flour, two chickens, and letters. It was, for all of us, the most beautiful day so far on the expedition.

Everyone was doing well at home, and Marion had sent pictures of Elias, who had grown noticeably in my absence. Only Ismail received terrible news from his family: his brother had fallen, killed in action while serving as a soldier close by. Ismail sat silently in the kitchen tent, staring at his cup of tea. Perhaps because we were brothers, Alexander and I could relate to his pain better than most. We put our arms around him and sat with him in silence. The muffled cannon salvos in the distance henceforth took on a deadly, new dimension. After the first shock, Ismail came to us asking to return home with the porters. His wish was more than understandable, and we bid a sympathetic farewell to our faithful friend.

We felt like we had been jinxed. Last time around at Latok II, we'd had several devil-may-care arguments, and yet, in the end, we were able to complete our project in the mountains. This time around, the team's vibe was on point, but nothing seemed to work out in terms of climbing the Ogre. An old mountaineering proverb sums up the dilemma well: "If it's going well, you can't do anything wrong, but if it's not going well, you can't do anything right."

This war had indeed gotten to us all, and the longer we thought about it, the more contradictory our actions started to feel. We were voluntarily risking our lives climbing, and yet not far from us, young men had to fight for their lives. After the death of Ismail's brother, we could no longer ignore this war. It felt like each of us was waiting for someone to say what everyone was thinking: "It doesn't make sense anymore; let's abort."

Two weeks later, when two more porters arrived at basecamp with letters, flour, and vegetables, Toni and Jan packed their bags. They decided to return to civilization with the Balti and hire for us fifty porters, who, if all went well, could be here in about ten days. We agreed to this plan, and in the final days of waiting at basecamp, Alexander and I climbed Latok IV to finish the job.

Latok IV was a sublime final climb, a mellow walk up snow and ice, the rope just for safety on the glaciers. At the summit, inhaling the beauty of the range, I shouted my son's name—*"EEEEEELLLLLIIIAAAASSS!"*—because I knew I would soon be able to push him through Berchtesgaden in his stroller again.

Back Home

We left behind the mountain, this endless waiting for better weather, and this senseless war, washing it all down with a cheap can of beer during our long flight home. Somehow, we still didn't know how to explain our failure. Was the Ogre perhaps beyond us, or had we just not wanted it enough? Had we really given our all, or had we missed a good chance? Regardless, this experience was not one of our proudest moments. The only good thing about the story was the mountain itself, which had once again shaken off another expedition and lived up to its name: Ogre, the Man-Eater.

Only after arriving at the Munich airport could I mentally leave the expedition behind, even though all my questions around it remained firmly unanswered. In front of me, in the crowd of waiting people, the loves of my life: Marion cradled Elias, who fixed his gaze on me in amazement as I walked toward them. Had he been able to speak, he surely would have said, "Hey, Mama, why is that overgrown savage looking at me like that?" "Ahhhh, my little Elias, it's me, your daddy; come here." At first, he was visibly uncomfortable in my arms, but when I elicited that first smile from him, I was his daddy again—just with a full beard, wildman hair, and possibly smelling a bit off.

Finally, I could let go of the unsuccessful expedition and celebrate reuniting with my family from the bottom of my heart.

Even my upcoming knee operation in Innsbruck and the three-month rehabilitation period could not shake me. Family bliss had gotten to me. There was Elias's first Christmas, Elias's first time crawling, his first time sledding, first babbling, and hearing him utter "Daddy" for the first time. To top it off, an interested party wanted to buy our property, with the prospect of us continuing to live in our house. Good things were happening.

While racing ahead at full speed on the Highway of Life, my thoughts tend to get lost when I'm not engrossed in the moment. On our last expedition, all my thoughts had belonged to my family—I missed them every second of every day. But soon, as time sanded the edge off these agonizing memories, the mountains inside gradually started to grow again, the granite towers singing their siren song, pulling me in with their bizarre shadows, and crowns of ice and snow. Slowly, they became more specific; among them, the Ogre stood out, its ultra-difficult, if not impossible, challenge as captivating as ever.

I was ready to rumble, but Alexander had been in a foul mood since injuring his fingers while working a 9a sport route. A renowned finger doctor had prescribed six months of complete rest, dampening Alexander's enthusiasm for future climbing objectives; he had to come to terms with his first real injury. But I was able to motivate him, as my experience with injury-related breaks was living proof that you can always come back stronger. In the meantime, I suggested we go on an expedition—to distract ourselves. This would be easy on the fingers, and getting up a summit would surely prove a cathartic experience. Alexander quickly got excited, and soon we had fashioned a master plan for the turn of the millennium. It would be a mix of an expedition and proper climbing, highlighting our joint portfolio: climb a mountain somewhere in the Himalayas in the spring, and then establish a new free climb on El Cap during Yosemite's Indian summer.

Pretty quickly, we agreed on Shivling in India's Garhwal Himalayas, which had a still-unfinished climb splitting light and shadow along the

6,543-meter (21,467-foot) peak's northeast ridge.

But before getting back to climbing, I initiated the planned band with Manni and three other friends. We named our stoner-rock combo after one of the hardest and most dangerous techno routes on El Capitan: the A5 *Plastic Surgery Disaster*, itself named for an album by the punk group Dead Kennedys. Two guitars, one bass, one drum set, and me as lead vocalist. We wrote the songs ourselves, basing our lyrics on my escape within the vertical realm, accompanied by the thundering riffs of my musical friends. It was rock 'n' roll at its best!

CHAPTER SEVEN

The Millennium

Shiva's Line

My family celebrated the traditional raising of the maypole on May 1. Marion was dressed in her dirndl, me in lederhosen, and Elias in a homemade cardigan. The next day, Alexander and I set off on our expedition. Saying my goodbyes was becoming more torturous with each new departure. Elias muttered, "Papa," while I held him in my arms, tearing my heart apart. Only ten more minutes. All of us standing in our living room, only the steady ticking of our wooden wall clock breaking the silence. Incessantly, on and on, and with each "tock" this clock was slicing down the time I had left with my loved ones. Back and forth and back again, just like the way I'd chosen to live my life: "At home, you want to get away; once you're gone, you want to return home."

As paradoxical as this approach to life might seem, it was also addictive. If only it weren't for the emotional pain when parting. Though, in a way, making these moments of departure intensely special was for me the only way to recognize what was important in life. Behind all the departure drama, I knew I owed this privileged life of having a family and living free in the mountains solely to Marion's trust and understanding.

After those ten minutes, time would remorselessly start ticking again: a last embrace, the pictures of Elias and Marion quickly stashed close to my heart, and then I was out the door. At the airport, we said our last farewells, keeping with our tradition of drinking one last Bavarian beer and wolfing down white sausages with sweet mustard.

Hours later, the sweltering, sticky air of India's capital, New Delhi, smacked us in the face. Thankfully, warring tempers had cooled somewhat this year, and firefights at the so-called "Line of Control" had been kept to a minimum. Perhaps both parties had learned that there could be neither winners nor losers in this war—only death and suffering. We spent two days in New Delhi, a city that, from our Western point of view, was at its limit. Too many people lived in far too little space, and it felt like more than half of them were traveling by car. If these endless traffic jams—this senseless honking coming from all sides—plus the unbearable heat, the acrid, coal-oxide-laden air, and the leaden sky heavy with dense smog spread across the entire globe, ours would be a bleak, frightening future indeed.

We crisscrossed the city, signing dozens of permits, until finally we had permission to climb Shivling, the Matterhorn of the Himalayas. For the Indians, the peak is the symbolic representation of one of their most important Hindu deities: Lord Shiva, the god of destruction and renewal.

After all these formalities had been taken care of, we drove a minibus toward the mountains, always following the holy Ganges, the mother of all life, past statues of gods, ashrams, yoga sites, and stray, feral holy cows, foraging in the accumulated roadside garbage. The farther behind we left the chaos of New Delhi, the bluer the skies turned, and the more everything corresponded to my preconceived notion of spiritual India. Everything was now much more colorful, glittery, and mystical, and the smells of spices, incense, patchouli oil, and marijuana were everywhere.

Barefoot pilgrims wandered along the side of the road, clad only in wraparound cloths, having apparently taken on the role of their gods.

They call themselves sadhus, the "enlightened ones." Their appearance is often mystical and ascetic: long beards, artistically tied-up Rasta locks, and faces painted with holy symbols. These pilgrims were walking in the same direction as us, up into the mountains to the sacred sites of their gods.

Unsurprisingly, this must have seemed like heaven on earth to the hippies more than fifty years ago. With The Beatles discovering Rishikesh, a small town on the Ganges, and John Lennon putting this magic into words with his "The Happy Rishikesh Song," this place at the gates of the Garhwal Himal had become famous worldwide. Melodic Hindu mantras spread around the world, and even in downtown Munich one could hear the ecstatically chanted *"Hare Krishna . . . hare, hare . . ."*

As a devout Christian, I'd be lying if I claimed that I was not captivated by this pictorial form of religion, overloaded as it is with its deep, mystical truths. The higher the mountains to the left and right of the road rose, the more sacred everything around us seemed to become. Striking rocks had been painted in colorful patterns. A spring that gushed almost unnaturally from a rock face had been framed with great effort and decorated with a blue effigy of Shiva. Basically, all the whims of nature that deviated from the norm had a divine origin and had been turned into spiritual places.

In the hillside town of Devprayag, the Ganges forms from the two individual headwaters: the Alaknanda and Bhagirathi, originating from alpine glaciers up high. We turn left, follow the Bhagirathi, and reach the village of Gangotri in the evening. Hotels, restaurants, and small stores crowd the narrow valley, while the wild Bhagirathi rushes over a water-polished rock step and provides the background music for this holy place. On a small hill, a whitewashed temple dedicated to the holy Mother Ganga, the source of all life, overlooks the sanctuary. Inside this simple building, we find a brightly painted deity and a round stone set in the ground, buttered and covered with flowers. Shiva's lingam is often interpreted in the West as a phallic symbol, and, as is custom, this lingam, in turn, has its own fanciful, mythical origin story.

Come nightfall, we experience hundreds of pilgrims undertaking ritualistic, sacred worship—a mystical dance of fire accompanied by the deafening ringing of bells. It's surprisingly like a Christian service: there's a priest in a festive robe, then the sermon, then chants, prayers, and rituals, the incense flavored with ganja, all while everything focuses on a holy symbol, a colorfully painted round stone—the lingam.

Behind Gangotri, the valley opens up. Everything now seems lovelier, gentler, and greener, and even the Bhagirathi, which roared wildly downvalley, settles down to flow smoothly through its wide riverbed. Framed by the glaciated mountains, which rise like luminous sentinels to form the left and right walls of the valley, the mighty 6,856-meter (22,494-foot) Bhagirathi looms over the vista. No wonder, according to legend, that this place is the key to salvation and liberation—the gateway to so-called nirvana.

Our porters hike us along a well-trodden path that Hindu pilgrims use to reach one of India's holiest places: the spring of Bhagirathi. For us, it is a big glacial cave from which icy water gushes forth, but for devout Hindus, it is the source of all life, the beginning of Mother Ganga. They lovingly call this place Gaumukh because it looks like a cow's mouth from which their holy water springs. Every Indian lucky enough to be reincarnated into the highest caste takes a full bath here, cleansing themself of sin in the icy-cold spring and booking a ticket directly to Nirvana for the moment when Lord Shiva ends their earthly life.

We wash our faces briefly and take a sip of the icy water—because who knows? Maybe it will help us summit Shivling. We fill our water bottles for the steep, gravelly climb up the lateral moraine to Tapovan. Even though the Gaumukh 650 feet below us is the gateway to nirvana, this is heaven for us because nothing on Earth could really be more beautiful to a mountaineer: a huge meadow full of flowers, littered with gigantic granite boulders perfect for climbing, and then crowning it all the Himalayan Matterhorn, rocketing into the infinite blue of the Garhwal sky. Right in the center is our prospective line, drawn by the light and shadow directly up the mountain. Everything seems so balanced and preternaturally beautiful that one immediately understands why the Hindus see Shivling as holy.

As if from nowhere, a sadhu who must have been living in a small cave throughout the summer months suddenly materializes. He greets us with a silent smile and a peace sign. Then he scribbles his needs onto a piece of paper, briefly outlining his story in English—he is not permitted to speak because he's taken a spiritual vow of silence. This "Silent Baba" sees himself as a spiritual guardian, and asks for something to eat. We are happy to share our provisions. He is then quick to highlight the importance of Shivling.

In Hindu mythology, Shivling it is not a mountain, but Lord Shiva himself.

I have the highest respect for this small, lanky man who lives here at 4,000 meters, dressed only in a thin gown. He asks why we have come. I blink up at the Shivling and start explaining our intentions. He closely watches my hands as I mime our line of ascent: down through the snow gully, out left to the sharp ridge, up to the col, diagonally left following the pillar, and then straight up to the summit. He flashes his white teeth at us through his full black beard in a cryptic smile, winks, turns around, and starts praying in silence, hopefully appeasing Lord Shiva with his prayers.

Days later, Alexander and I are finally approaching our dream climb, initially ascending slippery grass slopes, then boot-packing through a steep couloir until we reach the first rock band. Old, tattered, fixed-rope remnants from previous attempts mark the entry point. We climb two more pitches, sleep in a small tent at the bottom of the couloir for better acclimatization, and descend to basecamp the next day.

In the meantime, we have made friends with a Swiss team—Bruno, Iwan, and Irma—that also wants to bag this infamous summit. Two of them plan to reach the summit via the Japanese Route, a line just to the right of our scouted climb. Subsequently, they plan to climb the normal route as a party of three.

We are more than lucky with our newfound friends. They are entertaining, sociable, and humorous; should we get ourselves into a bad place on the mountain, they will surely have our back. There is no mountain rescue you may call; no helicopter like in the Alps. Only one rule dictates progress in these mountains: help yourself, because no one else will.

Then I get sick and end up tent-bound. Alexander, however, is ready to go and wants to push our line farther with Bruno and Iwan. They climb along tattered fixed ropes, slabs, and cracks in dubious weather, and complete another significant section. This positive news alone, in conjunction with the fact that should high pressure set in, we stand a really good chance of succeeding, miraculously seems to cure me.

After several days of bad weather, the sky clears in the evening, the last snow clouds dissipate, and the fine needle of the Thommen altimeter shows fifty meters less, which means the air pressure has risen and hopefully implies good weather for several days to come. It is not long before the stars come out, framing the majestic Shivling, and then, dreamlike, a full moon appears just above the summit. It's an image that immediately recalls the blue painting of Shiva we encountered during our approach. I get goosebumps all over, and an inner voice tells me that now is the right time to get going.

Bruno and Iwan are also ready, and the four of us find ourselves standing next to each other shortly after midnight, already wearing mountaineering boots, and shouldering our backpacks loaded with food for the next three days. Bruno and Iwan head toward the Japanese Route, while we set off to the pillar's base.

When Alexander and I arrive at our fixed ropes, the sun is already peeking over Bhagirathi and the weather could not be better—no wind, and the sky is azure. Only, Alexander does not feel it. He feels weak and lethargic, and pretty soon, it is clear to us both that this needs to be our high point for today. We deposit our backpacks behind a boulder and rappel, frustrated. Iwan and Bruno, on the other hand, continue to climb and manage to push out their ropes.

Back at basecamp, I worry we have missed our window—in theory only, it turns out, because Alexander begins to complain of a strong fever and sore throat. Meanwhile, the weather changes for the worse, slightly putting our minds at rest about losing valuable time on the mountain. The sky still shines in that almost unnatural gentian blue, but swirling plumes of snow whip off the ridges, and our Swiss friends are surely not having an easy ride.

I alternate between binoculars and Alexander. Iwan and Bruno are making very slow progress because of the high-altitude winds, and Alexander is lying on his mat in the tent, sleeping. This obviously does him well because the next day he he's overcome his infection. Plus, the wind dies down toward evening, and we decide to go for it again at midnight.

Back at our backpacks, history repeats itself: Alexander is falling behind again, powerless, empty, and without any energy. Pretty quickly and without commenting on the situation, we pack everything up and rappel again. This time with the backpacks, because we are both aware that there will not be a third attempt.

Iwan and Bruno also give their all on the mountain, but it is not quite enough for a summit bid, primarily due to the gale-force winds. Back down in Tapovan, our cook invites us to a common dinner. While we sit around the table, Alexander, visibly distraught, announces that his tonsillitis has the better of him and that a further attempt would be pointless, both from a mountaineering and medical perspective. He knows he can only hope for improvement if he descends to lower altitudes as quickly as possible.

There is an awkward silence. Even though I had an inkling of how everything would come to pass, at this moment, I don't want to give in, and I'm not convinced by his decision to leave the next day.

Somehow, deep in my heart, I still hold out hope that everything could take a turn for the better. But now, it is official. Goodbye, Shivling; there goes our dream line! Lord Shiva, the destroyer and creator, has killed off our dream with his trident. Is that why this Silent Baba was grinning so mischievously—because he knew what would unfold? Such are my moronic thoughts, searching only for an explanation as to why Alexander and I struck out once again on a Himalayan expedition.

Our cook serves us rice with curried vegetables, garnished with a tomato artfully carved like a rose. Tasty Indian food, but both of us have lost our appetite. Iwan bawls out a cheerful *"A Guadn zamm!"*—"Enjoy your meal!"—to our dreary little group. Then, with his very next breath, he blurts out a bombshell: "Well, I have a suggestion: If Alexander is going to the G'sundwern, I could team up with you, Thomas—if it's okay with both of you, naturally. Bruno and Irma will ascend via the normal route; that way, we still have a chance to bag this summit!" Iwan's suggestion puts me and the group at a loss initially. For a moment, I stop breathing. I cannot send Alexander down alone while I decide to get all heroic with a new partner. Only when Alexander tells me that it doesn't matter to him what I decide while reassuring me that he's doing just fine on his own do I jump on the opportunity. The mountain has captured me yet again, and I fail to hear my brother's silent cry for help hidden in the subtext.

The next morning, Alexander hugs me goodbye, heading home to sort himself out. In contrast, I'm heading up the mountain for an unbelievable adventure. "Hey, Thomas, be safe, and please take care of yourself, and I'll see you back home!"—"Yes, Alexander, see you there." All I really want is to raise his spirits and say something motivational—"Hey, Alexander, it'll be all right!"—but I fail to think of anything appropriate or meaningful. I quickly swallow my rising sadness and say: "Look, the good thing is, you'll soon get a proper beer again!" His spirits buoyed, Alexander laughs, shoulders his backpack, and leaves. By God, I don't have a good gut feeling as I watch him stroll alone across the Tapovan meadow and then disappear behind the moraine. But the fire for adventure has been rekindled, and I put my focus back on this singular ridgeline where light meets shadow.

Iwan is a lanky, tall Swiss man with buzz-cut hair. He is an experienced mountaineer and motivated to experience adventure in its purest form, with me as his partner. A few days later, we are already in the middle of the steepest terrain of our magical line; Shiva stops us in our tracks, offloading thunder and lightning while we hunker down in our warm sleeping bags at our exposed high camp. Axes, pitons, and all our metallic gear start buzzing, the adrenaline in our bodies making us as nauseous as if we were cranking difficult moves 60 feet above our last reliable piece of protection.

A thunderstorm is probably the most unpredictable event in the mountains and one that nobody needs. We deposit our equipment a safe distance from the tent under a slab of rock and then hunker down, wearing our mountaineering boots inside the tent to insulate against a ground current, should there be a lightning strike. After an hour, the storm passes and we can finally sleep. Yes, Iwan is cool; even in this extreme situation, he stays calm and focused, and above all, he keeps his black sense of humor. He doesn't replace my brother, but we work well together in this German-Swiss climbing synthesis.

Another forty-eight hours in the overhanging world of Shivling, and again I am forced to put life and limb on the line: We have been climbing for hours, at first in bright sunshine and pleasant temperatures, but then later in fog and through thick clouds, and then finally in snow. But because everything above us is overhanging, the miserable weather doesn't bother us much. However, the climbing challenges me completely. I am stagger upward, using Cliffhangers and shallow pitons to ascend a brittle, exfoliating flake; all placements can barely hold body weight, meaning a fall would zipper the gear straight from the wall. This feels like the trickiest thing I've ever climbed, and only madness could have got me this exposed.

Just sixty-five feet in two hours, and there's no turning back once I'm climbing. The only way is up. There is still ten feet left to go, then it looks like the climbing eases off. Above, I eye a compact crack feature where I can certainly place a bomber piece. But these final ten feet—a chossy hairline seam—look even trickier, more difficult, and more dangerous than what lies below me. I finger a Knifeblade from my harness and place it in a small crack. With three hammer blows, I sink the piton into the hollow-sounding rock. Now I take a deep breath and load it slowly, as I have done dozens of times in Yosemite and on Latok II. The pin seems to hold my body weight.

As I step higher in my etriers, I feel something shift—I'm moving down! Adrenaline rushes to my head; my blood pressure skyrockets. *Shit, my piton is going to blow!* Then, by some miracle, the eye of the piton lodges on a tiny flake. Lord almighty, I do not want to imagine the consequences of a 100-foot whipper here. "Take a deep breath," I tell myself. "Stay cool, be cool now, just like the time back when you were 17 on *Rauhnachtstanz*"—that first route my brother and I ever put up, the runout VIII- (5.10) in the Berchtesgaden Alps. I climb back up, pull the loosened piton out of the crack by hand, and reposition it. Again, I pray aloud: "Stay cool, Thomas, stay cool now." From below, Iwan joins with a motivating, "Thomas, you're doing great."

"Whether I'm going to be great, we'll find out right now; watch out, Iwan, it's going to get really hot out here."—"Thomas, what are you talking about? There are no ladies close by!"

I have to smile. This Swiss humor really helps calm my nerves. I take a breath and weight the piece again. I find a tiny crimp up to the right, bear down on it, and hence manage to get some weight off this dodgy placement. Avoiding all jerky movements, I slow my breathing, my heart rate drops, and my placement stays put. Now the same game starts again. Jam the Knifeblade above me, sink it with careful blows, take a deep breath, tense up, and spread my weight across the holds as much as possible. Finally, when I sink a bomber piton with singing blows in a solid crack, I feel victorious beyond belief.

"Yeeeeaaauuu, Iwan, I got it!"—"Great, Thomas, when it gets spicy, you get even better!"

I must laugh—a Swiss with a sense of humor, a rare species indeed. Ten minutes later, I reach a small ledge and set up a belay using cams in a perfect hand crack. Below lies 100 feet of psychological torture, the likes of which I have never experienced. Shiva seems to have a lot in store for us.

Although the weather is far from perfect come morning, we leave nothing to chance and go for it, all guns blazing. The climbing is overhanging but manageable, and in the evening, we summit, the sky bursting with clouds laden with snow.

Days later, I meet Silent Baba in Tapovan and recount our story. He wants to know every detail, and then he starts laughing and says that we found Lord Shiva through the way of the heart. I sketch Shivling into his notebook, trace our new route up the wall, and sign it "Shiva's Line!"

Apart from finding a wonderful, new climbing partner who never lost his sense of humor even when the going got tough, I take home far more than the story of a difficult first ascent. Rather, it becomes a spiritual expedition to my inner self. I have been immensely touched by the encounters with people in Pakistan and India during these two expeditions, realizing that there is no one right, wrong, better, or pious way to God.

As contrasting as our paths may feel, in the end, they all lead to the same summit! It's merely the choice of route that sets us apart. No one person is better, worse, or more pious, but everyone is a mountaineer, trying to reach the summit via their purest path. A path in space, where there is nothing above you or beside you, one that lets you be truly immersed in the presence of God.

Everyone who believes in the divine is a mountaineer at heart.

The Spirits That Called to My Brother

When I returned to civilization, I went straight to see Alexander. He'd recovered from tonsillitis and congratulated me on Shivling, but also announced that he needed time to digest this second unsuccessful expedition. Returning from India, he'd fallen into a deep mental crisis. Everything that had meant something to him in life had become his greatest enemy—speaking frankly, he was in a shit place and felt sick at the thought of embarking on a new project in the mountains. After this failed expedition, only a void was left. Everything that had freed him before now trapped him like a wild animal.

Back in Berchtesgaden, my own life was becoming all-encompassing, so I did not catch on to Alexander's plight, as he was still living in Traunstein some distance away. The new owner of our former property gave us an eviction notice without any warning, and we were literally out on the street from one moment to the next. We packed everything we owned, moved to Oberau near Berchtesgaden—back to where Marion's parents lived—and set up our temporary abode in a small apartment they had previously rented to holidaymakers. Now there was no longer any place to remind me of my past. Everything was gone for good: our farm, the apartment building, our apple tree, the property, everything.

After this financially nerve-wracking time, I was glad for a fresh start in a new place. After all, when you have nothing left to give, you also have nothing left to lose, and Oberau wasn't the worst place to start over. Truth be told, Oberau was a gem, located above the tiny town of

Markt Berchtesgaden, with a small church, an inn, a grocery store, and a premium view of the mountains including the Untersberg, the Rauher Kopf, the Reiteralm, the Hochkalter, the Watzmann, and the Göll. Somehow, I felt like I could finally unpack my boxes, plant a family tree in the garden of our new home, and put down roots for real. I hoped so much that this could finally become our *Dahoam*—the Bavarian word for "home." Actually, it was a bit atypical for an original Stone Monkey, because a Monkey ought to fight for every bit of freedom and independence. But I needed this grounding; I needed this base, a place from which to launch my alpine visions, to anchor me to the here and now as I focused on my goals.

Meanwhile, our parents had created a new beginning for themselves in a small wooden house in Oberau, which they lovingly renovated. So, they, too, found their new home, and at least a little more peace returned to the Hubers after these years of turmoil.

Golden Gate

Two months after India, Alexander asked if I'd like to go back to Yosemite, perhaps to try something new on El Cap. Of course, I couldn't say no. We were supposed to go in mid-September, but at the end of August, I crashed my motorbike and dislocated my elbow. Once again, I needed the whole shebang before going on a trip: hospital, a plaster cast, etc. When I asked the doctor how long it would take until I would be up and running again, since I was flying out to Yosemite in two weeks, he could only mutter: "That's probably not going to happen with Djosimeit!" "No, it's called Yosemite!"—"Yeah, well, Yosemite it is!" He pointed out that because the capsule and ligaments on my arm were badly injured, there was no guarantee it would return to the way it was before. I had heard something similar from the big-headed staff doctor at the Bundeswehr hospital in Munich when I had a herniated disc at age 20. Statements like these always seem to ramp up my fighting spirit, and as a default, I avoid self-pity.

Max Reichel, a good friend who had often accompanied us with a film camera, stood in for me as a climbing partner at short notice. He helped Alexander on El Cap scouting out a new free climb while I was once again a regular at the local physiotherapist. My physio, Sigrun, got me back to my original condition in no time, and I flew out to the States two weeks later in the hot pursuit of my brother. Of course, I couldn't resist informing my former physician that I would be flying out to the "Djosimeit" the next day.

Indian summer at last. I inhaled the smell of the Yosemite Valley, so unmistakably flavored with the scent of the pines. The thermals off El Cap were creating gentle waves in the golden-yellow grass of the El Cap Meadows, and here we were, Alexander, Max, and myself, swigging beers and eating nachos. Alexander had finally made peace with the events of the Shivling expedition and was a changed man. Full of enthusiasm, he told us about a near-perfect free-climbing route on El Cap. It looked awesome. The first part followed the *Salathé* to El Cap Spire, then veered out right into a golden granite ocean, following the aid line of the *Heart Route*, which had free-climbable features all the way to the top-out. Alexander had thoroughly prepared the line and felt it would go at 5.13; now all that remained was to redpoint this beauty—to lead each pitch without falling.

And off we went! The climbing surpassed Alexander's description. En route to El Cap Spire, we had to get past the formidable-looking and torturous Monster Offwidth, a sixty-five-foot-long eight-inch offwidth, slick, vertical, and strenuous throughout. For us Europeans, this section posed the physical crux, as offwidth climbing is nearly nonexistent in the Alps. After a comfortable bivouac on El Cap Spire, we embarked upon the climbing proper, virgin territory consisting of technical slabs interspersed with tricky boulder problems, chimneys, splitter cracks, and a spectacular traverse above butt-clenching exposure on the thirtieth pitch.

Overall, we had a superb time on El Cap and while hanging out in our portaledge camp. Dangling in space, Alexander could finally open up and let me know how much he he'd been on edge—"This exposure here on El Cap is nothing compared to the anxiety I was feeling after the Shivling expedition, Thomas—I can tell you that." He had lost all direction and was psychologically burned out, and the only solution was to drop all expectations and do what he loved: pure rock climbing. Two consecutive failed expeditions had been at least one too many! And now this experience high up on El Cap was literally healing his soul. As long as Alexander's psyche was still in turmoil, he would continue along this trajectory—following his own passions, and not trying to live up to others' expectations.

On top of El Cap, we sealed our redpoint with an emotional handshake. "Hey, Thomas, what do you think of the *Golden Gate* name?"—"Yes, Alexander, that is exactly what I want to call it!" We rolled another cigarette, shared the last of our beers, and gazed into the distance. The warm wind caressing my face reminded me of our recent days on the wall. I had to smile; there was no name more fitting for this route. For Alexander, it really was his *Golden Gate* back into life.

CHAPTER EIGHT

My Way

The Decision

After this trip to the United States, I knew I could not count on Alexander as a climbing partner for future expeditions to the big mountains. He had had his share of the Ogres, the cold peaks, and the thin air; he wanted to focus on climbing, feel his fingers, and trust his body. He had been dreaming of the overhanging wall of *Bella Vista* on the Western Zinne in the Dolomites for quite some time, a route he had solo aided two years earlier in winter. Of course, it would have been cool to climb these amazing roofs with Alexander because we were brothers, crafted of the same clay, so to speak. But for the moment, we were walking on different paths.

It was still wintry at home in Berchtesgaden that season of 2000/2001. We had settled in well in Oberau, went sledding with Elias, and built snowmen; in between, I was doing talks focused on my successes in the year 2000. But in my mind, I was already pitching my tent below the Ogre with Iwan and packing my backpack to set off into the unknown. I was utterly obsessed with this mountain, just like Alexander was obsessed with the yellow, overhanging roofs of the Western Zinne. Our lives were directed toward specific goals, driving our every move and decision. There was no room for compromise, and because we were so similar in this respect, there was a silent understanding between us that we would be following our individual aspirations in the coming year.

When you are burning for a single goal, you feel that there's only this project in the world, this one mountain, and that everybody else around you must feel the same. In my case, it was the Ogre, and I was sure that soon the international mountaineering elite would be lining up at the base because, in my mind, the second ascent of the Ogre was nothing less than a first ascent of sorts. It is essential to know that the route taken to the summit by the English when they first climbed the Ogre in 1977 had become unclimbable due to a vast serac collapse, so any repeat would essentially be a "new" line.

The cards had truly been reshuffled on this infamous mountain. In 1987, the French climbed the south pillar for the first time but failed farther up on the summit ice field. Nevertheless, from then on, the massive granite pillar was soon seen as the best and safest way to tackle the Ogre. And yet all later attempts had failed, as had ours in 1999, merely reaching mid-height on the pillar. If we take the sum of all failed expeditions as an indicator, this mountain has become one of our planet's most challenging and desirable—well, at least in my humble opinion.

Like me, Iwan had been motivated for the Ogre ever since Shivling, but all attempts on my part to find a third partner had failed. Jan, Toni, even Michal had already cut their teeth on the Ogre and needed a break from this Man-Eater, who liked to gobble up climbers' stoke—well, maybe everyone's but mine!—like it was his favorite food. Although the search was not easy, in the end, we enlisted the Swiss Urs Stöcker, who was still, fortunately, completely unbiased toward the Ogre.

Finally, our gear was topped off by a golden ice axe—the Piolet d'Or, the most prestigious award in alpinism—for our climb of Shivling. In mid-June 2001, I could finally catch up with my racing thoughts and pitch my tent in the meadow at the edge of the Uzun-Brakk Glacier, with a view of Latok II and the Ogre's Thumb. In the kitchen tent, Ismail and Quasim were cooking again while Urs, Iwan, and I packed our backpacks for the following day. But this time round, we were not alone: as feared, the mountain had become a much-coveted prize.

Besides us, there were three other expeditions on the mountain, each hoping to bag the second ascent. The Südtirol climbers Hans Kammerlander and Luis Brugger were at basecamp, trying to find a way through the serac zone to the right of the first-ascent line. Then there was a three-person American team who, like us, wanted to climb the south pillar. And, on the other side of the mountain, i.e., in the Choktoi, the Slovenian Silvo Karo with his team was taking his chances. Hans Kammerlander was quite relaxed. He didn't think he had much of a chance of reaching the summit and wanted mainly to acclimatize for K2, but he was also there to get acquainted with the mountains far from the well-known 8,000-meter peaks. The Americans were ready to give it their all. Straight from the get-go, the race was on as we battled for an alpine pole position. However, we soon agreed amongst our team to give way to all other expeditions because this mountain was too difficult, too dangerous, and too beautiful to be the setting for an "Alpine Extreme Race." Such exploits have all too often ended in tragedy. Just take the Eiger or the Matterhorn, where climbers set aside common sense and died for it, their decisions spurred on solely by the actions of others.

I could not and did not want to climb a mountain such as the Ogre like that. I firmly believe in destiny—that everything happens for a reason—and so I was okay banishing the Ogre from my thoughts. Moreover, deep in my heart, I knew that the Ogre would not make it easy for us. While Kammerlander and the Americans continued their preparations, we focused on the still-unclimbed Ogre III, which rises to nearly 7,000 meters directly above basecamp. Even though this mountain was overshadowed by its big brother, it was, perhaps, next to Latok II, the most striking mountain in this valley—symmetrical and sharp, a Swiss mountain from a picture book, looking as perfect as the Matterhorn logo on a Toblerone chocolate bar. The mountain is guarded by a labyrinth of broken glaciers, the sharp, steep southwest ridge being the most alluring line to the summit.

An Italian team had attempted an ascent but failed before the rock-pyramid section, so this peak was totally virgin alpine territory. After all the turmoil around the Ogre had been worked out, we finally got a forecast of good weather for the coming week. This time not from our Thommen altimeter or by a subjective meteorological interpretation from Ismail, who liked to send us off with a "Tomorrow, Inshallah, good weather." No, this time the good news came directly from the alpine weather center in Innsbruck, from our friend Charly, transmitted via a satellite phone—our new trump card stationed in our basecamp tent.

Charly, whose real name is Karl Gabl, is a relatively short, lanky Tyrolean with a cheeky French mustache; he's a passionate mountaineer and meteorologist who uses various weather models to interpret the weather globally, in our case for 35 degrees, 56 minutes, and 53 seconds north latitude and 75 degrees, 45 minutes, and 12 seconds east longitude. So, we knew when a five-day high was approaching or when the next cold front was heading toward us, and could plan accordingly.

Once we had the sat-phone technology, it was hard to imagine going on an expedition without this friendly Tyrolean voice coming through the earpiece. Charly has been instrumental in the success of many an international expedition, using the satellite phone to help revolutionize alpinism. This invention, meanwhile, brought another big change to my expedition climbing: I no longer had to sit for hours on the moraine waiting for porters to bring letters from home, but could instead just dial home to talk to Marion and hear Elias babbling.

In this first period of good weather, we got after Ogre III, establishing our camp on a small shoulder at about 6,000 meters. Above, we fixed the tricky mixed terrain to the steeply rising southeast ridge, reaching the base of an overhanging, somewhat monstrous dihedral.

Hans Kammerlander and Luis Brugger, meanwhile, had realized that their route to the Ogre was too dangerous and moved their tents to K2 Basecamp. The Americans were already in the middle of the pillar and wanted to go all in come the next spell of good weather. And what Silvo Karo was planning stayed an enigma. Everyone had had enough time to acclimatize and prepare, so now it was time for our summit bids.

And the good weather did indeed come. According to Charly, four days without wind and clouds were on their way. It was going to be nippy, but not unsafe or so cold you'd get frostbite. The summit days we had all been waiting for were upon us. But then, I began to doubt: *Were we on the right track? Had we given way on the Ogre without having put up enough of a fight?* There it was again, the Ogre, tormenting me from the inside. Finally, these doubts were dispelled by the hissing of our kerosene stove. Ismail was sitting in the kitchen tent, smoking a cigarette and casually proclaiming, "This time, Inshallah, no problem, I will pray to Allah, then, Inshallah, summit!" Quasim cooked up our breakfast. We had coffee with porridge, and afterward we said goodbye with a heartfelt embrace, and they gave us a "*Bismillah*"—"In the name of God"—to go.

For the next three days, everything went as Ismail had predicted because, from his point of view, Allah wanted it that way. Around noon, the three of us were 2 meters below the summit. It was windless. Only light clouds mottled the blue sky, and behind us lay the best, steepest climbing, which would easily befit El Cap, interspersed with sharp alpine ridges and exposed mixed terrain. Only the plod up the last 100 meters in sugary, baseless snow had almost seen us throw in the towel. But we did not give in, even if one step forward often meant two steps back. And now, so close to the top of Ogre III, we paused. "Hey, Iwan and Urs, guys, I think we've got it because we can't go any farther. Why don't we take the last step together?"—"That's great, Thomas!" replied Iwan, and Urs added:

"Ahhh, I can't believe it!"

I couldn't believe it either, because it was so close to my heart—something completely different compared to all the other summits I had climbed. No human had ever stood on this snowy peak; we were the first. I felt like a true explorer and a pioneer, just like my childhood heroes Hermann Buhl, Walter Bonatti, Reinhold Messner, and Wolfgang Güllich. I was smiling from ear to ear. Some discover a continent, others take a massive step for humanity, but really we have achieved nothing. Still, this was one of my most crucial moments as a climber.

I consciously focused on the last feet as if crossing the threshold of our front door, uttering a quiet, humble "Thank you." We then cheered and sealed the first ascent with a handshake. As sacred as this moment was, I nonetheless felt like a little devil was scratching inside me, even though I'd sworn to be grateful for this climb and not obsess over the Ogre. Right before we'd summitted, we'd stopped at a vantage point to observe the Ogre more closely, scanning its summit ice field to see if the Americans or Slovenians had left any footprints. I was sure they would also summit today because the weather was too good. We realized how pathetic and obsessive our behavior was when we found no evidence of their passage. I was ashamed of my greedy thinking, and we'd turned our backs on the Ogre and looked toward Latok II, Masherbrum, Broad Peak, and almighty K2.

A day later, we were back at basecamp, and our Pakistani friends had once again outdone themselves. Our goat had been slaughtered, and on a beautiful tablecloth in the middle of the meadow artfully arranged a paradisiacal menu, with braised goat meat over rice, a pizza, roasted vegetables, baked bread, and even a cake. If there had been any beer, it would have been heaven on earth. The Americans were also back at basecamp, visibly drawn from their exertions up high. They congratulated us on a successful climb and told us that at about 6,500 meters, just above the top of the pillar, they had gotten stuck in the bottomless snow and abandoned their ascent. There would be no second round for them. The Ogre had challenged them beyond belief, and they were satisfied with their effort.

If I had said out loud that our food tasted all the better for our success, it would have been insensitive—though brutally honest. Even if I was secretly pleased that the Man-Eater had bared its teeth at them, I was glad they were back at basecamp safe and sound. A few days later, the Yanks left, and we enjoyed our time with Ismail and Quasim in basecamp. We still had some time left and a realistic chance to climb the Ogre. As we had done in 1999, we climbed to about one-third height on the pillar, fixing ropes to around 6,000 meters and thus giving us the ultimate high point to launch for the top.

The plan was good, except that the weather played Wagner's *Götterdämmerung* for over a week. The snow clouds in the mountains were heavy and thick, and had we not had the satellite phone linking us to the outside world, we probably would have wandered home like the Americans. But the almost daily contact with home shortened the nerve-wracking wait for better weather. Marion and Elias were fine, enjoying summer in Bavaria! And the phone also delivered news of climbing developments across the Karakoram. On K2, all the climbers, including Hans Kammerlander, were waiting for better weather at basecamp. There was also news from the Ogre: Silvo Karo had made it to 6,200 meters with his team, but the risk of going farther was too high, and they had ended their expedition. This was the news of the day for us, and it motivated us to sit out the bad weather because we were now the last team in position to close the bag on the Ogre this season.

After eight days of eating, reading, playing cards, and sleeping, we got news from Charly about the weather finally calming down: four days of viable weather might be on their way, our last possible chance this year. At 3:00 a.m., as we stood in front of the kitchen tent to be welcomed by Ismail and Quasim, our backpacks loaded and ready, something inside me resisted leaving. I'd slept poorly and dreamed fitfully, the stars twinkled conspicuously above us, and my bad feeling was reinforced by Ismail throwing a "Maybe better stay in basecamp and wait." We were back in our sleeping bags after half an hour of back and forth, weighing facts and gut feelings. In the evening of the following day, a heavy thunderstorm and low-pressure system set in.

What You Do to Sleep Well

The clouds looked jet-black high up in the mountains as three dots of light moved farther and farther from the brightly lit kitchen tent. If we hadn't had Charly's weather report in our pockets, which promised a fine, five-day weather window starting now, plus the excellent gut feeling on my part and Ismail's "Inshallah this time summit, I will pray to Allah!" in my ear, none of us would have set off—or we certainly would have turned back when it started snowing. Because I wanted to make light of this seemingly senseless mission, I started singing quietly to the rhythm of my breath–"Hey, Charly, I go, because you say, it goes, hey, Charly!" until it became a melody that drove me on.

Because of all the "Hey, Charly!"-ing, I didn't notice that we were almost knee-deep in fresh snow on the Uzun-Brakk Glacier. I was surprised that the boys, Urs and Iwan, followed me so stoically, in total silence. It was moronic what we were doing; our glacial ramble was only leading us into a whiteout. Maybe we needed to hike on a ways until reason finally got the better of us and someone spoke up. Our initial gut feelings and the errant weather report were returning to the forefront of our minds. By an almost magical coincidence, we found our gear stash in the middle of the by-now deeply snow-covered glacier: the helmets, the climbing harnesses, and a rope. Everything was iced up and stiff.

Then came the first, obvious comment from Iwan: "What are we doing here? Do you really believe we will climb Ogre in this weather—it's nonsense!" He had finally said what we were all thinking. Although he was right, and there was no sign of Charly's five-day symphony of sun, we decided to wait up here another three hours, given that we'd be at basecamp long enough in the coming days and would have nothing better to do but eat, read, play cards, and sleep.

I found a cavernous crevasse very close to our stashed gear. We knocked the icicles off the ceiling into the black void, and then huddled together on a tiny, square patch of ice so as not to get completely soaked. I was desperate, grumbling, "This damn weather! Ogre's doing in my head." Urs said: "Yep, we won't have a chance with this snow. I think it's better that we get off this mountain. I could eat breakfast; I'm hungry already!"—"Okay, if we go, I want *paranthas!*" But Iwan insisted on pancakes. Ultimately, Urs and I overruled Iwan, and there would be paranthas.

Amidst our animated conversation, we had completely overlooked that it had stopped snowing, and peeking out of our icy shelter, saw bits of blue shimmering through the dark clouds. Had Charly been right about dream weather being on its way, only off by a few hours? It was worth a try!

Even though the mountains were blanketed in snow from the past few days, we continued on and broke trail up to the south pillar in the ever-deepening snow. I was in front, Iwan behind me, and Urs in the rear.

In the meantime, the sky was opening, and the sun was flashing through the gaps in the clouds. Despite these glimpses of hope, I remained plagued by doubt: "This damn couloir up here leading to the south pillar could be pretty darn dangerous with all the snow and sunshine, but so could the snow-covered rock above it." And: "Is this even going to be climbable in these conditions?" If we put all the facts on the table and looked at them realistically, we had no chance of succeeding. And yet, we fools marched on, if only to be able to tell the folks back home we'd left no stone unturned.

We walked silently, taking it slowly, and I was sure I was not alone in my doubts. Then I felt a little jerk on the rope, followed by a torrent of Swiss expletives. I didn't understand much in the flurry of comments, but a *"hure Schissdreck!"*—"Fucking shit" in English—was included for good measure. I looked back to see Iwan mired to his knees in the ice water of a snow-covered glacial lake. The snow cover had held me, but Iwan had punched through and now had soaking feet. I interpreted it as a sign to turn around: "Hey, guys, I don't think this makes any sense. Let's have breakfast, eat paranthas or even pancakes!" But Iwan only said: "We don't have to turn around because of wet feet. I've already lost my appetite, and besides, I've got spare socks. Fuck it—they will be dry again on the summit!"

I laughed out loud at Iwan's optimism and said that if we were going to continue, we would have to hurry before the sun emptied out the entrance couloir. The first small avalanches had started to shoot off the walls around us, forming debris clouds, an impressive display of the dynamic energy latent in these massive mountains.

We picked up the pace, crossing a flat, snowy plateau below an imposing, overhanging granite wall that towered 500 meters above us. To the right of it was the notorious 300-meter snow flank that would take us to the south pillar. The sun was already smacking the snow in the upper third of the couloir, and it was only a matter of time before all the white stuff came down in one fell swoop. We were panting, walking faster, suppressing thoughts of this ticking time bomb that was ready to go off at any minute. Iwan crossed to the right, to the beginning of the snow gully. Then, near the bergschrund, we halted in our tracks. Iwan sank in the bottomless snow, and pretty soon the Swiss, who had been so highly motivated earlier, gave up and reiterated that this was all a "hure Schissdreck" and that it was also much too *"huregefähr-lich"*—"fucking dangerous."

Despite the tense situation, I laughed again, charmed by the uniquely Swiss fusillade of swear words —these mountain people would easily win the World Championships of Profanity, if such an event existed. With this laugh, I gave myself another jolt and said, "Hey, Iwan, let a proper Bavarian try his luck, then I'll show you how it's done in our neck of the woods!" However, I soon recognized the hopelessness of moving forward and called back: "Shit, Iwan, it does not work one bit! Just push from behind . . . !"

At the last moment, my ice axe stuck. Gently I pulled myself out of this snow swamp and then helped Urs and Iwan across the bottomless crevasse. We'd reached the base of the deeply snowed-up, 300-meter flank. Only now did it hit home how crazy and dangerous our situation was. A half meter of snow covered the fixed rope we had left behind in the couloir, and without this theoretical line of safety, we were entirely at the mercy of the forces of nature.

The sun was creeping farther down the couloir, and it felt like we were on the count: twenty, nineteen, eighteen . . . Mortal terror bubbled up under my helmet. I would have loved to scream my thoughts and worries out loud, immediately. I felt that this Ogre had robbed us of our senses and threatened to eat us whole: *"We were blind to all the warning signs, to Iwan's mishap; we have simply gone too far. What a fucking mess—what are we doing?"* In this silent despair, Iwan set off, traversed left, and said dryly, "Now we're already here; let's give ourselves another ten minutes. If we find the rope, then off to the top we go. Otherwise, in two hours, paranthas for breakfast!"

It didn't even take five minutes, then Iwan held the red fixed rope and shouted at the mountain, "Ogreeeeee, here we come!" It sounded like a warrior's battle cry, and I replied, "You're nuts, bloody cheese-muncher!" We traversed over to him, clipped into the rope with our ascenders, and started upward. When we were hanging free in the fixed ropes up the south pillar, an avalanche cleared out the entire gully. When we arrived at 6,000 meters in the late afternoon at our gear cache, we could hardly believe our luck. The sun, low in the now-cloudless sky, sent us some evening warmth, conjuring up a crazy light to transform the south pillar into a golden-yellow ocean of granite. As if by magic, the sun had also swept all the slabs free of the freshly fallen snow, and only now, in this mountainous idyll, did we have time to reflect on our day. We could not believe what had gone down. It was surreal, and we asked ourselves whether diabolical madness or divine fate had brought us this far. We could not find an answer.

We cooked, ate dinner, and set up our portaledge, just like in 1999, when we had watched monsoon clouds gathering behind Nanga Parbat and did not dare to continue climbing. This time, thanks to Charly, we knew that we could continue. And there was another big difference: back then, there had been four of us, and we had had two portaledges. Today, there were three of us, and we'd all squeezed into one to save weight.

This had already been rehearsed at basecamp. Everybody had his position because, on an area only four by six feet, we had to stack three full-grown men like sardines. Iwan lay on the inside, I on the outside, and Urs, our smallest and lankiest, squeezed into the middle with his head at our feet. Between, we positioned our steaming liners, cooking utensils, climbing helmets, and headlamps. It was absolute chaos, plus the aluminum frame was bending suspiciously—it was a miracle that this contraption held our weight along with all the gear.

Everything was fixed to a piton and backed up by a Camalot so that we could rest easier. Sleeping in this cramped space, however, was out of the question. It was simply too claustrophobic, and everyone was gasping for air. Looking back, these moments in our hanging tent were the biggest challenge of our climb. Everything else was pure bliss: climbing on primarily solid, slabby granite, a maximum difficulty of 5.11, easy to protect, plus the weather on both days could not have been better. "Papageno's Aria" from Mozart's *The Magic Flute* would have made for the perfect background music.

The pillar summit at 6,500 meters, culminating in a sharp ridge, was a flat, snowy plateau. It was our third night on the mountain. We made a makeshift tent out of our portaledge and fly, and after a short night, we started again at 2:00 a.m. for our final leg up toward the summit. The stars were out, but a strong, gusty wind kept whipping up plumes of snow before us. Doubt set in once again, as we couldn't imagine summiting the exposed summit tower in this wind. Nevertheless, we pushed on through the snowy plateau. Firstly, we were experienced at this kind of senseless walking, and secondly, we hoped that the nocturnal winds would subside at daybreak. We moved quickly, soloing the final icy slope, and by 8:00 a.m., we're standing under the massive, final granite tower of the Ogre.

The air was getting thin at 7,000 meters. An old piton marked the start of the line the English took in 1977 up the summit tower, which, according to Doug Scott's descriptions, offered interesting climbing, meaning it likely threw everything that alpinism had to offer at you: difficult free climbing, tricky aid, pendulum traverses, and rugged mixed terrain.

Things started immediately with an almost-vertical rock gully filled with ice and snow. Not only was the climbing technically challenging, but the Ogre decided to send spindrift our way. The wind had picked up, and I needed to hunker down repeatedly due to all the stuff coming off the mountain. In addition, it was icy cold, so our water bottles had frozen solid. But to turn around now and hope for a better day, that choice was off the table; we had already pushed too far. I hooked my ice tools on a slight lip, protected only by a dodgy placement, and hauled my utterly exhausted body over an iced-up overhang. This was borderline behavior.

My entire being—my sole focus—was on upward progress, and I'd left all fear behind. I was uninterested in what was below, only on what was above.

I climbed on without fear, just as Scott must have two-plus decades earlier. What a crazy achievement for back then. After an hour, I finally reached a stance. Iwan and Urs followed with ascenders. No laughter passed their lips. How could they laugh? They had stood in knee-deep snow for an hour in extreme temperatures to belay me.

We would be up on the ridge with a few more easy meters. The wind smacked ice crystals into our faces. Even though the elements were hammering us, it was still beautiful: the steep flank of the north face plunged down to the seemingly endless glacial plateau of Snowlake, and ahead of us, there was yet another golden, smooth granite face, so perfect it looked machined. A hairline crack, which disappeared after twenty meters, split the granite block. That was our way up. Aiding, I bumped myself upward using micro-cams until I could clip an old piton. Scott himself must have placed it twenty-four years earlier. I gave it another few blows with my hammer to set it deeper in the crack. Above lay only crackless granite—a blank wall.

And yet we were on the right track. Ten meters to my right, a fat hand crack reared upward. Overcoming this blank passage was part of the classic school of "Yosemite Climbing": Urs lowered me back ten meters off the piton, and I started running back and forth along the vertical wall, like the pendulum of a clock. This kind of sheer acrobatics is also known as a pendulum traverse. With ever-increasing momentum, I eventually caught the hand crack to my right. Now came the most exciting moment: I fought against the pendulum swing yanking me back, jammed the back of my hand into the icy crack, plucked a red No. 1 Camalot off my harness, and slammed it into the crack. Taking a quick breath, I clipped my rope. The piece held.

Only now did I feel that I was utterly spent, and as if the exposed climbing, the wind, and the cold were not drama enough, my left eye clouded over 100 meters below the summit. Was this snow blindness? Or perhaps a symptom of altitude sickness from complete dehydration? We hadn't had anything to drink since 1:00 a.m. because all our water had frozen up. But I didn't feel bad; all my vital functions were still fine, and we could continue climbing as long as my right eye still had full vision.

My visual mono-perception made everything even more complicated; I could no longer estimate distances correctly. All movements were more tentative, slower, and more angular. I desperately searched out smears and handholds, while placing gear was highly troublesome. I circumnavigated a final roof on the right and found two old pitons in an iced-up gully, this time connected with tat—old slings. The English must have used this belay for rappelling. I fixed the rope and shouted, "Iwan, Urs, rope's fixed. I think we're almost there!"

In front of me was stair-stepping rock, above it a snow slope on which perched a square granite block. Was this the summit? I was too curious, and climbed on carefully without a rope. A little later, I was standing on this mighty block. Urs and Iwan followed, and only when they were standing next to me did I realize that we didn't have to go any farther. We were finally there; everything around us was lower. Only the summit cornice overhanging to the east was that little bit higher, as if the Ogre were taunting us: "You may climb on my head, but not on my crown." We humbly touched the highest point with our hands but kept our feet anchored on solid rock.

It was 3:30 p.m. It was windy, visibility was poor, and the clouds shot by like wispy rockets. Everything felt surreal—the climb, the exertion, the exhaustion. I felt empty. This was it? It was the end of a long dream, but what came now? Had I found what I was looking for? Probably. I was indeed happy to have arrived, but that was as far as I could go then and there. The ride on the Ogre was not over yet. The long and very demanding descent still lay ahead of us. Only forty meters below us was where Scott and Bonington's descent drama had begun, and the two Englishmen had survived only by the skin of their teeth.

We embraced, and from the bottom of my heart, I thanked Iwan and Urs for this moment of being here with me. We descended past Doug Scott's accident site, where he had broken both legs, and then onto the ice field below. I had long forgotten the cloudiness in my left eye because of the emotion of summiting. We downclimbed step by step, focused and slow, back to our tent pitched at the top of the pillar. It was nighttime when we finally reached camp. Iwan heated water, and we greedily slurped up warm soup. At that moment, it was the best food on Earth. Pretty soon, the three of us were lying in our mini tent. Again, a strong wind set in, blowing from the west. But we couldn't have cared less. We didn't have to go up anymore because we had been up today, and tomorrow it would only be down to basecamp and then home. The warm sleeping bag and the cozy tent gave me a sense of security, and I incorporated the tent walls rattling in the wind into my dreams, sleeping straight through until sunrise.

The storm swirled great plumes of snow off the summit ice field, and our tracks from the day before were barely visible. Now we knew that yesterday had been the best day for summiting. We stowed all our gear in the haulbag and dragged the fifty-plus-pound "pig" up to the edge of the overhanging wall. One strong push and it was off, free-falling down the entire south face. We hoped to find it intact in the glacial basin a few hours later, after we'd completed our descent.

Equipped with only the bare essentials, we abseiled pitch after pitch and cut away the old, rotten, fixed ropes from the wall with our pocketknives. Toward evening, we stood at the bottom of the basin. But our haulbag had exploded. Our ice tools, cams, stove, and tent had vanished. Only our sleeping bags had survived. So, in the end, we lost most of our gear. But what was this material loss when measured against our health and survival?

We reached basecamp four hours later. Ismail and Quasim came running. "So great to see you; we pray all day to Allah, but we are sure Allah likes you!" We celebrated this moment with loud laughter, appreciating what we had experienced with every fiber of our bodies. Late that evening, as the stars again set the backdrop to our camp, I crawled into my tent, my eye finally recovering, and dropped into the deepest slumber.

A week later, we left basecamp, a place where I had spent three-quarters of a year of my life. A place so full of longing, where I'd experienced the most incredible adventures, made difficult decisions, and undergone intense strife. A place that could stand as a metaphor for my life. Because not everything is always as beautiful as it might look on paper, but if you persevere, you might find paradise after all. I was sad to leave; I knew that no goal would bring me back to this place again, my self-created little green prison in paradise. In silent prayer, I said goodbye and bowed to Latok II, Ogre III, and the Ogre, these three mountains that had enriched my life beyond belief.

Brothers

A journalist once described us as: One is born a brother and thereby made a brother. A climbing partnership, on the other hand, doesn't just exist; it's a conscious relationship you need to create.

Yes, we are brothers, two dumplings from the same dough. So alike and yet so different, one climbing team, and yet we often follow different paths. While I'd stretched my hands to the sky on these expeditions, Alexander had climbed 5.14 on alpine rock on the giant, exposed roofs of the Westliche Zinne. We had both had a *Bella Vista*—a "beautiful view"—in our own way. And both of us made it onto the cover of several climbing magazines at the same time.

With these simultaneous successes, we once again proved ourselves internationally in the world of mountain sports. We boys had pushed the limits, managing the tightrope walk of the "State of Vertical Art." Although, for the moment, our partnership was defined only in terms of our brotherhood, we still surfed as the Huberbuam on the wave of success. Even the grandmaster of Himalayan mountaineering himself, Reinhold Messner, recognized our achievements.

When you stand in the limelight, you cast a long shadow, and shadows don't please other sun worshippers. First and foremost stood Stefan Glowacz, whom the public recognized as the indisputable king of the vertical arts, primarily due to his success on the early competition circuit. And now, suddenly, we brothers were climbing into his realm. He criticized Alexander's performance on *Bella Vista*, specifically for, in the crux section, clipping a bolt at a hanging belay while linking the two pitches to climb from ledge-to-ledge, while also claiming the first bolt-free alpine 8c. Stefan also criticized me for using expedition style on the Ogre. From his point of view, there was only one honest and authentic way of expedition mountaineering. He had developed this "fair means" benchmark himself: everything must be human powered and you need to be a purist—no porters were allowed. While his was certainly a good idea on paper, it was difficult to implement for mountains like the Ogre or Latok that lie deep within an inaccessible range.

But in the end, it was about something other than the actual climbing. Far more, it was a competition of strength and competence, so often prevalent among elite mountaineers. A last Darwinian relic, which can still be seen today when observing gorillas in the wild. This behavior is as old as mountaineering itself. Bonatti/Maestri, Messner/Kammerlander are just a few prominent examples—and us and Stefan. This conflict would stay with us, a long-smoldering discord we were only able to resolve many years later.

Because blood is thicker than water, Alexander and I possess an intrinsic understanding of each other, and we wanted to continue this elite performance in both realms of climbing as the Huber Brothers. In the meantime, Alexander was preoccupied with a new project on the smooth walls of El Capitan, while I had focused on alpinism again in Pakistan, on perhaps the most beautifully shaped wall on Earth, Masherbrum's East Face. There, wild mixed terrain leads to a monolithic golden-orange diamond of compact granite and a summit 8,000 meters above sea level.

I was determined to convince my brother that this wall was the biggest, the best, the highest, the most beautiful, the most magical, and the wildest place he could imagine. These superlatives could only be topped if we tackled it together as brothers. Alexander didn't have to think for long: "Hey, Thomas, the wall looks amazing. But from my point of view, it is perilous, and I feel too young for projects of that caliber. I can still crimp down hard; I want to keep rock climbing for a few more years. Expedition climbing, I can do when I am too old for hard climbing!" This answer echoed within me repeatedly, until I questioned the path that had led me to the big mountains.

It's natural that we all prefer to do what we're best at, since being successful is an exhilarating feeling that gives you the confidence to push yourself further. It's also precisely why we go places where we can realize our potential 100 percent, and why we give our all, train like madmen, and sacrifice so much. But if this was the case, Alexander and I could no longer exist as a climbing team, and the word "Huberbuam" would exist only on paper. Then, behind the Huber Brothers, Alexander, the climber, and Thomas, the alpinist.

"I can do expedition mountaineering when I'm old!"

Because of this proclamation and my romantic longing to be on the road again with Alexander as a real ropeteam, I packed away my boots, crampons, and ice axes. I was again systematically training, fingerboarding, and bouldering. Just playing catch-up with my brother's level motivated me so much that, within a very short time, I became stronger than ever. I was ripped, didn't have a gram of fat on my body, and went flying through my most complex route yet: *Adrenalin* (8c+) at Karlstein. Finally, I was again a climbing partner on par with my brother.

Our family also grew in the fall, and our second son, Amadeus, was born. On the surface, everything seemed perfect, yet my brother's persona demanded a lot from me. I could relate somewhat to how Alexander felt—overshadowed—when I was standing on Shivling. Alexander was in top form after climbing *Bella Vista* and seemed to have overcome his crisis. He celebrated his regained zest for life by climbing Fitz Roy and Cerro Torre in Patagonia in January 2002, and then made two first ascents in Yosemite, free-soloed the *Hasse Brandler* on the Große Zinne, and was personally honored by Reinhold Messner as a worthy successor to Paul Preuss, the historic pioneer of modern mountaineering.

Ultimately, Alexander finished the year with a winter ascent of Cerro Standhardt in Patagonia. During this time, I was at home, training diligently, rejoicing over our little Amadeus and my brother's successes in the vertical realm. At the same time, it hurt and scratched at my ego when I was told from all sides that Latok II, Shivling, and the Ogres were ancient history, and that everything concerning the Hubers was now focused on one name alone: Alexander. Nevertheless, this spurred me to train harder and push myself even further.

The journalist continued: for a climbing partnership to exist, both parties involved have to decide to want it, and above all, they must do one thing—climb together.

A New Horizon

"Hey, Alexander, that just looks wild, and if we're being honest, it feels pretty impossible to top the bar set by Hans Florine and Yuji Hirayama. The 3,281 feet of the *Nose* in 2:48."—"Two hours, 48, minutes and 53 seconds to be exact!"—"Yes, but the seconds don't matter. If we want to make it, we must reach the limit."—"It's possible!"—"Yes, it's possible."

I never thought we would compete on the Stars and Stripes' sacred vertical racetrack, because we had always smiled down at speed climbing. Besides, the idea always seemed too American and not Bavarian enough for us! But let's start at the beginning.

Spring 2003. We were back in the Valley, the golden granite wall of El Capitan in front of us, a can of beer in one hand, binoculars in the other, trying to piece together the rock features, cracks, and slabs on our objective, amidst the lush greenery of El Cap Meadows, embraced by the quietly moving Merced River, watered by the torrents of the High Sierra, which plunge into the Valley as the world-famous Upper Yosemite and Bridalveil falls. Next to these vibrant waterfalls, "Uhhhhhh, uhhhhiiii, ahhhh, ahhhh!" could be heard from all sides. The Stone Monkeys were communicating.

The morning meeting was in the cafeteria, at the table in the left-hand corner. This is where they could be found, the Stone Monkeys, and in the middle reigning supreme: Chongo, our spiritual leader. Beyond his philosophical and quantum-mechanical theories, often interspersed with stories from the vertical realm, he was a fountain of general life wisdom, often sounding like a prophetical scholar eager to give his students something to take out into the world: "It always depends on how intensively you want to shape your own life. To make it rich, you must be exposed to risky elements. With risk, you are putting your life on the line, but how boring it would be without it, and how great it becomes when you dare to do it. But experiencing it doesn't come for free; it comes at a price. Without risk, nothing is real; life is not real. This makes life on El Capitan as real as anything you'll find. It's a trip like no other."

We got him instantly because we already knew this life, and now we were "ready for the wall" once again! After coffee, hash browns, eggs, and Chongo's philosophical insights, we continued to the "Center of the Universe": a now-defunct bus lot close to Camp 4. Here is where the Stone Monkeys gathered to plan their next trip into the vertical realm, without getting in anybody's way. No rangers were snooping about; we were by ourselves, lounging on the hot tarmac, chatting, drinking beer, and sorting gear.

It was a wonderland, this ranger-free space, and when the "Green Dragons" tour buses drove by we could hear the guide commenting: "To the left, sitting in the dirt, you can see climbers, getting ready to climb on El Capitan!" We brothers were sorting our gear for a first "go" on our "Free *Zodiac*" project, a double set of cams, tiny wires, and some pitons organized at our feet.

Ivo cruised by on his longboard. He was rolling a cigarette in one hand, a ghetto blaster perched on his left shoulder playing Linkin Park's "Numb": "Hey, Thomaaaas and Alex, monkeys are raging! If you need help, just let me know!" Squinting, he took a deep drag from his cigarette and casually surfed past our sorted gear. Ivo was a crazy story in his own right. The Bulgarian had been in the United States illegally for over four years, living out his rebellious Stone Monkey existence to the core, and we could always count on his unlimited willingness to help. He was like a brother to me, one day older, apparently filled with the same thoughts and blood pulsing through his veins. His ghetto blaster provided the soundtrack to our time in Yosemite.

It was noon when Alexander and I reached the base of *Zodiac*. It was clear to both of us that we were not going to free-climb the original first pitch. It was too slippery and blank, and the sun was blinding. Not the best conditions for a first day on the wall. We headed to the right via the established aid climb *Bad to the Bone*, looking for a free-climbable approach to the meat of *Zodiac*. I climbed; Alexander belayed. After three hours, I sent him positive signs from above: "Hey, Alexander, I'm at the belay, and the terrain on the right below me looks climbable; we can free it—at least, I hope so!"

With the rope running through the belay anchor, I lowered myself hand over hand for ten feet, gripping the rope in my right hand and leaning out as far as possible to scan the rock. "Hey, Alexander, this will be awesome; I'm sure it'll go!" I said. Then, out of the corner of my eye, I saw Alexander strolling along the base of the wall, unaware of anything going on above. I was shocked that he'd taken me off belay and that I was now holding onto my life with only one hand. The chorus from Linkin Park's "Hit the Floor," omnipresent on Ivo's ghetto blaster, ricocheted inside my mind: "One minute you're on top/The next you're not . . ."

My heart was pounding, blood pulsing through my veins. It can happen that quickly. One slight miscommunication, and everything is over. I'd wanted to signal Alexander with "I'm at the belay!" that the endless belaying was finally ending, but he'd only heard the word "belay," which implied that it was safe for him to take me off—a minor nuance in climbing language, but with a considerable difference in the messaging! Ultimately, I was fortunate that I'd realized I was off belay and caught myself at the last minute, before I fell 200 feet to the ground. We both knew that something like this could not happen again!

The early California summer spoiled us with warm nights, and cloudless skies during the day—the blank granite reflected the strong sun, and within no time, we were bronze, as if we had fallen asleep in a tanning salon. We had been on the wall for days now, wearing the same T-shirts, underpants, and socks, drenched in sweat day in and day out. Our tattered trousers had blackened from the aluminum of the carabiners, our long hair was disheveled by the constant thermal winds, and our fingers were taped up and bruised from the cracks and crimps. It was dirty, dusty, and sweaty, and I don't want to know what we must have smelled like, but it felt great and pure, our new horizon of life, twisted by 90 degrees, smooth, steep, exposed, and hostile, just as Chongo had put it: "To live up there on that wall is a trip—it´s like nothing else"

And yes, it was a trip—natural LSD—and we were both entirely into it, turning increasingly into real monkeys, utterly alienated from "real" life down in the valley. We were part of this wall now, and it demanded everything from us: our skills, our ingenuity, our endurance, and even some "psychedelic" problem-solving to find the free line. Slowly but surely, we solved sections that had seemed impossible upon first inspection. The route was challenging but just doable. We could climb around the intricate, very compact lower wall until we reached the "Grey Circle," a circular gray granite zone approximately 985 feet in diameter, with a hairline crack through the middle—the heart of the *Zodiac*. It is incredibly steep, compact, and perhaps "the sexiest structure on El Cap!" because the rock forms beautiful, breast-like features in the center of the Grey Circle. Meanwhile, because the pitches had so many individual characteristics, we started them as well. When we were done, they almost reminded us of settings for a Tim Burton movie: the "Black Tower," "Flying Buttress,"

"Open Book," "Nipple," "Mark of Zorro," and "Devil's Eyebrow." The Nipple stood out as the spiciest ropelength, comprising a rightward traverse on fingery, low-percentage moves with barely any footholds, certainly up in the lower-5.14 grade range (later downrated to 5.13d on a repeat ascent by Tommy Caldwell).

No matter how hard we tried, the high temperatures fried us to the bone on our "Free *Zodiac*" attempt. Again and again, we were spat off the Nipple onto the rope, the intense heat making the rubber soles on our climbing shoes too soft to stick to the microscopic edges. We tried everything—swapping in shoes with a harder rubber compound and looking for other climbable features—but we kept slipping off, cursing, and with every failure, our doubts grew. By now, we were questioning everything. Were we too weak, or was it simply that the heat was making us fail on this sweaty "nipple"? No matter how we looked at it, we realized that further attempts were going to be futile, and so buoyed our spirits with the hope of returning in the autumn for cooler temperatures.

With some time left in the Valley, Alexander came up with the idea of trying our hand at speed-climbing *Zodiac,* a form of climbing that was totally novel for us as a ropeteam. Two years earlier, Alexander had climbed the *Zodiac* with Ammon McNeely in a record time of six hours. Now he could envision shattering his record. If we applied our strengths as free climbers and combined them with American speed-climbing techniques like simul-climbing and short-fixing, we could be faster than anyone before us. (In simul-climbing, the two climbers move roped together without stopping at belay anchors, placing intermediate protection to keep them from being stripped off the wall in a fall. In short fixing, the top climber reaches an anchor, pulls up slack, and fixes the rope to the anchor so his second can jumar below him while he continues leading, self-belayed, on the slack he's pulled through.) The *Zodiac* was the perfect venue for us to try speed climbing: no one was more familiar with the route, and the knowledge we'd gained from trying to free it would help us pulverize the standing record.

That evening with Dean, Winky, Ivo, beer, chips, and binoculars, we sat down enveloped by tall grass in the middle of the El Cap Meadows. We debated our new plan on the *Zodiac*. We quickly realized that we knew nothing about speed climbing on El Cap. Ivo gave us the lowdown on the rules and ethics, and introduced some technical and tactical shenanigans, like the ones described above. The teams themselves take the official time, so the times are therefore always based on honesty. The clock starts running when the lead climber leaves the ground and stops when the second reaches the last belay. All quite logical and straightforward. Further, you may not prep the route with added protection, which might speed up the ascent.

To put the pedal to the metal, Ivo said, we would have to depart from our tried-and-tested method of belaying each pitch, and instead move as a team simultaneously, simul-climbing and short-fixing. These were new concepts for both of us, but we were ready to familiarize ourselves in theory with these new tactics and then go for it on the day. We would learn by doing!

By now, the sun was low, barely cresting the grass in the meadows. Shadows crept across the *Dawn Wall*, and Winky took pictures of this incredible mood with his little analog black-and-white camera. Dean's eyes seemed captivated by this play of light, or perhaps in his mind he was already climbing high up on El Capitan. When Ivo finished his sermon on speed climbing, Dean spouted a loud "Baaabooom!", disrupting our conversation and wearing a broad grin. His alert eyes flashed beneath his frayed cap, and in a confidant but calm voice, he said, "You have to understand, speed is exciting, but also crazy dangerous, because one mistake, one fall, can be one too many, and you're lucky if you only get hurt. Speed is perhaps the most dangerous discipline in climbing because the rope gives you the illusion of safety, which is never really there in the first place. This makes speed even more dangerous than soloing. It is Zen, the highest art form in climbing. Speed climbing, you have no time to think; everything runs on intuition. The cutting edge is defined only by doing. That's exactly where the fascination lies. Thomas and Alexander, start slowly, be humble, feel your way into this speed, and discover a new world that will always remain invisible to everyone else."

The sun had set, we packed everything up, and the five of us strolled back to our car. Alexander and I now knew a little more about what speed means. It didn't just mean being fast; it was a new game. That made us more than curious!

One day before our first "go," Alexander and I planned our speed tactics, sketching out a gameplan on a piece of paper and going to a small crag to familiarize ourselves with short-fixing and simul-climbing, optimizing our systems, and getting our rope commands sorted—agreeing on "Fix," "Belay," "Secured," and an "Okay," words that were clear, simple, and easy to shout. We also worked on our rack: it must not be too big, because then we would have too much to carry; but also not too little, because then we would have to resort to time-consuming trickery. In the end, we agreed on the following sequence: I would lead the first block, while Alexander took over on the upper part of the wall. So far, so good. We were mentally well prepared for our first speed experience. All good on paper. Would that be enough? Time would tell.

We are standing at the start of the 2,000-foot mega-classic in the late afternoon. Only Winky has come with us, and he shoots a few photos shortly before we set off. We are ready to give it our all today, fully immersing ourselves in this new world. Winky also feels this energy and whispers, "It's so nice and peaceful here. I can feel a great energy, and there must be something seriously off if you're not going to make it!" He grins at us and quickly takes another photo, and then Alexander starts counting down.

Twenty seconds: I place one foot on the rock and focus on the first move. *Ten seconds:* another short breath, chalk up, breathe. Then *five, four, three, two, one,* and at "Go," I'm propelling myself off the ground into the vertical realm. I acrobatically haul myself over the first few fixed rivets, in between a dicey hook placement, and after ninety feet, I clip my first piton and shout "Beeeelay!" Alexander throws the rope out of the Grigri. I quickly pull up sixty feet of slack, clove hitch it to the piton, and yell, "Fiiiix!" Alexander jumps into the jumars and sprints up the fixed rope while I continue leading out on the slack.

From now on, we're on the move at the same time, and it's spectacular: any fear of taking a massive whipper has dispersed, and each of us knows automatically what to expect from the other. I'm always ahead, gradually placing all the protection on my harness. Alexander collects the pieces while following, taking care to sort them strategically on his own harness in preparation for his block. All the gear should take us to the middle of the wall—we'll be doing the entire climb in only two ultra-long pitches.

After two hours, I reach our strategic switchover point, 1,000 feet above the deck, and our gear has been sufficient. Alexander climbs past me, taking over the lead, switching between technical aid and free climbing, and from free back to aid. He flies through the extensive interlocking crack systems of the Grey Circle, shimmies from nut to nut on the Nipple, and swings over the overhangs on the Mark of Zorro and Devil's Eyebrow. I follow, sometimes doing spectacular pendulums clipped to our rope with ascenders, sometimes free climbing simultaneously. We pass a ropeteam that has been on the wall for several days and who can't believe we've only been going for 3:15. "Fuck, yeeeaaah, you are on speed!" I laugh and explain that we are merely speed climbing, not high on amphetamines. They too must laugh, and cheer us on: "The Monkeys are raging!"

Alexander flies over the final ropelengths, and I sprint behind him with the jumars. In the end, he pulls me over the edge after 4 hours and 7 minutes. We are exhausted but exhilarated, and it is hard to believe that we made it in such a spectacular time—and that, above all, it was fun. Around sunset, we celebrate our new record with some other Monkeys down at the Meadows. But we have a nagging feeling that we still haven't tapped our full speed-climbing potential. Next time, we want to find out how far we can push ourselves as a team.

Every two days, we climb an evening lap, and its pure rock 'n' roll each time. By now, a horde of spectators gathers to cheer us on from El Cap Meadows, and we get faster every time. Afterward, we celebrate another new record at Camp 4. It's nuts out there, intoxicating, and we're becoming addicted to speed. In the end, we put down 2 hours and 30 minutes. But we both know there's still room for improvement, but we do not have enough time left in the Valley!

Alexander and I were completely in sync with the *Zodiac*, and everyone knew that we would return in autumn, during the famous Indian summer, when the meadows glow yellow, the temperatures are cooler, and the friction is perfect. We would take our time and hopefully free the *Zodiac*.

Back home, the two of us spent the hot summer days on the Feuerhorn Nordwand on the north side of the Reiteralm massif, climbing two new incredible routes to the right of *End of Silence*: *Monstermagnet*, an IX (5.12d), and *Firewall*, an athletic X (5.13d).

By early October, we were kicking back in the Grey Circle and working the Nipple again. It hadn't gotten any easier, but the friction was second to none, and we finally managed to free all of *Zodiac's* pitches without falls. We celebrated our two-day redpoint back at Camp 4 until late at night. The beer cans piled up to a small, tinny El Cap, and shortly before midnight, I got the crazy idea that one should do justice to *Midnight Lightning*, as befits a real Stone Monkey. Although some camping tourists had already complained about our boisterous celebration, Ammon, Ivo, and Alexander still cheered me on. A little later, I dangled off the exit jugs of *Midnight Lightning*—precisely at midnight. The mood was jubilant but a bit too boisterous. A little later, the rangers ended our celebration—with much luck and persuasion, this time without imprisoning any Monkeys.

At that moment, Chongo came out with the following: "Happiness is a very short moment—it´s a fragile thing. Once you get there you are stuck, no matter what happens. I suppose in the end happiness is a matter of luck—to be lucky enough to be there in the first place. And once you are there it´s so cool, [and] you couldn´t not be there But you can't understand that unless you've been at the top and really experienced it."

Chongo was right: that feeling of being at the top is addictive, and for us at that time, Yosemite, this rebellious community, and the granite walls of El Capitan were the foundation of our happiness. We didn't want to and couldn't let go, so we returned to the Valley the following spring. Not to seek another free-climbing line, but for *Zodiac* on speed again. To push our speed to the brink, to squeeze out the last few minutes and seconds.

This time, we set the bar high: *Zodiac* under two hours. It was unimaginable for everybody else, but we had faith that we would break this barrier. Dean had already told us at the beginning that speed is a world that cannot be penetrated from the outside; it's an intangible thing that's hard to explain in essence.

Our target "Highspeed" went a little like this: There are two doors, one at the entrance and one at the exit. When we leave the ground, we open one of the doors and are inside. At the top, we close the second door behind us and leave that world behind. Everything in between is crazy and happens automatically, intuitively. And yet everything is dictated by a meticulously rehearsed plan. We always know what we are doing on each section of the climb. From belaying to simuling to short fixing, every climbing move, aid move, and placement is mapped out in detail, practiced and practiced again and again until it all becomes second nature—part of our DNA as climbers—and nothing is left to chance.

Or let me put it this way: when you start thinking, it's already over. Only our shouts of "Beeelay," "Fiiiiix," and "Okay," and our panting give this vertical vacuum, in which we function as automatons, a certain humanity. It's a weird world that doesn't reveal all its secrets, not even to us. Why we ended up going so fast, we didn't know. Behind it was this mysterious, magical world of speed. It lies outside of space and time, or in Chongo's words, it's "a trip like nothing else!"

After our fifth "go," we are already close to our personal sound barrier, and today—in autumn 2004—we want to shatter our record. We hike up to the tie-in point, moving slowly to save energy. In the meantime, El Cap Meadows has become a small outdoor arena for climbers and non-climbers alike, certainly more than 100 spectators who, instead of sitting around the campfire in the evening, want to witness our adventure firsthand. We have the best possible conditions today: except for one party high up on the last pitch, there are no other ropeteams on *Zodiac*. Thus, we do not expect to encounter any time-consuming overtaking maneuvers.

We rope up. I'm still sorting out the gear on my harness; on the left are all the bigger cams, and on the right are the small ones and the Stoppers. Five minutes to go. I quickly pop another stick of gum in my mouth, stashing a spare piece in my left pants pocket. It's a recipe against thirst from the Native Americans, who would suck on a pebble when crossing the desert. "Hey, Thomas, you know what? We'll catch up to those two today; that should be our goal!"—"Okay, Alexander."—"But this is an unfair race."—"Unfair for whom?" I ask, and he winks at me. Another minute: "Hey, Alexander, let's do this, safe and fast!"—"Yes, Thomas, step on it and hold on! Twenty seconds to go!"

I put my left foot on the familiar first foothold. "Ten seconds." Breathe deeply, chalk up again, a ritual. "Five, four, three, two, one," the gates drop, and the rope flies through the Grigri; a little later, my first command: "Beeeeelay." Pull up the rope, "Fiiiiix" to the bolted anchor, continue climbing on the slack rope, a No. 2 cam whistles into the crack, and now I start free climbing; Alexander, jumaring, simultaneously sorts the cleaned gear to prepare for his block. Arriving at the anchor, Alexander puts my rope back in the Grigri, unties the knot, then immediately I'm on "Beeeeelayyy" again. Alexander throws the rope out of the Grigri by the armful; I quickly pull up thirty feet, hitch, "Fiiiix," and continue climbing.

Fifty minutes later, I reach the middle of the wall, where we'll swap leads. Alexander is already only thirty feet below me. This will be the only moment I get to take a deep breath until we're on top. Alexander rushes past; the changeover takes seconds, then we're off again. Simul-climbing, a little later short fixing again; at the Nipple, he yards across using the fixed wires, even faster than last time, and then runs out the rope for sixty feet without placing any protection. I follow behind on the jumars . . . past Mark of Zorro and the Devil's Eyebrow into the exit dihedral.

The ropeteam above us on the last pitch is still climbing. Unbelievable, but we will decide the race in our favor. In the blink of an eye, Alexander climbs past the belayer, who is visibly frozen in shock, cheekily climbing into their pitch without asking. A minute later, he reaches the exit at the same time as the leader. The climber is petrified, perhaps afraid of doing something wrong, clinging to a jug and quivering. Alexander, between them, fixes the rope and shouts: "Fiiiiix!" I follow with the jumars and haul myself over the edge. The door slams shut behind us in an incredible 1 hour, 52 minutes, and 38 seconds.

A "JEEEEEAAAHHHH, uuuuuhhhhh" resounds from El Cap Meadows. The Monkeys are celebrating our record time, while the climbers we were having a secret race with can't believe we've just ran through the entire *Zodiac* while they only climbed the last sixty feet. "Now you know, Thomas, why it was an unfair race!"—"Yes, because they didn't know about partaking in one in the first place."—"Well, because we were just too fast for them!"—"Yeah, you're right!" We laugh and grin down from El Capitan, and before dark, we reach "El Cap Bridge." Once again, we celebrate our speed, and once again, the rangers are called in to end a raucous Stone Monkeys get-together.

We spend our last evening in the Valley with Ivo, Winky, Ammon, and Chongo, lounging in Sentinel Meadows. Chongo dances on his slackline, Ivo supplies the tunes from his boom box, and Winky holds a walkie-talkie in one hand while scanning the surroundings. In addition, Ammon takes his bike for a spin to ensure that no rangers are in the immediate vicinity. Come sunset, as twilight blurs our surroundings, we hear Winky speaking into the walkie-talkie with a strange German accent: "The bag is ready to haul!"

It doesn't take long for the silence to be interrupted by an increasingly loud hissing noise, until after ten seconds, a loud "*Waaawumm*" pierces the gloom. A short time later, a black parachute floats above, makes a steep, banking spiral, and lands next to us. Dean and his eyes shine even in this dim light: "Thank you, Winky, thank you, brothers—it was so great to fly. Baaabooom!" Now I finally get what trip he was on back when Ivo tried to explain speed to us! I have to laugh: "Baaabooom! The monkeys are flying!"

And yet, even as I say "Baaabooom," a cold shiver runs down my spine because it feels like I've jumped myself. "Hey, Winky, there's one thing you'll have to explain to me about the 'ready to haul' and the extreme

German accent!" He laughs and says, "We learned that way of speaking from you, brothers. 'Ready to haul' is our code for no rangers snooping around. They'd put any BASE jumper in the pokey for a long time!"—"Yeah, we get you now!"

Winky, who has always been more of a silent observer with his camera, suddenly goes off: "And because tonight is our last night together, I want to give you something to take home with you, back to Bavaria. You will come back because, on the one hand, you are Stone Monkeys, and on the other because you should try your hand at speed on the *Nose*. This game is longer, more dangerous, crazier than the *Zodiac* and loaded with history. Jim Bridwell, John Long, and Billy Westbay started it, and after that, the best of their generation always saw the *Nose* as their personal racetrack. For a while now, the record has been firmly held by self-proclaimed 'speed king' Hans Florine, who smashed up through the 1,000 meters with Yuji Hirayama in 2:48:52. I would love to see their record tumble. If anyone can do it, it's you guys."

Dean, still hyped from his jump, can only agree. By now, the walls to our left and right are mere black shadows, the sequoias in front of us are ghostly sentinels, and a starry sky twinkles above. We're standing still in the middle of it all, silently celebrating these incredibly intense moments. Dean finds the best words that night, explaining why we do what we do: "All of us here are so powerfully guided by what we do that we have almost no choice but to follow this one path. And when I look at our world and see that so many are not living out their dreams, what we do makes sense: to make the world a better place by encouraging everyone around us to live a life full of passion and love."

Grounding

It reassures me that we are not alone in our worldview. We are not obsessed but are courageous adventurers who can enter an incredibly intimate relationship with this vertical space defined by Mother Nature, balancing on the precipice to find the deepest personal fulfillment. The only frustrating thing about living by this mantra is that everything messy, incalculable, and dangerous vanishes in the periphery.

It is thus even more important to break out of our sterile society to connect with nature through climbing, using all the senses, observing and reacting, and allowing oneself to be guided by instinct alone—and by doing so, pursuing one's own happiness. For me, this is magic, real art, almost poetry. An art of living. And because art knows no boundaries, climbing higher and higher is the way to freedom; at least, that's how I feel.

The alarm rips me out of my early-morning dozing and straight into the daily routine of preparing breakfast, changing Amadeus, taking Elias to kindergarten, cleaning, cooking, washing, and just about everything a household of four requires. In between, I give a lecture because the money we spend must be earned in the first place. In the little time I have left, I tax my fingers on a sport-climbing project near Berchtesgaden, trying to stay fit. In short, I don't get bored, and my everyday life is back in full swing. It's a life of opposites—on the one hand, fully functioning and family focused, but then again adventurous and freedom-loving.

As different as these two ways of life may seem, that's where I find meaning and inspiration. If I had total freedom all the time, I would lose myself. But if I always had to work and be a dad, after a while I would be sucked dry, ready to be recycled. But through this structure I've created, these two forms of existence feed off and balance each other. In the spring, Yosemite; in the summer Dahoam—back home, where I can give a little of the freedom I so uncompromisingly demand back to my family. This soothes my guilty conscience.

Come autumn, it's "stucko time" in Berchtesgaden. These dark, baked rolls flavored with raisins and cinnamon—i.e., the "stucks"—are a valley specialty and, at this time of year, a foretaste, so to speak, of the dark days to come, which, especially in Berchtesgaden, are full of magic and dark energy. A time of year highlighted by the changing of the sycamore maple, the larches burning with yellow leaves amongst the green mountain spruces, and the region's men preparing local holiday traditions like our traditionally crafted, handheld firecrackers with black gunpowder, which vibrate the valley with their thunderous noise.

The other frenetically celebrated custom is for bachelors only: the Buttnmandllaufen—the march of the alpine demons.

The Buttnmandln are men bound in fur and straw. They are fitted with large bells on their backs, and their hands are blackened with tar; they don a demonic mask—a *loafn* mask—that's usually carved from wood and fitted with faunal horns. This heavy mask is precisely fitted to the face and has the most diabolical features, including razor-sharp fangs. The men run in specific packs, ringing bells, shouting bloodcurdling screams, and slapping their willow rods. They march from house to house, following St. Nicholas visiting the local children. Their presence and powerful anarchic energy are meant to drive evil spirits away from the area's homes and farms. The whipping of the willow rods has another meaning, rooted in fertility rituals from pagan times. It comes as no surprise that the blows are primarily addressed to single girls. The posher and more aloof the young ladies act, the blacker their faces are sooted, and the more blistering their lashing. For non-natives, this custom can seem barbaric. For us locals, it is normal.

This archaic custom has such importance with the area's youth that because of the Buttnmandllaufs, a wedding has been postponed on more than one occasion—so a man could run wild one last time before getting married. I partook until 1993 as part of the Ganghofern, a *Strohbass*, as the whole group is called, but was retired due to my old age. As part of a team of other, older former Buttnmandln, I am now a *Bindter*, tying a Buttnmandl together with forty feet of sturdy hemp rope. Large bundles of long-cut straw and three Swiss bells complete the costume using a traditional tying technique. All this takes part in a hay barn just outside Berchtesgaden. Of course, each *Bass* guards its Bindter secrets with their life. Every year there is an unofficial competition among the *Bassn* to see who can tie the most potent and beautiful Buttnmandl.

Before the group starts moving, they commune through the Lord's Prayer. The mother of the household gives the final blessing with holy water. But then, this peace is abruptly crushed by a fearsome, guttural scream: "*Gaaaanghooofer Buttnmandln*" from the Buttnmandl master. "*AAAUUUFFFGEEEHT'S!*"—"OFFFFFFF WEEEEE GOOOOOO!"

Then everyone erupts. Runs wild, screaming, ringing bells, charging toward the congregation of spectators. Gone is the romantic idyll. The times ahead are anarchical, demonic, archaic, and dangerous. They will last late into the night.

On December 6, the actual St. Nicholas Day, the second Buttnmandl day, it's the same procedure as before: The master, who takes over coordinating the group and ultimately bears responsibility for everything that transpires, comes to me first thing in the morning, visibly tired from the previous days' events: "Hey, Thomas, yesterday we lost a young man—he got hurt. Say, would you like to jump in, because you're not married anyway!" He grins like a naughty schoolboy because he knows I cannot and will not say no. It is also no coincidence that I have everything in the trunk of my car: my bells and loafn mask, which my trainer Rudi Klausner carved for me when I was still a young man. It's a demon with bared teeth that bears a certain resemblance to me when one stops to think about it.

Sunlight cuts through the slits in the barn wall, casting a mystical light. As the oldest, I am the last to be bound in straw. As so many times before, I inhale the grain smell, feeling the straw on my body and the rope that tightens around my belly until I am almost unable to breathe. But the tighter, the better when running wild later on. Then come three bells tied to my rear, face, and hands. Last is the loafn, and, transformed, we set off. Slowly the town gates are pushed open, and we all walk devoutly out behind St. Nicholas and up to the meadowed hill outside town.

It is another beautiful, pleasantly warm late-autumn day. Unfortunately, there is still no sign of winter; only the higher peaks are covered with a dusting of autumn snow. At the top of the hill, we line up again. We pray as the farmer's wife sprinkles her holy water, and then there is a short moment of silence. Everyone takes another breath and adjusts their costumes one last time. But above all, silence prevails. This is true dark magic, and I lose myself in the backlight of the early-winter sun, staring into the mountains of my homeland. Everyone waits as if electrified by this bristling silence. Then, finally, a profoundly archaic, primal scream erupts, far beyond any social norms: "Gaaang-hofer Buttnmandln. Offffffff weeeeee goooooo!"

To describe what happens to you at this moment is impossible because you need to experience it firsthand: You transform into a Buttnmandl—an alpine demon—go wild, become indestructible, scream off all the energy pent up within your inner self, and rage into the night. You move ecstatically in a specific fashion, letting the bells ring perpetually. You ignore the hemp rope chaffing and cutting your skin. You block out all pain, partly anesthetized with beer and schnapps. But you are not drunk when wearing the loafn because you have already gone far beyond your physical limits; you are climbing through another realm, running wild, unhinged, rebellious. Come midnight, back at the Stadl, you finally break free of this spell of possession. And even though it leaves you feeling utterly destroyed and drained physically, you are happy.

The next day, I hang up my loafn costume for good, and it feels like the right thing to do. Maybe my sons will run with the demons one day, or perhaps they will have sons of their own. I don't care at this precise moment. More importantly, I'm able to shed my melancholy over this being my last run because I know I can find the place beyond the limits anytime in the mountains. Because I know: when I set off, I march till the end!

CHAPTER NINE
Patagonia

Somewhere-Nowhere

After Christmas 2005, I head off across the Atlantic. I have never been as far from home as I am now, yet this foreign land feels somehow more familiar than any other far-off place.

"Riders on the storm," along a gravel road to nowhere, stormy skies, driving into the wind. Our dust plume hangs behind, still visible in the endless plain. In the middle of it is an *estancia* (ranch), the *gauchos* (cowboys) with their tanned faces and sharp knives herding sheep on their horses in an unpredictable environment. A guanaco carcass lies in the dust next to the gravel road—a feast for the condor, the most primitive bird on our planet.

Lenticularis billowing in the sky look like oversized UFOs. My body is crammed between backpacks, panniers, my brother, and the Swiss climber Stephan Siegrist. Carolina sits up front. She is a doctor in a hospital somewhere out here and is steering the Land Rover—not a status symbol urban car out here, but a utilitarian vehicle dinged-up and dusty from Patagonia's dirt roads. Her co-pilot is a local mountaineer with a slim face. The two are constantly sipping yerba mate from a hollowed-out gourd with a silver straw. To me, the drink seems tart, bitter, and undrinkable, but to them it's indispensable. Carolina floors it down the straightaway along the windswept Lago Viedma toward a black wall of clouds on the horizon. Hidden within are the steepest granite needles, towers, and walls of golden granite, interspersed with surreal formations of ice and snow.

At the gates of this world, hidden from us for the moment, stands a last bastion: the village of El Chaltén. "Riders on the storm . . . into this world we're thrown." No song could better describe this part of the world. Now I understand why Wolfgang Güllich and Kurt Albert named their route, on Torre Central del Paine in this land of notorious storms, after the famous, mysterious song by the Doors. But I don't know why it has taken me this long to get here myself. After all, I have loved this song forever, sung it on stage myself, empathized with Jim Morrison, and even lived by it. But "The Doors of Perception"—these gates of perception—have remained closed to me until now. Maybe because, from Bavaria's point of view, this really is the end of the world, or perhaps because these mountains have all already been climbed and the highest peaks reach a mere 11,155 feet.

In comparison, in Pakistan's Karakoram, I was served peaks above 22,000 feet, some still unclimbed, on a silver platter. Stephan has been down this road five times previously, and Alexander, who has climbed the region's two most famous mountains—Cerro Torre and Cerro Fitz Roy—has convinced me to come with epic stories of those ascents. As we ride along this road toward dark black nothingness, it almost feels like a revelation, one that vibrates through my soul with the lyrics looping in my head: " . . . into this world we're thrown . . ." Thrown into this world indeed—I cannot wait for this road to the end, and my very own relationship to Cerro Torre to begin.

Suppose you were to squint while looking at a map of South America. It would be easy to imagine a giant relic of prehistoric times lying there—a fossilized spine from the north all the way down to the farthest reaches of the earth.

The Andes, geographically the longest mountain range in the world, is a coastal range that connects most South American countries, from Venezuela to Tierra del Fuego. At the ass, that is, at the level of the sacrum, Argentina and Chile share the region of Patagonia, the land of storms, gauchos, Estepa (plains or steppe), great lakes, glaciers, and bizarre mountains: a wild, vast, lonely land, and one so full of beauty.

On the Andean ridge, creation has once again gone to great lengths for us alpinists, it seems, and fashioned a paradise of rock, ice, and snow like no other in the world, with massive granite towers and sheer walls interspersed among glaciers, mysterious forests, and winding valleys of unspeakable beauty. The granite colossus Fitz Roy towers above them all. It is the highest peak at 11,155 feet and, in good weather, can be seen from far out on the Estepa, often with a small cloud clinging to the summit. Because we humans like to imbue every striking natural formation with some mystical secret, the Tehuelches, the indigenous people of Patagonia, called their mountain Chaltén, the "smoking mountain." The Chaltén is a sacred mountain that their god Elal was the first to climb. From high up there, he gifted the people with his wisdom. In my imagination, the peak is a petrified condor sitting upright, spreading its mighty wings to form the outlines of the adjacent *agujas* (rock needles, or spires) l'S, Saint-Exupéry, San Rafael, Poincenot, Mermoz, and Guillaumet.

On the other side stands Cerro Torre, juxtaposed to the valley's left, in a seemingly more modest position. And yet, this granite tower, embraced by storm, is the undisputed king of this region. Mythical, elegant, slender, and crowned by ice and snow—although lower than Fitz Roy by 1,312 feet—it is of far greater alpine standing. For many, this granite tower is THE mountain of mountains, and its profile should read: "Most Wanted! Reward: Immortality."

Cerro Torre, affectionately called Torre by us climbers, is the most exposed to the vagaries of nature simply by its geographic location. As the first bulwark growing out of the tremendous Patagonian ice sheet, this granite tower receives the full force of the weather along with its satellite peaks, Torre Egger, Punta Herron, and Cerro Standhardt. After a storm, the towers are often glazed with a fat layer of ice for weeks. In addition, the Torre is steep, forbidding, vertical, and inaccessible from all sides, and was long deemed an "impossible mountain" after its discovery by mountaineers.

This statement alone was a magnet for many top alpinists of the postwar era to come see for themselves. The Torre turned many of them mad but also reverent, creating anger and resentment on the one hand, but, on the other, a longing for and obsessive devotion to the peak and its beauty. Thus, throughout its alpine history, the Torre had endured much from man. The confusing and bitter story of the first ascent, involving Cesare Maestri, Torre Egger, and Casimiro Ferrari, mythologized this mountain for all generations to come: when Maestri, the Spider of the Dolomites, made his second attempt on the Torre with the exceptional East Tyrolean mountaineer Egger in 1959, time literally stood still in the Torre Massif.

Maestri was under enormous pressure to climb Cerro Torre. He had already failed the previous year, and his Italian competitor Walter Bonatti also had plans to attempt the Torre that season. In addition, Maestri's ego had been badly bruised when he'd been rejected as a member of the expedition for his Italian colleagues' successful first ascent of K2, and he wanted to polish his alpine CV by climbing the Torre. Put bluntly, he had to deliver.

But the story ended in tragedy. An avalanche cut Maestri and Egger's rope and swept Egger into the depths. Maestri survived. In his despair, he told a story that to this day raises many questions—questions concerning the ascent to the Col de Conquesta, the most extreme climbing over the heavily iced-up north face, the summit bid, the descent, the avalanche, the death of his comrade Toni, and finally Maestri's own struggle for survival.

He took this tragic success story back to his native Italy, where he was celebrated frenetically, his achievement put on a par with the first ascent of K2. Meanwhile, Egger, who as his heroic tomb now had the most iconic mountain on Earth, was lionized in an obituary: "Cerro Torre, Toni's last and greatest victory. A giant of granite in the Patagonian Andes, a beacon of courage, unwavering faith, and the will to win of a Tyrolean climber. The tombs of the kings will once again turn to dust. Cerro Torre will continue to defy the storms for millennia as a heavenly beacon!" Maestri and Egger's story become immortal, a tale of two heroes who had spiritually connected with the mystical world of the Torre, defying all risks, facing impossibility, chins up, breaking barriers, but paying the ultimate price.

However, as time went by, Maestri's story became increasingly more tangled, and doubts arose about the authenticity of the climb. So he returned, because Maestri did not want to leave any questions unanswered. This time, in 1970, he went with various climbing partners and a 220-pound air compressor. With the help of a 60-foot hose with a percussion drill attached to the end, he engineered his way up the east face. In the end, he placed more than 300 bolts and reached the upper edge of the granite headwall, without climbing the summit ice formation above.

Maestri hated this mountain, this summit, and his actions brought this alpine monument to his level, punishing the Torre for everything it had done to him. But the *Compressor Route* did not bring him the peace of mind he had hoped for; instead, this route became an alpine memorial, the much-discussed "murder of the impossible"—as Reinhold Messner labeled it. In a later interview, Maestri, close to tears, came out with the following statement: "In the beginning, the Torre was a dream, then it became a nightmare. And if I could wish for anything, it would be for the Torre to collapse into a thousand pieces!"

Four years after Maestri removed Torre's veil of impossibility, Casimiro Ferrari and his team climbed the icy west side to the highest point, becoming the first official ascensionists! When asked how he liked the Torre, the lively Italian replied that it could be compared to an enchanting woman: beautiful, capricious, and you had to take her as she was. Otherwise, you have no chance with her. For him, the Torre was simply the hottest mountain on earth, the most sought-after alpine trophy! No matter how you look at it, it always depends on the perception of the person observing. One thing is certain: Cerro Torre is a mountain like no other. It is the screen onto which each individual projects their hopes and dreams, a mirror of a person's soul.

Carolina eases off the gas and carefully steers her Land Rover across the last steel bridge over the Río de las Vueltas. From now on, the road winds downhill in gentle curves into the valley. To the left are gentle, forested hills; to the right, a 300-foot vertical cliff; and in front, the slopes to the torres disappearing in the black wall of clouds. Only now, up close, do we understand the dynamics of the weather. Dramatically, a granite tower will tear open the cloud cover, wispy cloud hissing through a narrow, rocky gap—one of Patagonia's many cols—before a mighty, dark cloud rolls in and swallows up everything again. This is the hell of Patagonia described in all the literature, lousy weather that only exists here and is affectionately called "Patagonia": snow, rain, and tempests in the mountains, but sunny and windy down in the plains.

"You're lucky you're just now getting to Patagonia, because it can only improve. The storm has been raging in the mountains for a month! A terrible time for the Torre but a good time to drink yerba mate."—"Hey, Carolina, we don't have to drink mate! You know, we packed good weather en masse. We're going to camp; hopefully, we will be on the mountain soon! I can only tell you one thing: I have a good feeling!" Carolina smiles at Stephan's optimism. "You and your feeling!" she replies, sipping her tea with gusto.

Between the Río Fitz Roy and the Río del las Vueltas, a symmetrical road grid has been laid over the gravel, resembling a small, planned American township. El Chaltén's wide streets seem oversized compared to the small, corrugated iron huts, shacks, playfully twisted houses, and old caravans, but the place has its charm, like a ghostly, semi-deserted town from a Hollywood Western. Everything looks provisional, as if it were just being built. Yet, the most necessary things are already there: a hospital, a school, stores, a bakery, restaurants, a *chocolateria,* a camping site, a gas station, and a large diesel generator that supplies the village with electricity. Only a cemetery is nowhere to be seen. The town is still too young for people to have died here.

The wind sweeps over the village from the valley, and the light-blue and white Argentinian flag at the entrance to the town stands crosswise, billowing in the wind. We pass a promising-looking restaurant called Patagonicus and then turn left. We have arrived at the end of the civilized world. Beyond, there are only mountains and glaciers.

Our destination is Hostería da Lago, a small hostel with an even smaller campground in the front yard. A wiry man with a curly afro and alert gaze lounges at the entrance. "Hola, Stephan. Hola, Alexander!" It's Luis Soto, a native of Brazil who, with his brother Hector, made his money in the literal creation of El Chaltén and is known by all. Luis starts speaking to us joyfully in Spanish. Stephan and Alexander, who seem to speak fluent Spanish, nod in agreement; I, however, understand nothing. "And what did he say exactly?"—"Yes, that everything has already been organized, and tomorrow, if the weather permits, we will set off for Campo Bridwell with Don Guerra's horses. But now he wants to drink mate with us, and he's looking forward to getting to know you too!" Luis immediately switches to English when he learns of my lack of Spanish. He's a person with a high level of social competence. With his brother, he has such a winning aura that even the storms of Patagonia cannot hold him back.

Late in the next morning, Don Guerra stands in the front yard with ten horses. He's a gaucho straight from a romance novel, stocky, relatively small, and his face tanned by wind and weather, sporting a cheeky mustache. Because of the permanent wind, he's bound his hat around his chin with a cord; he's also tucked a large silver knife into the back of his broadly wrapped cloth belt. His posture and callused hands reveal a lifetime on horseback. At 60 years old, Don Rodolfo Guerra is undoubtedly the area's most senior inhabitant, his time here pre-dating the establishment of El Chaltén, when he worked as a gaucho on the estancia of Andreas Madsen, a Danish pioneer who was the first to settle this valley. It was not until 1985 that the first huts were added at the behest of the Argentine government, to demonstrate a presence in this part of the country to Chile. They named this place El Chaltén, the village in front of the smoking mountain.

With Don Guerra and his horses, we hike across the Estepa into the scenically rugged Torre Valley, passing through gnarled lenga forests sculpted by the Patagonian wind. For Alexander and Stephan, who have been up and down this trail umpteen times, it is familiar terrain; for me, it's a mystical new frontier. Behind every bend opens a unique perspective on the surrounding mountains; only the Torre remains hidden, standing out slightly against the black cloud wall as a dark shadow. In the end, we are lucky. Except for a few raindrops, we reach the camp still dry.

Campo Bridwell is somewhat protected behind a large moraine in a small forest, right on the banks of the wildly rushing Río Fitz Roy; it feels like Camp 4, only in Patagonia—a campground for hikers, nature lovers, and climbers. In the middle of it stands a small hut, lovingly crafted by climbers from wood from the forest. The attention to detail in the handmade furniture and the stone-built stove make it clear that time must be relative here. Behind the rocky moraine rises a vista past the glacial expanse to Cerro Torre, the view stunning on the rare clear day.

But today, there is nothing to be seen. All the mountains are walled in by a black bastion of clouds; the hurricane-like wind whips the ice water of Lago Torre into the air and drops torrents of rain 600 feet away in the Campo, practically the forecourt of hell. This upper edge of the moraine marks the threshold of a world defined by the brute forces of nature, where it is not you who decides how far or how high you can go.

Alexander and Stephan know this game of Patagonian mountaineering. The endless waiting through storms and rain; the constant observation of wind, weather, and pressure on the altimeter, so that you're ready to roll in an instant, coiled like a tense spring about to go off. If the needle on the altimeter drops by a couple of feet because of rising atmospheric pressure, then the wind will surely die down somewhat later, and you must be quick—very quick. Put on your boots, shoulder your backpack, Tyrolean traverse across the river, walk alongside Lago Torre, and hike across the Torre Glacier to the high camp, under the towers, called Noruegos. That's a whopping ten miles with lots of ups and downs. Three hours if you move quickly. Then maybe a short break or a bivouac under the granite blocks and then straight on to the mountain because time without wind is in short supply throughout Patagonia.

Sometimes you have two days, rarely four—and, if you are unlucky, only a few hours. It takes only a blink of an eye for the weather to swing from steel-blue calm to a jet-black inferno. If you're still high on the mountain, you're in for a wild ride and a significant challenge when trying to rappel. The wind cancels all gravity, blowing the ropes horizontally away from the wall and sometimes vertically upward. They often get stuck behind flakes and blocks and must be freed; you feel like a plaything for the forces of nature. Ultimately, you must give everything to escape this hell in one piece. In the moment, you curse these mountains, mountaineering in general, the wind, and the weather. This is "*Puta*-gonia."

Alexander has given me a heads-up. As beautiful as the Torres are, they require extreme patience, mental serenity, and a willingness to outright suffer before they make you a hero. But above all, success is defined by the power of your legs. You must never pass up an opportunity to climb, no matter how miniscule; sprint up the hill and give it a whirl, even if you get washed out and blown off the mountain more often than not. If you're unlucky, you'll slog hundreds of miles but still come up empty after two months in Patagonia.

But this time, everything is going to be different. Today, we won't start running up the hill at the first blue gap in the clouds. Today, we have a trump card in our back pocket: a satellite phone! The direct line to my friend in Innsbruck, Charly, our weather god. He already gave me the meteorological information crucial for success on my Ogre expedition, and now he'll try to interpret this fluctuating Patagonian weather using state-of-the-art computer models. If he is successful, he'll be able to tell us when to get going and, above all, how long we have until the next storm smacks the Torres.

Even though we've been stuck in camp for over a week due to the weather and I have yet to glimpse Cerro Torre, I'm still fascinated by this surreal landscape. Somehow, I maintain a good feeling that we will get to climb the Torre via our extravagant traverse route, which no one before us has ever dared to attempt. For now, we must stay patient. Finally, I have time in abundance, the time I never get at home. Some might call it boredom. But I enjoy finally not having to do anything, being able only to breathe, explore the woods, and stand on the moraine in the storm, facing it, and let myself be carried by the sound of the thundering, rattling rain slapping my jacket. It's a familiar sound, one that takes me back to high up on El Cap, when a BASE jumper plummeted past our bivy site. I close my eyes and start to fly.

Days later, a glimmer of hope: Charly gives us the green light for twelve hours before it becomes stormy again. We take advantage of the weather window and haul all our gear over the Torre Glacier to the Noruegos. Then I'm standing there, mouth open, under these mountains I've read so much about and seen so many photos of. The sky is azure, and it all looks even more powerful, impressive, and wild than I have imagined in my wildest dreams. No matter which direction I turn, there are towers, walls, pillars, and towers again. The Stonehenge of Climbers is a sacred, mystical circle of the most beautiful mountains in our world. An ancient world, practically a Jurassic Park of mountains. In contrast, the Alps are a cultivated landscape.

The most massive among them is by far Cerro Torre. It is impressive how defiant and almost gracefully serene this Torre stands, how it carries and embodies its history with silent dignity. The Col di Conquesta can be found between Torre Egger and Cerro Torre. Far below is where the drama of Maestri and Egger played out. Above the ominous north face, crowned by a massive ice mushroom, is the summit. On the far left, the southeast edge, the bolt ladder. The frozen compressor is in the middle of the headwall, only dimly visible to the naked eye—the tool with which Maestri murdered the impossible. Between this ridge and the north face is a smooth big wall, close to 5,000 feet in height, the still-unclimbed east face. It shines monolithically due to the bright, reflective granite and resembles El Cap—a visionary climbing goal, but not ours for this trip.

Our goal is something else entirely: for me, the most beautiful, the longest, the craziest, the only true objective is the skyline, the EKG readout of a climber, a line drawn through heaven and earth across all four Torre peaks, the entire traverse, pure rock 'n' roll. The only problem might be that our project will no longer be a secret once we start. Then suddenly, everyone will want to do it, and everyone will claim that the idea was theirs initially. In alpinism, there is no such thing as intellectual property, no red tag on the first bolt to mark a closed project like in sport climbing. Up there in the world of rock and ice, elbows come out, even if a friendly beer was drunk together in the valley beforehand.

So, we are cautious with our treasure. When asked what we will tackle during the next weather window, we always say: Cerro Standhardt over the ridge from north to south, on the route *Festerville*, because of its beauty—which isn't even a lie. However, what nobody knows is that on *Festerville* we will carry bivy gear and provisions for at least two more days and that after Cerro Standhardt, we will carry on toward Herron, then further to Egger and finally up the Torre.

We stow our backpacks under a large granite block and stumble across the glacier back to Campo Bridwell. Again and again, I turn around and look back at the Torre. Now I can understand all the climbers who have become addicted to it. Because once you've seen the tower, you've also heard its demand to be climbed. This mountain is more than just a mountain; it is the mirror of a climber's soul.

These are not good times in the Torres. Our hopes of riding over all four ice mushrooms soon crumble come Charly's latest forecast: at least a week or maybe more of storm. That's too much for Stephan and Alexander, who have already spent too much time in Campo Bridwell in their mountaineering lives. Back then, they relied solely on hoping conditions might improve. At that point, waiting still made sense. But with the new weather oracle via the satellite phone, we can't gloss over the truth anymore. Puta-gonia will not become sunny and stable through mere "hope" alone.

We descend to Chaltén because waiting here for another week in the tent makes no sense anymore. In town, you can at least make the eternal waiting a little more athletic: you can go sport climbing and bouldering, and there are pubs and restaurants. Pretty quickly, our little group settles into a good rhythm. We quickly learn the best bouldering circuits, and then, come afternoon, visit the Patagonian "Kugelbach-Haidi," a pub run by the chocolate-store artist Anabel, for the day's first beer.

In the evening, we go to a restaurant, Patagonicus, for a divine Bife de Chorizo with lots of chimichurri, and the final stop is always El Puesto—the best bar in town, run by local climbers. Here, people party excessively every day of the week until the early-morning hours. For those hours, we banish the Torre from our minds.

Biding our time is exhausting, draining, and slowly making us soft, while Charly can still report nothing new except more Puta-gonian weather. Alexander decides to get his arse out of there. He no longer sees any sense in staying, and heads back home. Stephan, who is faring well with the "Triple B"—bouldering, biking, and bar—will remain until his official departure date in a week. And I'll remain as long as I feel like the Patagonian life suits me. It's a good plan that each of us can live with.

Just four days before Stephan's departure, at the last minute, a gap in the clouds appears amidst the foul weather. It's now or never, and with a new, highly ambitious game plan, we need to get going! Our objective is Torre Egger, which Stephan tried in years past but failed at repeatedly—had he succeeded, he would been the first to climb all four peaks in the range, a small record for him and a pat on the back from his sponsors! We break trail from the village past Campo Bridwell to the Noruegos. After a short pause, we hasten up to Col Standhardt, and then in the pitch dark traverse across the ice fields toward the north edge of Punta Herron.

At the razor-sharp col of Col de Sueño, the sun finally rises over the Estepa. The granite towers glow a fiery red, set ablaze by the morning light, and we are right in the middle of it all. To get the momentum going, we now divide the leads into tactical blocks. Rock is my forte; the ice goes to Stephan, who has far more experience climbing the rotten ice mushrooms barring the way to the summit. I climb fast, zigzagging between blobs of rime ice and icicles stuck to the wall, up flakes and cracks, until finally I reach the mighty, bulging, ice mushroom of the Herron. Aesthetically, it is the most beautiful alpine structure I have ever seen. A work of snowy art, anarchically sculpted by the wind, curved, overhanging, and unclimbable upon first inspection. It's rime ice: snowy, porous, and often bulging with overhangs. But the Patagonian gods have a soft spot for climbers and have, with painstaking dedication, playfully milled a few runnels and "tunnels" from bluish, shimmering ice into these ice bulges, making passage just feasible.

Despite this assistance and the aesthetic appeal of the features, they offer the most terrifying climbing experience. Stephan digs, fights, curses, and needs an hour for the first ninety feet. As I'm following, the ice screws he labored to place in the rime ice pluck right out of the wall, zipping down the rope to dangle against my harness. At the top, I pat Stephan on the back: "Well done, Steph! Rime-ice climbing is a completely different discipline than ice climbing back in Germany, and it's a miracle that it works at all. It's more like dancing on raw eggs, because nothing really holds!"

These ice mushrooms are often the crux of the Torres. They are ever-changing due to the wind, and the more horrible the weather, the more massive the mushrooms become. There have been times when the Torre was unclimbable until climbers spent days excavating a way through the ice mushroom to reach the top. "This is crazy. But, Steph, you should probably know this. All the screws fell out just by me looking at them. They wouldn't have held your body weight!"—"Yeah, I figured as much, but you know, I climb a little more relaxed when there's a carabiner clipped underneath me!"—"Yes, then you like to fool yourself, or how do you see it?"

We both laugh, if only because the worst is already behind us. Stephan digs through the last cream roll of ice, and at four in the afternoon, we stand on the summit of Herron. It is pleasantly warm, with no clouds and no wind whatsoever, and the view is phenomenal. The endless, icy expanse of the Helio Continental to the west, the broad Fitz Roy massive to the east, the Estepa and Lago Viedma to the south, and Egger and Cerro Torre directly in front of us. It is Herron's fourth ascent, yet I search in vain for a smile on Stephan's lips. His goal was not Herron, but Egger, whose slabs have been iced over and made unclimbable by the weeks of bad weather. Once again, my Swiss friend has to give up before the summit of the Egger. We make a bollard rappel anchor, stuffing snow into an empty sleeping bag, wrapping it with a sling, and burying it. As we rappel, Stephan grumbles to himself, "Patagonia!"

From now on, I'm alone and will move my tent back to Campo Bridwell just to be closer to these mountains. Flying solo opens a door for me to get to know Patagonia in a new, intimate way. I walk for hours on end through spellbinding, twisted forests, where small, thick-trunked trees stand close together, bracing themselves in communion against the storms. I lose myself in this jungle, merged with Patagonia, and discover many new things.

I find the former camp of Maestri and Egger on a wooded moraine ridge at the right edge of Lago Torre. It's a paradisiacal place—from there, a new view of the Torre, visible briefly after it cuts through the billowing clouds like a warrior's sword. Today, I've seen the Torre many times, even up close, but the sight remains breathtaking each time. What a mountain! Compared to the Ogres, Latoks, and Shivlings—which are undoubtedly beautiful, mighty fortresses of rock and ice—none can match the aesthetics of the Torre. It is the monumental wonder of the alpine world, and I understand Maestri's infatuation. And yet, simultaneously, it is incomprehensible how a mountain of such beauty could symbolize hatred. What happened to him up there?

Adjacent to Campo Bridwell, directly on the raging Río Fitz Roy, is a small shelter in a small forest, temporarily built from branches and tarpaulins, and stocked with cooking utensils and provisions. It's the hut of two Austrians, one young and one old. The younger one, a Carinthian, is muscular, looks determined, and is sharpening his ice tools with a fine file. The older one is an East Tyrolean. His long, straight blond hair hangs over his angular face, but his piercing ice-blue eyes are fixed on the Torre. When he finally notices me, he slowly turns and directs these words at me in a somewhat haunted, heavy voice: "I know you. You're Thomas. You are here for this mountain, just like us."

He pauses momentarily, and with his intense stare, he seems like the

Torre reincarnate—dramatic, wild, aloof, mysterious. He takes another deep breath and, with a slight smile on his lips, utters, "I'll keep trying until I find the way I need to take it!" He is referring to the controversial line taken by Maestri and Egger through the north face. His first name is Toni, but not with a surname of Egger—it's Ponholzer, and he lives in Debant, as Egger did in his day. He seems as if he were carrying the whole burden of the Egger story on his shoulders, as if he had to solve the mystery of 1959 by climbing the north face route to help the soul of his namesake finally find the peace it deserved.

Curious, I ask Toni the question that every Patagonia newcomer wonders about: "And what do you think, Toni? Were they really up there?"—"Thomas, no one can say! Only Torre knows the truth. If we're lucky enough to summit Torre via the north face, we've done it for Toni. Maybe we'll find pitons from back then hidden under the ice; perhaps we'll find nothing.

"But that's not important. Finally, we climbed his way, and no one will have to ask that question again!"

The younger Austrian inspects the perfect teeth of his ice tools, "Hey, Thomas, now I have to introduce myself, too. I'm Markus—Markus Pucher!" He is a perfect partner for Toni's mission on the Torre. He has the edge, the focus, and the look. He has level-headed energy and seems determined to solve the historical riddle of the north face.

Toni, as I learn, is so much more than a climber obsessed with the Torre. Through his ten years of experience with this mountain, he has amassed countless quirky stories and bits of lore—from making "mouse goulash" to ghostly encounters in these very woods. At the end of our first encounter, he adds: "Thomas, I can see it in your eyes. The Torre is already very close to you; you can feel and understand it. And if we are quiet now, we can even hear it because it is always present!" At this, he laughs loudly, and I'm initially lost. "What do you mean—where is the Torre supposed to be?" I understood only when he directs his ice-blue eyes toward the raging glacial waters beyond: the river, rushing past us, is part of the Torre summit in molecular, liquid form.

Because of the permanent sour weather, I move my tent back to El Chaltén, pitching it in the front yard of the Soto Brothers, and become a regular at the Chocolatería, Patagonicus, and El Puesto. During the day, I train my fingers on the blocks, and develop a deep friendship with many locals, especially Luis. We are brothers in spirit, and Torre soon connects us. Even if Luis will never have ambitions to climb this mountain, he is excited about this crazy traverse over the four rime-ice mushrooms. "Thomas, this is a divine path. It doesn't get any better. When you climb over these towers, I will be with you in thought for every foot. Your dream has become mine, even though I'm just standing at the bottom!" he tells me.

As much as I would like to make it to the top this year, our project has to be postponed for another year. Alexander and I have the idea to return with Stephan, with the added bonus of our spiritual ground support, Luis.

In the meantime, it's now mid-February, and some Stone Monkeys from Yosemite are in town. Dean Potter; his girlfriend, Steph Davis; Winky; Kurt Albert; Leo Houlding; and Silvo Karo grace El Chaltén with their presence. All are waiting for the excellent weather to get after it finally. Only I don't have a partner (yet) and no real idea of what to do when the weather turns good. But soon, word gets around that I carry the weather gods in my pocket.

"Hey, I'm Thomas!"—"That's what I thought—that you are a Huber. I'm Andi, a Swiss from the Valais." Somehow, we Hubers have a name now wherever we go. We're sitting in a bakery early in the morning, and Andi has just arrived from the Río Blanco, the camp at the foot of Fitz Roy. This year already has seen him summit Cerro Torre, but with his Swiss colleagues, he was riddled with bad luck when trying to get up Fitz Roy. For now, he is fed up with the bad weather and the senseless waiting in his lonely tent. We hit it off immediately and quickly imagine being on the mountain as a team. In my personal history, a Bavarian-Swiss partnership has always worked a treat, and I promptly convince Andi to set off during the next good weather window. Toward Egger, precisely on the same route as three weeks earlier with Stephan.

Finally, the weather takes a turn for the better. Charly promises meteorological perfection for three consecutive days. Because we go, all the other teams follow suit, knowing of my connection to this ace weather forecaster which I carry in my pocket. Toni and Markus launch their mission on the north face, Leo and Kurt head up toward Fitz Roy, Dean and Steph head toward Standhardt, and Andi and I head up Herron toward Egger. And three incredible days, with a flawless deep-blue sky and zero wind, really do materialize. This means the sun scorches the mountains, and the Torres are soon covered in water, snowmelt drenching all the climbable features. It is simply too beautiful and sadly too warm for these ice-crowned towers.

Toni and Markus bail on the approach because of the falling ice, while Dean and Steph manage a new route on the Standhardt, weaving between the waterfalls. Andi and I make good progress despite the heat, harmonize as a team, and laugh a lot about communication problems; we reach the summit of the Herron in good time. Afterward, we abseil into a col where no human has ever trodden, naming it Col de Luce. We continue over compact slabs toward Egger, to the base of the ice mushroom. But the heat precludes a traverse underneath this mighty ice overhang, and we get out of there. Even without a summit, I am satisfied, because I have learned more about the traverse terrain with our route up these new slabs, which we call *El Espejo del Viento* (*The Mirror of the Wind*).

After these warmer days, everything turns dreary again—rainy and gray, the mountains washed black by rain, dripping wet clear to their summits. Even Charly cannot summon a new window of sunshine for now, so things are over for Toni and Markus. It isn't their year, but they know they'll be back the very next Patagonian summer. And so will we!

Dean wants to parachute from the top of Cerro Torre, but, at least for now, he lacks a partner for such an undertaking. As he meticulously packs up his parachute in front of his tent, he winks at me and says that I should start BASE jumping because that would give mountain climbing a new dimension, and the two of us could realize the craziest alpine objectives. "Baaabooom! That's the way we have to go," he says. Dean's eyes light up as I signal that I plan to follow him down this path!

Unexpectedly, the rainy, mucky weather breaks, and Charly issues a good-weather alert for four days—zero wind, zero precipitation, and ten degrees cooler than the last window. We're not sure what to do with this fantastic weather. Another try at Torre Egger? Dean and Steph are immediately off in the direction of Egger. They want to tackle the tower via the *Titanic* route, a plumb line up the east face. Andi and I get together with Luis in the best weather possible in the Torre Valley, and while out hiking, finalize our objective: Cerro Standhardt, the first part of the traverse, in a one-day push with a very light backpack. This will be the best preparation for next year!

Both Andi and Luis are enthusiastic about the plan. We cannot believe it when we reach the Noruegos in the late afternoon. All the rock is ice free and dry, without the typical water streaks, even though the sun has shone all day! The air up on the mountain must be cold. Absolutely stellar conditions. Did we blow our chance for the full traverse? I don't want to waste any thought on that right now: it is what it is! Dean and Steph are already bivying halfway up the east face, while we will start at two in the morning, heading toward Col Standhardt. As the sun peeks over the Estepa, we climb the glowing red granite of *Festerville*, bathed by morning light. It is a demanding climb, but still well within our skill set. A grand adventure in an incredible setting, precisely on the border between Chile and Argentina, between the inland ice and the Fitz Roy Massif. In less than nine hours, we are both standing on the summit of Cerro Standhardt.

"Thank you, Thomas, for having me with you; this is great!"—"Yes, Andi, today is the day of days; even the ice mushrooms are frozen. The climbing was fun. These are the exact conditions we'll need next year!"—"Yes, let's ensure we get down safe and sound."

The sun is low, about a hand's breadth above the horizon, when we reach the Col de Sueño. I knot a new sling into the anchor for our next rappel. Andi says: "Hey, Thomas, do you think it's good what we're doing?"—"What do you mean—the belay is not sound?"—"No, no that. Let us keep climbing in this weather and the bloody-good conditions. I think we can summit Egger. Not today, but tomorrow!" I can hardly take him seriously: "Hey, Andi, you are nuts. We have only two cereal bars left, a liter to drink, and no bivy gear; how will you get up Egger with that? There's only one sensible option, and that's down, toward our warm sleeping bags. So stuff it!"

I am no longer motivated to continue climbing, because now I have all the information to get after the traverse come next year. But Andi, persistent, goads me on: "Hey, Thomas, I guess you guys from Bavaria aren't used to it. But for us from Schwyz, a bivouac without a sleeping bag is no problem. Besides, we have a Gore-Tex jacket, which should be enough, and you can have the two muesli bars. I don't need anything to eat because you will lead everything anyway!" With this challenge, I can no longer say no; otherwise, I'll lose my mountaineering honor, though on the inside I feel like giving Andi a good kicking. "So, Andi, on your responsibility, we'll go on. Take me up to the belay. If we're going to continue, we shouldn't lose any time!"

The first feet out of the col are covered with a paper-thin glaze of ice. This costs time and nerves. After that, everything happens very quickly. The shadows of the Torres projected on Fitz Roy deepen in the evening light, and if one were to zoom in on the edge of the Herron, one would see two small dots like ants scurrying at breakneck speed toward the summit. Even the summit mushroom of Herron, typically precariously steep and challenging, is easy because of the icing, and as we stand at the summit and lift our hands to the sky, over on Egger, Dean and Steph do the same just then. These are the moments I will never forget!

Meanwhile, the setting sun swallows up the shadows cast by the torres of the Fitz Roy Massif, and in the last light, the Egger heroes rappel down their route into our Col de Luce. We look for a favorable place for the night between the boulders but do not find one. At some point, we sit uncomfortably two by two on a small ledge. A light wind whistles from the inland ice across the col, bringing a bitter cold. Andi thinks he might pack it in. I laugh out loud, even through chattering teeth. "Hey, Andi, you were the one with this glorious idea, so stop whining!"—"Yeah, right, but it's still cold, even with an insulated jacket!"

I stifle any further laughter, triumphing inwardly that we Bavarians can take a bit more than the Swiss. We huddle close, looking for warmth, and wait for the night to pass. When Andi starts to snore, perhaps warm finally from huddling next to me, it's too much and I snap. A gentle elbow is directed at his ribs, and he is awake again. "Yes, what's wrong?"—"Andi, you've been snoring for ages!"—"No, Thomas, I'm freezing; it's much too cold to catch any sleep!"—"Sure, you are! But Andi, I can't stand the cold myself. Come on—we can get out of here at night." Andi nods in agreement, and a little later, we climb by headlamp up the slabs we first climbed only a week earlier.

Slowly the stars disappear. Above the Estepa, the sky turns a dark purple and runs through the entire red spectrum in a few minutes. Then, very slowly, the sun hauls itself over the horizon. By now, we're sinking our axes into compact ice, the rock slabs far below us. With unexpected ease—almost a sense of playfulness—we pick our way through the snowy, rocky slabs up toward the white crown of the Egger. We reach the summit earlier than expected, following in the footsteps of our American friends. It is incredible, the sixth ascent of the Egger! We also get the best and most spectacular viewing platform for the Torre's north face, the wall of walls. Putting aside the historical drama for a moment, we see a perfect rock face with significant cracks soaring skywards, plus clean lines and features, all topped by the mighty summit mushroom. Crazy ideal conditions that could not be better.

But as perfect as our flow has been up to here on the Egger, a "push on" is no longer up for discussion. Without food, we don't stand a chance, nor do I want to relearn the hard lessons from Shivling on the Torre. Both of us are overwhelmed, without regret, just genuinely happy. We've done our homework, and the whole thing will definitely go down next year. But Andi, especially, has reason to celebrate. For him, as for me, it's the first Patagonian season, and through this adventure, he is now the first person to have stood on all four Torre summits. A crazy success without a pat on the back by a sponsor, because he has none. So, he must make himself content with my humble person's firm pat on the back.

After forty-eight hours nonstop in the alpine world, we are back in the Noruegos. Luis cooks us soup, and we fall asleep soundly straight afterward.

It is the end of the Patagonian season. The forests have turned an autumnal reddish yellow, the mountains are once again walled in by black clouds, and we are all celebrating with an exuberant Argentinean asado in El Chaltén, in the Soto Brothers' garden. Kurt, Dean, Steph, Winky, and Leo have unique stories. We add ours, and I feel this is just the beginning of the following extraordinary tale.

Exit

Switzerland, end of July 2005: I'm standing on the edge of a giant precipice. My body trembles with fear. Below me, a vertical sea of rock, mottled yellow, reaches at least 1,300 feet to valley floor. "Yellow Ocean" is the name of this exit point—the BASE-jumper terminology for a launching spot. As frightening as the view into the void might seem, it is a great vantage point to observe the paradisiacal, crazy landscape below. It is

FREIHEIT

almost like a painting that the Romantic landscape artist Caspar David Friedrich might have envisioned. To the left and right, the steepest possible walls rise from a lush valley. Across the valley, water cascades over an overhanging wall, pummeling the basin more than 1,000 feet down, where gusts of wind pick up the water to create fountains spraying through the air—the Staubbach Falls. Below is the picturesque mountain village of Lauterbrunnen. Up-valley are small alpine pastures and farms, then, shining white, the glaciated Jungfrau—a dominant high-alpine peak of the Bernese Oberland—commanding the vista in the distance. It would be the perfect film set for a heroic epic directed by the Südtirolean filmmaker Luis Trenker.

To be more honest, the only non-heroic thing in this environment is me: I'm scared shitless. Ulli, my mentor, stands behind me and tries to ease my tension with calming words: "Thomas, take your time—breathe!"

I feel my pulse throughout my body. My knees vibrate with excitement, because I know that if I take the next step and screw something up, that's it for rock 'n' roll—the wild, rebellious, incredibly awesome life that I have fashioned for myself.

Do I need this? Isn't it enough just to be, or am I doing all this to please others, to be a hero, to not disappoint Dean? This world is much too beautiful, this Lauterbrunnen Valley, my home, family, and friends. Should I put it all at risk because I must take this next step? Who says I have to?

Ulli senses my nervousness, but stays cool and tries to build my confidence with more calming words—words that very deliberately don't pressure me to take the next step: "You know yourself what you have to do, Thomas. You have mastered everything so far in the best possible way. Take another deep breath, and you'll notice that your pulse is slowing down. And then, when you are ready, go through everything exactly as we discussed. Keep yourself stable and pull in five to six seconds!"

Ulli is right about that; we have meticulously prepared for this day.

After coming home from Patagonia with Dean's pipe dream of taking alpinism to a new dimension with BASE jumping, I immediately sought a way to join him on this path. That my family was not enthusiastic is an understatement. Nonetheless, one of my character traits which others around me occasionally find annoying and problematic came into play: when I set my mind on something, I do not deviate; I follow my heart without compromising. In such moments, I am no longer controlled by rational thought; instead, everything runs through my defiant heart of an outlaw, which fights to the death to get what it longs for, setting aside even empathy for what my family must be feeling and their fears over my risk taking. In such moments, I'm so caught up in my world that I can't find a way out by myself—primarily because I'm not looking for it.

I couldn't get the glow I'd seen in Dean's eyes after his Yosemite jump out of my mind, accompanied by the "Baaabooom" he uttered from his mouth. He was not stoned but high on the BASE experience. I knew there must be more to BASE jumping than mere danger and extreme risk. It is something you only understand when you do it.

By chance, I found Ulli Wambach. He was a skydiving instructor and BASE jumper at Skydive Colibri, sixty miles north of Berchtesgaden, and I was able to win him over for my project: to BASE jump from El Cap before the end of the year. It usually takes more than 1,000 jumps from a plane until you're ready to jump from a rock face. While a skydiver has a 99 percent chance of arriving safely on the ground, a BASE jumper faces too many potential dangers and has no guarantee of survival. The only way to minimize the risks is through practice, training, and self-discipline.

My first jump from a plane flying 13,123 feet above the ground was breathtaking, unusual, and electrifying. After 9,843 feet of free fall, I pulled the auxiliary parachute, which pulled the main parachute—the so-called "rig"—out of the backpack. The chute gave a slight jerk, and then I glided toward the ground. I quickly understood that I could shape the air with my body like a potter shapes clay on a wheel. Soon, I could control free fall stably across all possible axes of rotation. I did somersaults, rolls, spins, flew forward and backward, and leaned, sitting, against an invisible couch. It was enjoyable, and I now understood the skydivers' slogan: "Fall free, be free!"

Packing the base rig is an art in and of itself. The chute is meticulously folded according to a specific pattern—every crease must be smoothed out in a way that makes folding an ironed dress shirt seem like a doddle. Then all the lines are meticulously sorted, and in the end, everything must be carefully packed into the rig. This is where the initial mistakes can creep in, potentially causing severe consequences down the line. That's why every jump starts with packing. Quite literally, you are packing your lifeline. That's why it's a written law that no one else is allowed to pack your chute—everyone needs to be responsible for their own life!

Eight weeks after my first jump and after sixty completed skydives, the next step was to jump from a hot-air balloon, and then culminate in a leap from a high bridge. (BASE stands for "Building, Antenna, Span, and Earth.") In contrast to the skydives, in which an air cushion immediately takes effect because of the plane's forward motion, and you can "work" with the air, when you jump into the void your body accelerates at 32.185 feet per second, and the atmosphere only slowly begins to carry you. Everything is more sensitive, more delicate, and more dangerous than when you jump out of a plane. There's the jump, the acceleration phase, the handling of the "ground rush," and the pollen filling the air only 330 feet above the ground, knowing that impact is now only three seconds away if your chute hasn't engaged. Fatal mistakes can creep into each of these phases, triggering a deadly chain reaction: there's "head down," i.e., upside down during the exit; bad body posture during acceleration; asymmetrical pull; twisted canopy opening; and the worst-case scenario, a line twist, with the canopy opening twisted 180 degrees. If there were a wall behind you in such a situation, there would be a collision, a "wall strike," which you would survive in only the rarest of cases. But there is no wall when you jump from the balloon or the bridge. That's why I provoked these mistakes in these proving grounds, so that I would know what to look for when standing on the ledge before my first cliff jump.

Now, at the edge of the Yellow Ocean, these thoughts are pulsing through my head: *Exit forward, jump upwards, just no head down. Stay symmetrical. Don't tense up. Pull late because then you'll be farther from the wall. Is the chute packed professionally? Did I miss anything? Hopefully the chute opens straight. Just don't do a 180, Thomas. Or even worse: a line twist* . . .

This firework of thoughts on the precipice creates a short circuit in my psyche, forcing my entire body to vibrate. Only the baggy jumping clothes, which puff up in the air like the Michelin Man and thus improve your forward glide, mask my jitters. I try to banish this mindfuck and focus only on my breathing: deeply out, deeply in, deeply out, deeply in. Slowly, my stress level drops; my blood pressure drops, hand in hand, too.

"Hey, Ulli, I think I'll jump now."

"Yeah, well, have fun!" There it is again, my mentor's dry sense of humor.

If only he knew that any idea of fun I'm having right now has fled somewhere far up into the icy world of the Jungfrau, and that everything inside me is bitterly serious. I am in complete survival mode. I take one last deep breath, fixate on a point on the horizon, and start counting out loud: "Three, two, one!" And . . . I jump down toward Lauterbrunnen.

Ulli says, "See you!" hoping that everything will go well, and that we will meet again down in the valley.

Now I am in the air; I am falling. Then I hear it, first softly, then louder and louder: the sound of falling, accelerating at the speed of a Ferrari. I race past this yellow wall, getting faster and faster like an arrow fired from a bow. The air pushes me forward, far from the wall. After what feels like an eternity, but is in fact only six seconds, I pull the auxiliary chute, keeping a stable, symmetrical posture. I do everything right, without thinking, because now I am just acting. With a loud "Baaabooom," the chute opens without a hiccup. Then I glide gently over an alpine meadow into the paradisical Lauterbrunnen valley.

When I land, I can hardly believe what I have just experienced. As soon as you leave solid ground, all fears and doubts dissolve. The jump occurs in a vacuum, where it's not survival instinct running amok but a love of life making all the decisions. It is genuine and yet surreal because something is taking place that's not entirely rooted in reality. Then the "Baaabooom" brings you back to this world in one fell swoop. As soon as you land, you feel reborn, back into life. I understand now why Dean's eyes looked the way they did.

A short time later, Ulli lands beside me and pats me on the shoulder: "Well done, Thomas—a clean first jump. But that was just the beginning!"

CHAPTER TEN

The Movies and the Arts

At the Limit

Taft Point: one of the most beautiful non-touristy lookouts above the Valley, with a magnificent view of El Cap. The vista is simply crazy: round boulders as tall as grown men perch on flat granite slabs, and between the rock crevices, scattered pines shaped by wind and weather find their way to the light, redolent with the resinous smell of pine and thyme. Surrounded by the golden colors of the Indian summer, we sit on the precipice with our feet dangling into the void. The light of the setting sun casts a wildly romantic spell over the valley. The day's last thermal updrafts ruffle our long, unwashed hair, our gazes lost in the walls of El Capitan.

Pepe, a short man in a peaked cap, visualizes a cutout through a square formed with his thumb and forefinger, and looks satisfied. He has the 16mm camera next to him in position. While Wolfgang focuses one last time, Susan cleans the lens again and writes the scene's title on the flap: "Taft Point-1". Joe fishes for the perfect sound, using a long, telescoping rod fitted with a directional microphone that's has a wind visor: "Camera rolling, sound rolling, action."

Alexander starts speaking, making a powerful statement: "No one could ever replace Thomas as the perfect climbing partner; of course, this is also related to the fact that he is my brother, the person I grew up with."—"We are brothers, but we are still fundamentally different. Alexander is calculated and has clarity, I am passionate and wild—and precisely this mixture of our differences makes us the perfect climbing team. A team seeking to be challenged by speed."

After these opening statements, we both gather firewood, light a campfire, set up for a bivy, and continue conversing. Alexander summarizes our endeavor: "When you're standing in front of that blank wall, you feel like it would be a better idea to stay down on the ground!" We laugh, although we both know that behind this statement lies a dangerous truth about speed climbing. Primarily, that staying put is the safest option. But we are here to do the opposite: leave the ground, run up the frictionless wall, and accept the possible consequences, including taking gigantic whippers that could be even fatal. Consequences that do indeed sometimes haunt our dreams.

Scene 2, next day, early morning, same place.

"Camera rolling, sound rolling, shut up."

We slowly crawl out of our sleeping bags and relight the campfire, and then I start reliving my nightmare: "Both of us are sprinting up the *Nose*, climbing at the same time. While I'm seconding, my foot slips from the granite slab. I fall and pull Alexander off the wall. Both of us fly toward the void below. A single piece of protection holds the fall. Then the medium-sized nut slowly loosens and then violently pops due to our combined weight."

Alexander explains how we deal with these fears: "The fear encountered in mountaineering, free soloing, and speed can be intense. But when we deal with this fear, utilizing all our senses and overcoming it, we gain an unforgettable moment in life. A hard experience, if not impossible, to put into words!"

Scene 7

Dean bridges up a chimney without a rope and then free-soloes up a crack. Ivo, waiting for him at the top, greets him: "Hey, Dean, how's it going? Looks cool what you're doing; let's go see the brothers—they're over there!"

Scene 8

We laugh, talk, and tee up an emotional scene. Dean, his language forceful, explains the essence of our adventure: "The brothers will probably break the speed record on the *Nose*, but they won't be happy until they've given it their very best. Speed is the most cutting edge—it's just doing—and that's where the attraction is. A lot of my friends, especially Thomas and Alex, we are drawn so powerfully to what we do, so we almost have no choice about it.

"You don't put your life on the line to be better than the other guy; you put your life on the line to outdo your present self. We can grow through this motivation to seek and find our own limits. This also includes confronting our fears and overcoming them in the end. That's how we all grow.

"With climbing, it's [easy to see that it's] a metaphor for all relationships—friendships, love, or family. I think all of our life is full of little deaths, transitions where we change and grow. Right now, there is some lesson I haven't quite learned, and the answers are in the walls and in the mountains. That's why we keep going back—to try to figure it out, because there is a higher meaning in life."

Pepe cracks a satisfied grin and thanks everyone for these successful introductory scenes at Taft Point.

It all began with Winky's notion that the Huber Brothers ought to topple the American speed record on the *Nose*, attempt a new personal best time, and leave everybody awestruck. It sounded logical, of course; we couldn't resist the temptation and wanted to at least give it a try. This initially whimsical thought gained momentum, and we suddenly found ourselves on this film set.

Max and Franz, our faithful companions with the cameras, initially wanted to raise money to get a film off the ground. But this story—the Huber Brothers, the speed record, the *Nose,* and Yosemite—immediately attracted strong interest from major production companies. In the end, Max and Franz abandoned leading the project, and instead were engaged as a vertical camera team by the Austrian Lotus Film and the Munich-based Hague Moss Film, which financed the film with public funding.

Pepe Danquart, who had already won an Oscar, would direct, while Wolfgang Thaler, an award-winning documentary cameraman, would create a visual language transferable to the big screen Alexander and I were right in the middle of it as a team, wanting to realize a speed project amidst this preconceived, stylized dramaturgical project. This was the literal crux: two self-contained teams wanted to deliver benchmark performances dependent on each other—them on film, and us speed climbing.

Even though we knew the film would make everything more complicated, it was exciting to experience something new and to act on a professional film set. But, as was to be expected, this cinematic adventure had its downsides. Gone was the rebellious life in the Valley we once celebrated passionately. The spotlight was switched off. The rangers were no longer our bogeymen, having officially issued the permits for the shoot while our friends—the wildlife of Camp 4—were disenchanted by us all staying in the luxurious holiday homes of Yosemite West.

But we all had to bite the bullet. It was a chance to be known as professional mountaineers through a feature film, which would bring us more lucrative slideshows and lectures.

The Stone Monkeys could earn good money doing odd jobs like carrying loads up El Cap. Ivo was the undisputed outdoor manager and coordinator,

Winky's assistant, and photographer for the making-of. Dean and Chongo had fixed roles in the film, were our closest friends, provided their input, and philosophized about the sense and nonsense of being an artist within the vertical realm.

Our first "go" on the *Nose* would be new territory for us both. "Sickle Ledge," "Stoveleg Crack," "Dolt Tower," "El Cap Tower," "Texas Flake," "Boot Flake," "King Swing," "Great Roof," "Pancake Flake," "Camp V," the "Glowering Spot," "Camp VI," and "Changing Corners" were landmarks we had known only from stories. Everything looked even wilder standing at the base, especially considering that we would have to climb it all in 2:48 (or less) at some point. Alexander was right when he said it would be better to stay on the ground. We were both silent at first, and I suspect we would have said the same thing: "Are you crazy? It looks so far; it won't be easy to do now. But now we are here. We might as well set off!"

We get ready, tie in, rack our gear on our harnesses, and tape our hands. For us, this pre-climb ritual is always the same; this time around, however, everything is different. Pepe stands next to us at the base of the *Nose* and asks some final questions with the camera running. He wants to know what we expect, what we hope for, and what fears we have for our first quest up the climb, demanding an emotional striptease just before we set off into the vertical. "Right now, the joy of climbing the *Nose* for the first time, encountering all the classic pitches, of getting used to all the conditions, still dominates. Then comes the training, which will be fun for sure. Only give and take three weeks will we start to speed-climb, but I don't even want to think about that yet!"—"Thomas, don't talk so much; it's time. Let's go!"—"Yep, good enough!"

Wolfgang Thaler changes his position with his 16mm camera to get a wide-angle shot, keeping the aperture open. It will show us brothers towering tall and in focus, dominating the foreground, with the *Nose* in the background getting blurrier toward the top. Soon the camera loses us in the sea of granite. With a "Camera running, sound running," "Take," and, "Please," our adventure finally starts. We climb over the slabby but technically complicated entry cracks; the climbing takes a lot of time and nerves from the get-go. Only after two hours do we reach Sickle Ledge, 600 feet above the ground; at 2:48, we are only 300 feet higher, sinking in bomber hand jams up the Stoveleg Crack.

The mere idea of being 2,300 feet farther up the wall now, topping out, weighs heavily on us, compounded by the heat, the glaring sunlight that fries our skin, and the fact that the little water we have with us has long since evaporated in our dry throats. The sheer, endless, ever-steepening granite desert of El Capitan hammers our optimism then and there. Suddenly, everything doesn't feel that great any longer. We encounter subsequent famous sections, like the King Swing, the Great Roof, and the Pancake Flake, with far less enthusiasm. We smash our way up these cracks and deserts of doubt, and, after eleven hours, finally fight our way onto the summit plateau of El Capitan. We summit drenched in sweat, covered in dirt, and utterly dehydrated, feeling heavy, exhausted, and clumsy.

If we are honest, everything seems unreal. We are being sacrilegious; we are fulfilling none of our expectations. We are worn out, empty, our hands are swollen, and our bodies have taken a beating. We are done! We doze in the shade of El Cap Tree, gnarled by years of mountain weather, and our tired eyes are reflected in the black filter of the camera lens. Our story today was not heroic, but devastating, and we tell the cameraman that we are feeling more disappointment than euphoria or hope.

As dramatic as it may sound, ours is just one story of many that could be told by this tree, which has stood as the guardian of the "Big Stone" for several hundred years. Perhaps the native inhabitants of the Valley, the

FREIHEIT

Awaneechee of the Miwok Tribe, sat here around their campfire while hunting in the high plains of the High Sierra, feeling safe from bears and wolves on the edge of the precipice. Before they were driven from their homeland throughout the nineteenth century by White settlers blinded by gold.

It wasn't until 100 years later that there would be the first documented gathering of people up here near El Cap Tree. In the fall of 1958, large groups of journalists and press photographers from all the national newspapers waited here for their national hero, Warren Harding, a ruggedly handsome, charismatic climbing pioneer from California. At the time, he was the first to believe he could climb the 3,000-foot wall of the Big Stone. An unknown climber, Harding, with his team, tackled the eye-striking arête that divides the El Cap into west and east halves. Thanks to all the newspaper coverage, the wild-eyed climber quickly became a national icon—a modern gladiator who was an easy distraction from the unpleasant daily grime.

When Harding and his team reached the high plateau after forty-seven days on the wall, a flurry of flashbulbs blinded them. When asked how he felt at that precise moment, Harding responded: "I don't know if you can say we conquered El Capitan; rather it has conquered us, because it's definitely in a far better state than we are!" Their route, the most complex and steepest rock climb of its era, was subsequently named the *Nose*. A barrier had been shattered, and more and more climbers passed by the tree, grinning broadly after a week of "Wall Life," donning torn T-shirts and tattered pants, with skin stained black from iron and aluminum, filthy, taking a summit photo, and perhaps spending another night under this gigantic, starry sky, the scent of pine resin mingling with those of marijuana and celebratory beers.

Unspectacular for the tree, but still a milestone in climbing, was the moment in the mid-seventies when three hippies stumbled down the East Ledges into the valley. Down in El Cap Meadows, Jim Bridwell lit up a filter-less Camel, took a deep drag, and grinned up at El Cap. He, John Long, and Billy Westbay had just become the first to climb the *Nose* in a day: "Guys, we're going to do harder stuff, but you only do a milestone like that once—it doesn't get any better than that."

The trio then went on to take the legendary, heroic photo in front of El Cap, which has been copied by all subsequent generations of climbers. It involves standing side by side as a team at a specific spot on the Meadows, with El Cap as a trophy in the background, looking as cool as possible, casual, with legs hip-width apart and a somewhat arrogant, perhaps even pugnacious facial expression, with no smiling allowed. The camera is positioned near the ground, so the actors seem more prominent than the wall they have just conquered. There have been a few photos like this taken of us brothers, too!

In addition to these stories, there was another firework display in the mid-nineties, when a woman electrified the climbing world with the provocative phrase "It goes, boys," ushering in a new era. Lynn Hill had redpointed the *Nose*. It was crazy, unbelievable, and she had broken down boundary after boundary: a woman had free-climbed this bastion of hardened big-wallers, redpointing every pitch. Baaabooom! The entire climbing community took their hats off to this achievement, and it didn't take long for Alexander to get the first redpoint ascent of the *Salathé* soon after. In 1998, the year we climbed *El Niño,* we brothers were dozing in the shadow of El Cap Tree. I admired this gnarled and weather-beaten pine, twisted in on itself, the crown bent eastward by the wind, a silent observer of the Tu-tock-ah-nu-lah, El Capitan.

Although our first "go" on the *Nose* was sobering, we didn't throw in the towel just yet. Every other day, we took another lap. Max and Franz filmed snippets of our training sessions, gradually collecting spectacular film sequences. The film crew was more and more satisfied. And Alexander and I were refining our tactics as well: we would divide the route into four blocks, mainly climbing and short fixing; only a few sections would see us simul-climbing. Today, with the advent of the unidirectional pulley the Micro Traxion, there is an easy, perfectly functioning solution to make simultaneous climbing much safer—the lead climber puts the rope through the Traxion on a bomber piece, such that it, and not him, holds a fall if the second slips off. But, back in 2005, we didn't have these pulleys. Today, the Traxion is commonly used in speed climbing, especially mountaineering, where it's a huge time-saver.

I lead the first block, up the entry cracks to the end of Sickle Ledge, where Alexander takes over the lead. Cross to the right into the Stoveleg Crack, up to the Dolt Tower, Texas Flake, and to the top of the Boot Flake. Here Alexander passes me the baton. The third block starts right away with the spectacular King Swing, then continues over the most route's most prominent feature, the Great Roof, followed by the dream crack Pancake Flake, which turns into the utterly disgusting "Groove." Past Camp V to the Glowering Spot, the last belay, where we swap leads. Alexander heads into the grand finale, leading the steep Changing Corners and linking moderate features into a final roof. A finishing sprint over low-angle slabs brings us to El Cap Tree, our stopping point.

So far, everything has been well structured and planned out, but we have yet to implement our training. After 20,000 vertical feet of climbing, divided into six training sessions, we can imagine squeezing out a time of four hours, but probably no faster. The film production has perhaps deprived us of our usual peace of mind. Having to function always and everywhere, always having the cameras focused on us, even on our supposed rest days, has taken its toll. Or is it just our fear of not making it?

We have already proven that we can be truly fast, on the *Zodiac*. But then, it was more straightforward—we were only racing against our own record and had nothing to lose. Now, however, the time of 2:48 is on our minds constantly—during training, while climbing, during the post-climb beer, while eating, and even while sleeping. In addition, there is this pressure of expectation because everyone is convinced that we will and have to make it. After all, our athletic success defines the success of the entire film.

Moreover, everything is much more dangerous, wild, and complex than on the *Zodiac* because there are more ledges to smash into. Dean was right; speed climbing on the *Nose* is more akin to free soloing. The rope implies a safety net that is often not there; even the slightest fall could have dire consequences. The *Nose* is the actual arena of vertical gladiators: *El Capitan, we salute you!*

That is the key to this speed: consciously becoming aware of this deadly danger. Because when it comes down to it, you will give everything to reach the top in one piece; it only gets dangerous when you think you've got things under control and there is nothing to fear. We also learned that, to climb our best, we'd need to block out the distractions from the film crew.

At some point, we have practiced everything that needs to be done, and slowly but surely, a proper first attempt looms on the horizon. We need to give it a go, try it, to find out where we stand and where improvements can be made. Those vibes spill over to the film crew, and it starts buzzing like a hive with anticipation. We map out a schedule, while Pepe has crazier and crazier ideas to give the movie the most visual impact, with Max and Franz filming up on the wall, a camera at the topout, and one at the base. Ultimately, the only thing missing is a healthy perspective of the *Nose* from an elevated position. Alexander gets an idea: he climbs a loose, chossy gully with Max on the Cathedral Spires to get into position. Then it happens: a hold breaks, and my brother loses his balance, slipping and tumbling down a cliff band, falling thirty-five feet! He lands intuitively, like a cat, and survives. Still, Alexander has bruised both legs, so our filming plan goes up in smoke. The hive stops buzzing for the time being.

Life Doesn't Stick to Your Plans

Things often turn out differently than you think. As an example, I actually wanted to go through with jumping off El Capitan with Dean. But after the film shoot had to be postponed until the following spring because of Alexander's fall, I was strictly forbidden to jump. Had we been caught, I would have been kicked out of the Valley for good, and everything we had filmed so far would have been useless. But every cloud has its silver lining: the postponement opened up entirely new dramaturgical possibilities. A film portraying immediate victory would have offered a boring, well-trodden heroic storyline, but we wanted to show that we brothers never give up and return stronger after setbacks.

I also brought Patagonia into the mix. I raved about the crossing of the Torres, this line drawn in the sky as if by a divine architect—and with an alpine-historical significance rarely found elsewhere on Earth. It would, I told the team, make the perfect film project. And, based on my previous experience, we could even factor in a high probability of success. The whole production team was suddenly enthusiastic about my idea. The director tinkered with the script, and a new plan was drawn up: in February 2006, the film team, us brothers, and Stephan Siegrist were to go to the "Land of Storms," and then back to the Valley for speed climbing come spring. However, what makes sense on paper often has nothing to do with reality, which follows its own script.

We have been in Patagonia for five weeks now, waiting in vain for the weather and conditions I experienced the year before. With so much time gone by and no climbing, almost all of us start asking ourselves why we are here in the first place. Dean, who, like us, hopes for clear weather to jump from Cerro Torre, believes the wait is worthwhile: "We are here for the specific goal of breaking on through to the other side!" With these words, once sung by Jim Morrison, Dean confirms my feeling of still being on the right track. Only, for now, our hands are tied. No one is doing anything on the mountain, and if they did go, they would realize quickly that man is small and fragile compared to Mother Nature.

If the storms were to take a short breather, we could bag almost any mountain, though probably not push for our primary objective, the Torre Traverse. Our goals are so beautiful, an aesthetic work of perfection, that it is worth waiting for the right moment and not burning our energy or psyche on other objectives. After all, we are not here to add to our tick list but are hunters stalking the narrow ridge of impossibility. Sending this goal would be the most beautiful, wildest, most incredible, and craziest thing life could offer. That's why it's worth waiting: it opens new horizons and shows you a new reality.

The strength you need for such a path is drawn from the fire of your passion, which will demand everything: unconditional devotion, patience, and belief in yourself. Because love is the key, giving up the intended objective would be immensely painful. But suppose you lose this butterfly-in-the-stomach feeling for the mountains. In that case, this Patagonia would quickly become the enemy and call everything into question: We may have the freedom as climbers to set off wherever we want, but after setting off in one direction, we become prisoners, preoccupied spirits, practicing doing nothing and waiting for something that no feels longer tangible.

Ultimately, it's all for naught, and Patagonia this time is once again Putagonia, permeated by bad weather, a gloom that infiltrates the atmosphere within the team.

Three months later, we are back in Yosemite Valley. Patagonia, Cerro Torre, the storms, and our frustration are long forgotten. Now we are standing in morning twilight at the base of the *Nose*. Three days earlier, we easily climbed to the summit in three hours, leaving room for improvement. Today, we want to go all-out and finally break the record. Thus, open the door again, get in, forget everything, climb, do, make, shout, grab, climb, and work. And then, after 3,280 feet, fly back through the door into the ordinary world. Stop the clock at that precise moment. Job done. That's the plan on paper—simple and fast.

Slowly, the contours of El Capitan emerge from the night. Above us, Sickle Ledge, El Cap Tower, Boot Flake, Great Roof, and at the very top, the overhanging, bulging Changing Corners. Ten more minutes. Then we will have enough light and will get going. Early, because otherwise the yellow star in the sky will burn us to a crisp—we'll already be hot enough due to physical exertion. Everyone is in position: two teams with cameras on the wall, a camera with director Pepe Danquart up at the summit, and Wolfgang Thaler with his 16mm camera next to us. Joe Knauer is fishing for sound again; Susan focuses the lens and writes on the clapboard: "*Nose,* full speed, take one."

Only, my own vibe fails to match this perfectly organized set-up. I slept poorly and feel groggy. Maybe I'm even nursing a slight cold. But now, to cancel everything at the last moment because of a bad feeling with a "Sorry, I can't—I have a slight cold!" would trigger disbelief. So, I keep my doubts to myself.

"Alexander, let's do this; see how far we get today!"

"Don't doubt it, Thomas. We're sure to get all the way to the top, and with a little luck, even under 2:48!" Alexander grins at me encouragingly.

"Yes, if we're lucky!"

Alexander counts me down, "Five seconds to go, four, three, two, one . . ." then we are off, as a team, into this vertical madness. Into a world in which it's better to leave your brain at the base because you won't get far by thinking—you'd be much too slow.

Although I know what full speed all is about, I find it impossible to let go completely. My thoughts return again and again to this damn doubt, this shitty feeling in my gut. I cannot share my trepidation with anybody, not even my brother. Hence, I try to block it out and slip through unnoticed, fighting to turn my mind off and just climb.

Miraculously, my brutal tactics work, and I hand over the lead to Alexander after a record time for the first block. He sprints up the Stoveleg Crack, over El Cap Tower, and up Texas Flake to Boot Flake: 1 hour and 5 minutes, again a new sectional record. We are now competing for the record. Change of lead at the King Swing. Now I'm up front again and right into the heart of the *Nose:* the Great Roof.

But from now on, all is lost. I am exhausted, with nothing left to give. I feel like a boxer knocked out in the sixth round. I keep climbing nevertheless. I pick myself up again, trembling and fighting, my muscles cramping, while sprinting past the lens of the first camera operators. The cameraman cheers me on: "Thomas, you're on course. Get it done! Give it all you've got, ahhhhuuuuaaaa!" This motivation pushes me farther up the wall. Giving up is no longer an option. There is one way left: the single track up ahead and putting the pedal to the metal. So, I gather my remaining strength, pull up sixty feet of rope, fix it at the belay, and continue climbing on the slack rope. I push my way through a disgustingly frictionless section.

The nex moment, the silence is cut by a bloodcurdling *"Sheeeeeiiiiiiiiissee!"* from Alexander, who is hanging sixty feet below me on his jumars. Meanwhile, I am flying through the air at full speed, falling and falling until the rope snaps tight. Then all becomes eerily quiet. I hang on the rope, dumbfounded and somewhat traumatized, not comprehending what caused these events. Only when Alexander scans me all over do I realize I have fallen. I'm visibly battered—but nothing is broken. I'm sure I've suffered a massive bruise from the impact on the rope; only then do I realize that everything is over for now.

Probably my foot popped off the slabby rock, and I had no chance to compensate for this mistake. As a result, I fell the full sixty feet onto my coiled slack rope. Despite everything, I was lucky in my misfortune. It could have ended much worse. Alexander and I quickly grasp that there will not be a second attempt during our stay in the Valley. It's almost the mirrored scenario from last year, when I carried Alexander off the Cathedral Spires on my shoulders after his fall. Now my brother supports me as best he can while we finish the *Nose*.

When we finally reach the top, Alexander declares in front of the camera that what we are doing is against all common sense and, by definition, a kind of madness. But it is precisely these stories that enrich our lives. Without them, we would be dull and pallid, like a plant that gets no light.

Our friend Chongo has also been able to give meaning to this madness, explaining that the happiness you feel when you are at the top of your game is so great, so insane, shining so bright, electrifying every cell of your body, that you definitely don't want to go on without having experienced it. For just this fleeting moment, everything around you disappears. You can consider yourself more than lucky to have experienced this happiness, even if it lasted just the blink of an eye.

Chongo was right. I would give anything as a climber to feel this elation. In this case, it consists of breaking the 2:48:55 mark on the *Nose*. And though we are screwed for now, we will certainly not give up, but push on. Not this year, but next year, because we want this cinematic Huber epic to end with a success story. Precisely because we, as brothers, have always been a guarantee for success, at least when it comes to Yosemite!

The production team, however, can no longer go along with this plan. The money has run dry, and the film shoot is over. But instead of tossing the exposed film reels into the garbage can, Pepe has the great idea of letting the story end with the Huber Brothers on the summit of El Capitan. Standing tall as failed heroes. Even if we don't understand him at first, he assures us that in the end, the film will be great and, above all, honest, because it's real life, and not an author, who has written the script. And life doesn't always write success stories; it is often riddled with failure. In the end, it always depends on what you do with that failure.

Pepe is right, and we have our plan—with or without a film. We will return because El Capitan has become even more significant, more exciting, and more appealing to us than before. For the first time, I understand the saying that the mountains only look majestic when seen from the valley. Every success becomes more meaningful if you failed along the way. If you make it easily the first time, you merely have an unobstructed view from the summit—nothing more, nothing less!

As I waltz into seventh heaven with Marion on the Kugelbachbauern restaurant's wooden floor, the mantle of oblivion has long since covered our miserable failure on the *Nose*. In the closest circle of the family, with our climbing mom, Haidi, and with Dean, we celebrate our honeymoon in the place where it all began. This wild way of living will apparently be tamed a little through the marriage bond. But only a little, because Marion has said yes to a freedom-seeking mountain rebel. And thereupon, I say yes, giving her my promise to be a loving, responsible family man and husband. But my life does not change much; I remain a tightrope walker caught between two worlds, balancing on the knife's edge.

Dean and His Art

Dean may not have been the strongest climber, but he always thought outside the box, far from mountaineering's longstanding culture of hero worship and lionization. He was the one who defined our vertical life as art and broke new ground in an almost surrealistic way. He was a highliner, a free-solo climber, and a skydiver, and he was the one who wanted to combine these forms of play to find for himself the ultimate form of freedom. He invented free-BASE: free-solo climbing with a parachute. With this ultralight "survival" parachute lashed to your back while soloing a steep route, "If you fall, you don't die. You fly," said Dean, his dark and highly expressive baritone making the words sound almost like poetry.

Yet he also yearned to break new ground in mountaineering, because until now, the route itself or the summit had always been the goal, followed by a tiresome, often tedious descent. With a parachute, any adventure could be gilded by flying off the mountain. This art opened up a whole new world, with one tremendous advantage: in thirty seconds, you are standing back at the base. Dean was here now because I wanted to experience this magic of "Baaabooom climbing" with him on the three infamous peaks in the heart of the Dolomites.

These were the mountains where Alexander had celebrated some of his most outstanding climbing achievements. Reinhold Messner championed my brother, who, from Messner's point of view, had reinvented climbing with *Bella Vista*; two years later, his free solo on the *Hasse Brandler* finally knighted him as a true expert in the vertical arts. In the popular perception of the time, there was only one Huber Brother: Alexander. The golden roofs of *Bella Vista* shone far and wide, while the Ogres and Shivling had long since been shelved away in the archives of alpinism.

Subliminally, my brother's successes may have influenced me to make these Dolomite monuments the bedrock of our adventure. Still, on the surface, there was nowhere more suitable than the Tre Cime di Lavaredo—the Drei Zinnen—to realize Dean's vision with a parachute, climbing shoes, rope, harness, quickdraws, and chalk: three freestanding summits, three routes, fifty pitches, two jumps, all redpoint as a team, all within twenty-four hours. A vertical marathon, aesthetically beautiful, as if designed by the climbing gods themselves. Dean was thrilled.

Together we practiced the three routes. The first was *Ötzi Meets Yeti*, a VIII+ (5.12a) on the steep south face of the Kleine Zinne, then the *Phantom*, am IX+ (5.13a/b) on the Große Zinne north face, and as an overhanging finale, we went for the *Swiss Roof,* an X- (5.13) on the Westliche Zinne. Three routes that should not be underestimated.

In addition, we did both jumps in preparation, a tricky one with only four seconds of free fall from the Kleine Zinne and a relaxed, eight-second one from the Große Zinne. (The ending point of the feat was the summit of the Westliche Zinne, hence we wouldn't jump from there.)

In mid-August of 2006, shortly after my wedding, the time had finally come. Dean and I were standing at the base of the south face of the Kleine

Zinne at 1:00 a.m. Everything had been prepared, with two parachutes deposited at the respective exits, and we were determined to give it our all. Dean was on the move, climbing without a helmet, because today, any danger was banished—there were no limits, no compromises, and rationality had been placed on the back burner. Using headlamps, we climbed through the vertical to slightly overhanging wall of the *Ötzi Meets Yeti*. It could not have been any better. At daybreak, we reached the summit of the Kleine Zinne. Then it was time for our first jump. The wall stands 919 feet tall, but after four seconds of free fall, you are still damn close to the rock. A twisted chute would have fatal consequences. It is indeed a risky jump. We were both more than aware of that fact.

I got ready to jump first, stood on the edge, and fixated on a point in the distance. In the morning silence and with my heart pounding, I breathed deeply. Slowly I became calmer and began to count aloud. "Three, two, one," and with Dean's "Seeyhhhaaa," I pushed upward and beyond into the void. I began to fall, faster and faster, into the depths, three seconds, four seconds, quickly only 150 feet above terra firma—damn close to the ground already. I pulled the auxiliary chute, and then came the jerk; slowly and softly, the chute opened, thank God, straight, forward, without any twisting. A short time later, I stood on solid ground. Now Dean jumped, pulled at about the same height, and opened with a 180-degree turn; the chute picked up speed, hurtling him toward the wall. "Nooooo!" I held my hand in front of my face, not wanting to see Dean . . . but at the last second, he steered away from the wall, avoiding a life-threatening calamity. He landed next to me, both of us white. Damn, the adrenaline was boiling in both of us. Now we were both finally awake!

We marched to the Große Zinne's north face to climb the dead-vertical *Phantom*, a 1,970-foot route. As a Bavarian-Californian duo, we smashed out pitch after pitch to reach our second summit of the day, the Große Zinne, in seven hours. It has been energy-sapping, because the wall is always steep and never really eases off. But we've been successful as a team, climbing without falling and redpointing every pitch. After a short break, we got focused for the exit, and then both jumped over the north face into the depths. After eight seconds, we pulled our auxiliary chutes. The opening was more complex than before but more precise, due to our arrow-like flight position taking us far from the wall.

We landed in the scree at the foot of the north face and traversed to our last route: the *Swiss Roof* on the Westliche Zinne. We allowed ourselves only a short break. Ahead of us, we needed only to climb 1,640 feet to complete our piece of art. It was my turn for the first pitch. At the first small roof, my foot popped off a smear, but I checked my fall by tensing my body with maximum effort. Unfortunately, this led to a short-term dislocation of my right shoulder. With a quiet crack, my strength left me, and I had to let go, sagging onto the rope then having Dean lower me to the ground.

According to the rules of redpoint climbing, I needed to climb the pitch again, but back on solid ground, I could do nothing more. I held my right arm in a steady position. I was pale, shivering, not from the cold but from pain. Dean sat next to me and put his arm around my shoulder. His gaze seemed lost, far away from here. We both knew that this was where our adventure ended. I'd screwed up, and I was angry at my stupidity, for not letting go before I injured my bad shoulder, so that I could simply lower off and have another go—and for losing everything in the process. I felt ashamed, crying in front of Dean, not because of the pain but out of pure disappointment, especially for my friend. His gaze returned to me for a moment, and he calmly said: "Thomas, everything is as it should be—take a deep breath, breathe!"

I needed shoulder surgery in Berchtesgaden for a triple tendon tear of the rotator cuff, followed by three months of rehab. The season was in tatters, and looking back, it had been a disastrous year in terms of mountaineering. We could have achieved speed and summits; in the end, I, and therefore all of us, lost everything.

Apparently, I also lost my friendship with Dean. After the fall on the Westliche Zinne, we parted ways very abruptly. He cut off everything behind him with a sharp knife and disappeared without a trace. Was it disappointment with our failure that led to this behavior, or had he realized at the base of our last climb together that even this form of climbing could not give him the ultimate freedom he longed for? When we parted ways, Dean was already on a new path and wanted to walk alone. His vision was a pathway to himself, to fly and be free like a bird carried on the wind—jumping off a ledge far up in the mountains wearing only a large wingsuit, flying and landing precisely on sloping, snowy terrain. "Break on through to the other side!" as Dean would say. In his own way, this was his art, of making the impossible possible, a metamorphosis from man to the king of the air. That was Dean for you!

The Red Carpet

At a large cinema in Munich, our film premiere of *Am Limit! The Life of the Huber Brothers* is finally happening. The auditorium includes guests, journalists, celebrities, and friends. I'm standing before the hall door while cradling my real life. Philomea, our daughter, just two months old, fixes me with her blue eyes while we listen at the door, hoping the audience will like the film. In the vestibule, the guests have left behind a small battlefield of half-empty champagne glasses and half-eaten bits of finger food—relics of a world to which we don't really belong but through which my brother and I must pass.

A limousine dropped us off at the Film Palace an hour ago. When we got out, a wall of flashing cameras awaited us, while, just behind them, journalists scribbled in their notebooks. The red carpet is lined by fans vying for an autograph. Intimidated, we try to saunter casually through this illusory world in which everything seems just a bit too beautiful, rich, and perfect. We are being celebrated, even though we failed athletically.

What a strange world, far from the dusty everyday life of a Stone Monkey living in the dirt of Yosemite.

With the greatest disappointment of our climbing lives being presented to the public as a motion picture, Alexander and I agreed that we had our backs up against the wall. Even if they were beautiful pictures, a "fall" remains a failure and can't be stylized into an athletic success by talking it up at the end. However, Pepe conjured up an emotional story bristling with hope, emphasizing that even the best can fail, even when they do everything right. The lesson being that if you believe in your goal and burn for it, failure will always be an intermediate stage on your path to success.

When the premiere is over, loud applause erupts. Later, one reads in many newspapers that this film is an unvarnished and honest account of real life, that one should never lose hope, and that one should never give up.

This mantra reflects us Huber Brothers 100 percent. Giving up has never been our thing. And so, even though the *Nose* and Drei Zinnen projects brought me closer to my limit than ever before in my climbing career, I know I must return.

I am a master of new beginnings. This fall, of 2007, we want to get back on speed on the *Nose* without the distraction of camera lenses and sound engineers. We want to go for it precisely as we're used to: as real Stone Monkeys. And because I'm so motivated, I'd like to finish the Drei Zinnen project beforehand, this time without Dean, who is off writing his own story. Everyone lives in their cosmos—and mine on the Dolomites looks like this: all three routes climbed redpoint with three belay partners. Starting with a night climb of the *Alpenliebe* on the Westliche Zinne and a jump from Scoiattoli Ledge, followed by the *Phantom* on the Große Zinne with a subsequent jump from the same exit as the year before, and then a final climb through *Ötzi Meets Yeti* to the summit of the Kleine Zinne. Job done!

So far, everything has been planned to perfection. I have climbed all the routes several times for training, and now all that remains is one last practice jump off the Große Zinne: fantastic jump, eight seconds of free fall, stable tracking, symmetrical pull, opening straight—the jump itself could not have gone any better. But then I am hit by an unexpected tailwind while approaching the landing. With too much speed, I slam into the scree slope and get dragged into blocky terrain. Another complex, painful landing, and I find myself again in ER Berchtesgaden. Diagnosis: compartment syndrome of the entire left thigh, a fat bruise under the muscle tissue that can only slowly be drained by repeated surgical interventions. Bye-bye Dolomites, for now, but there is still enough time to get back into shape for speed climbing in Yosemite.

I am once again resurrecting the phoenix from the ashes. In fragments, my strength grows—unleashed, I rise from depths, having mastered my abyss. Three weeks before our scheduled start for another "go" on the *Nose,* my thigh injury has finally healed. Through a systematic training regime, I have washed the propofol cocktail of five general anesthetics out of my bloodstream for good.

At dawn, we again stand at the base of the *Nose*. But without a camera, sound, or stage direction. We are all alone, and it feels perfect for the first time. Shortly before we go, the ritual handshake, a brief look into my brother's eyes—a ritual that unites us as a team—and then the countdown. The last minute, the final seconds, and then we are off into the dimension of speed. We are immediately in the thick of it—"Beeeelay" . . . "Fiiiix" . . . "Tiiiiight" . . . "Fiiiix" . . . "Roooope" . . . "Beeeelay" . . . "Ooookkkaaay" . . . "Roooope"—in which everything is reduced to commands and upward progress. The next moment, we are outside the vortex and stop the watch.

Perhaps not everything has gone flawlessly, but we've still been faster than any team before us—if only by the blink of an eye, a mere 20 seconds. We have set the new record at 2:48:35. We've done it—broken through our

FREIHEIT

personal "limit"! The feeling is insane, almost surreal, yet rooted in the here and now, pulsating with life. Chongo was right when he said, "When you've made it, there's nothing like it in life. Therefore, not experiencing it in the first place cannot be an option."

We cement our record two days later without any hassle, clocking in at 2:45:45, shaving off almost three minutes. We celebrate this success late into the night around the campfire in Camp 4.

One year later, Hans Florine and Yuji Hirayama will shave a few seconds off our record. The press naturally expects us to get back into the race, but we have left the gauntlet in the venerable dust of Yosemite Valley. The Huber Brothers break their own trail and do not follow the path others lay out for them. Besides, as long as humans have the time and luxury to pursue such feats as speed climbing the *Nose*, there will probably never be a "record for eternity." This is because, living outside society, the Stone Monkeys have an intrinsic urge to define their existence by breaking down barriers. Addicted to this rush of life, and with the luxury of not having to fight for our survival as so many in the world do, we create scenarios to survive on the edge of the abyss. Thus, another new team will soon be racking up at the base of *Nose*, motivated to go beyond their limit and race against the standing record.

As beautiful and exciting as our time on the *Nose* has been, we have sacrificed enough for speed climbing. The vertical race is truly over for us brothers. We want to shift our focus to pure free climbing high in the Karakoram mountains, Patagonia, and maybe even Antarctica. Yosemite certainly also has much to offer, but after adding our record time to the list of speed records in the fall of 2007, we leave the Valley and never return.

After we leave, things change. The old guard is replaced by the young; the New Generation and the Stone Monkeys slowly migrate out of the Valley. Ivo Ninov returns to his homeland, banned from re-entering the United States because of his previous illegal residence. Dean Fidelman devotes himself exclusively to black-and-white photography and publishes several books. Dean Potter puts his focus on free-BASE, tinkering with his vision of landing from free fall without a parachute. And he breaks the speed record on the *Nose* with Sean Leary. Ammon McNeely has a BASE accident, which he survives with much luck, losing one of his legs in the process. And, finally, living up to his nickname "the Wall Pirate," Chongo is rudely ejected from the Valley by rangers and has since lived as a homeless philosopher under a bridge in Sacramento.

Meanwhile, our film *Am Limit* is awarded the Bavarian Film Prize but fails at all the other film festivals because it it's deemed long-winded and not spectacular enough. It won't be until years later that it receives recognition from the public and becomes the most-watched mountain film on German television. From that success, Alexander and I became the faces for a well-known chocolate bar. The result is a TV commercial that goes viral, primarily because it's authentic, funny, and full of self-irony. Everyone suddenly knows us as "the speed climbers from this one commercial," and the slogan "It's this way to the refrigerator!" becomes as much a part of us as our long hair, wild looks, and steep mountains. The red carpet, it seems, enabled us to make a living off climbing as Stone Monkeys, keeping it real all the way!

Silence at Last

Peter Anzenberger and I are sitting on a small, rocky ledge. Above us, the overhanging yellow wall loses itself in the black darkness of night. I munch on two bananas as a booster for what lies ahead and then tie in, while Peter places the rope in the Grigri. A firm handshake swirls up a cloud of chalk into the darkness, pulsing in the glow of our headlamps. "Peter, you got me safe?" I ask.

"Yep, Thomas. I've got you safe. I've got your back; let's go for it!" he replies, and then adds, "You'll do it for sure!"

As we both know, before us lies a long story with many ups and downs, fluctuating between hope, euphoria, and disappointment. It all started with Dean's artful idea of combining climbing with BASE jumping to create a surreal hybrid. My project on the Drei Zinnen would have been perfect had I not fallen near the end in 2006. After this disappointment, Dean and I went our separate ways. He pursued his goals, and I mine. But I held on to the Zinnen trilogy. And even though the renewed attempt the following year caused me to fail again, I will try this third time in August 2008.

This time, too, I start the vertical marathon on the Westliche Zinne with the *Alpenliebe,* a full-on 5.13 through the middle of the overhanging north face. I have timed the climb precisely to stand in the rising sun close to the summit—just above the Scoiattoli Ledge—for my first jump, and then I will head to the *Phantom* on the Große Zinne and my second jump, and thence to *Ötzi Meets Yeti* to summit the Kleine Zinne. All routes will be climbed redpoint, with a new belayer for each. The great advantage of my game plan: the most accessible route comes at the very end.

I switch my new battery-powered headlamp to full beam and climb into the darkness. Even though I feel good, I think about the weight of this incredible challenge, of all the madness that lies ahead of me—more than 4,920 feet of rock, two jumps into the void, and an ongoing fight against my inner demons. These doubts about my capabilities and the uncertainty of the challenge put me on edge. Am I even up for this? On *Alpenliebe,* the overhang traverses could become a problem for me as a prisoner of my own cone of light. Head to the left, back to the right, and climb down to be able to illuminate all possible holds and footholds. In such a moment, one can get fatigued and easily make a mistake.

After a quarter of an hour, my first of the day's many rope commands echoes through the Dolomites: "On belay, Peter. Rope's fixed!"

"Ha, lick my arse. You're crushing it, Thomas!" Peter calls back. This vulgar phrase is deeply ingrained in the Garmisch climbers and expresses the highest appreciation for what has just gone down. And yes, now I feel great. Every climbing move is smooth despite the darkness, and there is no more reason for doubt, even though the final pitches are still nearly a vertical mile away.

Peter jumars the fixed rope and pats me appreciatively on the shoulder: "Look, Thomas, I've always told you: 'Don't shit yourself—just be yourself!'" The people of Garmisch with their sayings . . . But somehow, they are right: *Don't overthink what could happen; just do it.* And if something goes wrong, you can reflect on it afterward.

Freed from all fears, I fly up the following ropelengths, and I'm standing below the tenth pitch sooner than expected. An overhanging athletic traverse to the right, a 5.13 for sure—followed by another strenuous, vertical forty-five feet up to the belay. I start traversing into this overhanging world, illuminated only by my headlamp. Peter's words echo through my thoughts. *How right he is,* I think. Things couldn't be better; I flow through all the tricky sections on my first attempt, and I already feel like a champion before reaching the belay. Then, suddenly, the lights cut out. Without warning, my headlamp has ceased to function.

"Thomas, where are you? Are you at the belay? I can't see you anymore!" Peter calls up.

"No, damn it, just below, and apparently, my headlamp battery is dead. In any case, this bloody thing doesn't work anymore, and I can't see a thing, absolutely nothing. Honestly, I don't know what to do now."

Stuck in place, I hold onto two small crimps and smear on a small, sloping ledge. No moon offers a glimmer of hope, and the stars, though sparkling beautifully, are far too dim. Out of sheer desperation, I shout my entire Bavarian repertoire of swear words into the night and then jump—the only thing left to do . . .

Back at the belay, I'm falling apart inside. But Peter always knows the right thing to say: "Look, Thomas, now you're just getting warmed up. All that has gone by went too easily, and only now can you show off what you are really made of!"

Once again, he's right. Up to this point, it was going almost too well. So, I change out my headlamp battery and traverse into the overhangs once again. After sixty feet, a jug snaps off, and I'm off again, sailing into the deep-black night. This time I stay calm; I don't curse, because now I'm on a mission.

I tell Peter, "Now I'll show you how it's done!" and set off for my third attempt.

After a quarter of an hour, only 600 feet of 5.11/5.12 stand between me and my first partial, little victory. From now on, I find only a handful of pitons to guide me, and the difficulties lie more in the route-finding than the actual climbing.

Small arrows I've drawn with chalk help me find the route, all part of my multi-day preparation, and at 4:00 a.m., Peter and I summit. Peter Gams, a BASE-jumping friend, is already waiting for me up there, and at six o'clock, the two of us jump off Scoiattoli Ledge. Instead of six seconds, I pull the auxiliary chute after only five seconds, the consequence being that I don't find the right balance in the air—my chute opening is imperfect. Still, I manage to correct my error and fly safely and soundly.

A few minutes later, I am standing below the north face of the Große Zinne, at the bottom of the *Phantom's* first pitch. Alexander, my next belayer, is waiting there with drinks, chocolate, sausage, and cheese—fuel for the next 1,969 feet. He puts the rope into the Grigri, and off we go. I feel at home on this route, having climbed it more than six times. Each pitch has something beautiful and unique, a feeling you can sense as you connect with the rock, all amplified by the fantastic backdrop. The Dolomites are really special—tall, looming grey and yellow spires that seem to kiss heaven rise from deep green valleys. Nothing close can be found anywhere else on this planet.

I easily climb to the section below the crux pitch. And although three BASE jumpers thunder over our heads in the middle of the most difficult passage, I send it on my first attempt: what madness! The Dolomites truly are a playground for adrenaline junkies from the world over. In fact, soon slackliners will be balancing from peak to peak, and I'm already curious to see how the next generation will realize their dreams here.

On the final seven, still-challenging pitches, my forearms begin to cramp with fatigue and lactic acid. But the motivation, the adrenaline, and the proximity of the summit push me on. At 2:00 p.m., Alexander and I stand atop the Große Zinne. I say goodbye and thank my brother, because Peter Gams is waiting with the parachutes. We get ready without haste and double-check each other: The auxiliary chute is in place, the ejection cord runs freely, the pin is in place, and the loops are all threaded correctly. *Ready?* Take a breath—I'm standing on the edge. Everything is calm; I start counting, and now there's no turning back.

"Three, two, one, go . . . !" The whistling wind quickly rises in volume.

I am already far out there, eight seconds of free fall, a short moment of limitless freedom, a hard jerk, the chute opens, and I float in a light headwind over the scree fields below. I touch down gently—no injury this time!

At 3:30 p.m., I start up the final climb of the day. Martin Kopfsguter, a good friend from South Tyrol, belays me. Although the Kleine Zinne's *Ötzi Meets Yeti,* graded 5.12, is quite easy compared to the other two routes, it still packs quite a punch. Martin must shake me awake several times at the belays. My body has already given up, but my soul continues to climb. I feel like Ötzi—the Iceman—being chased by the Yeti, is fully depleted. But in the end, Ötzi is faster; my will is stronger, and at half past seven, I embrace the summit cross of the Kleine Zinne with Martin at my side. Finally, silence; I have time to breathe. It's just like the famous book *Erlebnis Berg: Zeit zum Atmen* (*Mountain Adventure: Time to Breathe*) by the German mountaineer Reinhard Karl. I finally get what he meant by it, because now I don't have to go on. I have time to breathe!

CHAPTER ELEVEN
Expeditions Through Golden Granite

The Pink Crocodile

That's where we want to go, to these bizarre, reddish, shimmering granite towers that rise like fangs over 3,000 feet vertically from a seemingly endless sea of ice. Relics from a primeval world, and yet they exist on our planet today.

If only we could skip these farewells, then things would be much easier for all parties involved. My family is standing at the front door in November 2008, a last hug, and Elias begs me: "Dad, take good care of yourself. Come home again, please, before Christmas Eve!" Our eldest, now 9 years old, is composed, because he knows these "Dad is going on a trip" farewell moments. Amadeus's brown eyes, on the other hand, well up with tears, and all he can say is, "Daddy, I love you!"

With a throaty, "Papa, for you," Philomea presses a small pink crocodile from a Kinder Egg, which she has just eaten, into my hand. At one and a half years old, she can't yet appreciate the drama of this moment. I try to defuse the heartbreaking mood with a, "Yes, I will come back and celebrate Christmas with you all soon!"

To the outside world, I usually play the tough guy, and yet I always carry this painful feeling of goodbye inside me wherever my adventures take me. This time, however, it's not all so dramatic, because our expedition might be considered more like a seaside vacation than a high-risk battle. Mountaineering and climbing in Antarctica, especially in the region around Queen Maud Land, seem objectively quite safe. There are no predators dangerous to humans as in the Arctic, the rock is solid and steep, crevasses and seracs are almost nonexistent, and the avalanche danger is near negligible. In other words, it's an ice-cold package holiday for rock climbers. And yet, all this is just window dressing of sorts, making it easier to say goodbye—because, as we all know, the devil hides where you don't expect him.

At Munich Airport, we brothers meet our other "fellow freezers": Stephan Siegrist from Switzerland and Max Reichel from Bad Reichenhall, who will accompany us with his camera. After a last, traditional Weißwurst (Bavarian white sausage) as a send-off, we set off for Cape Town, South Africa. Our time on the ground there is perhaps the most dangerous part of our trip: A helter-skelter cab ride toward the city center takes us past a ramshackle array of corrugated iron huts and wooden shacks—the slums. These are poor people who, in addition to their daily struggle for survival, must live with extreme violence in their neighborhood. If we had to go in there, we would probably not come out. After dozens of miles, the landscape finally changes. Along a gentle chain of hills, we see the first villas and settlements, protected by walls, barbed wire, cameras, and massive gates complete with armed guards. In other places, these would be the entrances to penal institutions; in South Africa, luxury estates lie behind, the golden cages of the rich minority that protects itself from the harsh reality festering outside. Rarely do the contrasts between rich and poor, and privilege and oppression, collide with such force as they do here. With this demarcation by barbed wire, one moves ever farther from the possibilities of integration, tolerance, and empathy.

We spend two days sweating in the crazy heat of Cape Town, buying regional antelope, ostrich, and springbok meat, vegetables, rice, noodles, rum for tea, fuel, toilet paper, and just about everything else we might need for our self-sufficient life in the cold of Antarctica. We cross over to the iced-up continent in an aging Russian cargo plane whose interior is spartan to say the least: stacked in the back is all the cargo, about forty tons, roughly bound down with a net. In front of it is the on-board toilet, a porta-potty lashed down with come-alongs, and then come forty-eight old seats bolted to the floor. Flags of various countries hang from the sides of the aircraft, concealing the tangled cables and the dilapidated interior, and in the front, there is a screen with a projector, the Russian answer to Western in-flight entertainment. The ticket price of 15,000 Euros per person is also well beyond all international flight standards.

After four hours of flight time, this mighty aircraft lands on the bare ice of the Russian airbase Novolazarevskaya Station. Outside, the temperature is -15 degrees Celsius (5 degrees Fahrenheit), a drop of 55 degrees Celsius from Cape Town. We spend two days here before a two-engined Basler BT-67 propeller plane flies us to the remote Drygalski Mountains during a two-hour "panoramic flight." It has been a week since our last Weißwurst, and finally we are standing in blissful solitude before this dreamlike array of razor-sharp summits spiking from the ancient ice. Our mouths remain open, because what we see surpasses everything we have experienced so far as climbers: Holtanna, Kintanna, Ulvetanna, Midgard—mountains where we can write history, and a sight that none of us will ever forget.

What Philomea's pink crocodile, which usually snuggles in my jacket pocket, experiences over the next few days is a crazy story beyond belief—four climbers undergoing the most beautiful adventure yet of their already richly realized alpine lives. Yes, it's cold, even freezing cold, sometimes below -50 Celsius (-58 Fahrenheit). This iced-up paradise sees us live, camp, and climb our way up crazy walls. We have a blast! Even if it is unimaginable, humans seem to get used to many extremes.

After acclimating to the cold, the four of us first climb the sheer, blank west face of Holtanna. A few days later, we climb the tower a second time, free climbing over a knife-edge ridge to reach the summit. In the end, we bag Ulvetanna through a spectacular new route, *The Sound of Silence*.

To experience the profound silence before this never-ending horizon, to lose oneself in this vastness, to observe the bizarre rock towers, these dreams frozen in stone, to be watched by the angelic snow-white petrels—all this is a priceless privilege. To be so directly at the mercy of Mother Nature, to observe the changing explosions of light due to the different positions of the sun during the perpetual day, the friendship among us four climbers—it is all beyond words.

After one month, we are picked up again by the Basel BT-67, and at Novolasarevskaya Station, the Russian researchers suggest it's high time we take a shower. Water for washing has not touched our skin during the last month; it was simply too cold for any such hygienic shenanigans. The shower is followed by an intoxicating Russian-style feast. On Christmas Eve, singing "Silent Night" with my family in front of the Christmas tree, I finally feel healed from all the vodka we were made to consume. When Philo finds her pink crocodile among the presents, perched on a stone from Antarctica, a sweet smile appears on her little face. She holds it tightly in her hand. She suddenly turns very still, as if listening to the crocodile telling her stories from the eternal ice of Antarctica.

Eternal Flame–The Legacy of Our Idols

It had been eight years—going back to 2001—since I'd last set foot on Pakistani soil. After the Ogre, I was intoxicated by my success, feeling an alpine high. If I had followed my inner calling, I could have planned an expedition to this region for every year henceforth. The Karakoram is a world as if designed by my imagination: dream lines, all extremely difficult, unclimbed walls with sections of perfect, golden-orange, El Cap-like granite. And perhaps I would have climbed many of them by today, had I not decided to pursue my romantic notion of the Huber Brothers as the ultimate climbing partnership. I traded the stage of those cold, wild, dangerously beautiful vertical walls for the tiny crimps and splitter cracks of Yosemite Valley. Then, my brother's proclamation that our free-climbing clock was ticking hung over me—over *us*—like the Sword of Damocles. But he was right: we still had some gas left—and we would have plenty of time for high-mountain objectives later . . .

Come 2009, I'm 42 years old and back in Pakistan. Once again, I am enveloped by the overwhelming, hot, humid Islamabad, with all its bustling human energy. From all sides one is greeted with "*Salam alaikum*" and "Welcome, sir, how are you?" followed by "Inshallah." It's a lived spirituality that seems to float above the permanent sound of traffic and the smell of two-stroke engines permeating the overcrowded streets. How I missed all of it! After a twenty-four-hour bus ride from hell on the Karakoram Highway, thanks to a flight cancellation, we meet up with Ismail and Quasim in Skardu. They greet us with intimate warmth, as if our last "goodbye" were only a few days earlier.

Why have we brothers decided to come this far? Precisely because this expedition is also driven by our inner, ticking free-climbing clocks. We are here, indeed, seeking out the high mountains, but also with the intent to free climb at altitudes beyond 19,700 feet while we can still climb hard.

There are many things you could climb in the Karakoram, but there is one route that has a unique story: the *Eternal Flame*. The *Eternal Flame* bristles with several superlatives at once. If you believe the stories, it is perhaps the most beautiful climbing route, on the highest pure rock tower—Nameless Tower or Trango Tower (6,239 meters, or 20,469 feet), in the Trango Massif—on Earth. On top of that, it is considered an undisputed milestone, and even further it was first climbed by the idols of our youth.

Exactly twenty years earlier—in 1989—our heroes Kurt Albert and Wolfgang Güllich, teamed up with Milan Sykora and Christoph Stiegler, made the first ascent of this wild, alpine gem. They free climbed a good 80 percent of the route, primarily following crack features through the compact orange granite and sending pitches graded 5.13 above 6,000 meters. A true milestone that shook up the climbing scene of its day. It was the names Albert and Güllich, the photos of the first ascent, and reports from initial repeats that contributed to the 25-pitch *Eternal Flame* subsequently turning into the most sought-after high-alpine wall ever. The Nameless Tower turned totem of the climbing world, and the *Eternal Flame* the focal point of vertical pilgrimage. Of course, many a climber has dreamed of sending this route, and some even of freeing the remaining 20 percent—Albert and Güllich's legacy for the following generations.

In 2003, Denis Burdet of Switzerland redpointed all the pitches that were obviously climbable. He pushed 5.13 into the high alpine with his remarkable effort—a new record in hard free climbing at altitude! But 10 percent remained unsolved: a small pendulum traverse at the start and the bolt ladder of the tenth pitch up a rock step, which was frictionless and featureless according to all accounts.

In 2005, the crème de la crème entered the Karakoram: two top-notch climbing teams, the Basque Pou and the French Petit brothers, both vying to add firewood this eternal flame. By freeing it, they all wished to cement its place in climbing history. They fought with the elements, gave it their all, and both teams finally reached the summit, but without redpointing all the pitches. The pendulum traverse at the start of the route remained unsolved, though Iker Pou did find a way to climb around the blank tenth pitch out on the right: a short traverse from crack to crack, well protected by a piton, but according to the Basque constituting a "tough boulder on two micro-crimps." A bit painful, but beautiful. A 5.13a for a mere thirty feet. This was quite a revelation. The crack section thereafter was graded 5.12+, but that did not sound too problematic.

However, this variation posed—fortunately only in the superficial sense—a little problem: The end of the boulder traverse was either iced over, or, depending on the time of day, water was seeping out of the crack. As a result, the whole thing was redpoint-able for either the Basque or the

French. A year later, the Austrian Hansjörg Auer tried it, also reaching the summit, but failing to free the crux pitches.

Now we were here, the Bavarian version of a brotherly team, to take on the legacy of our idols and perhaps, with a bit of luck, become part of its history. We were on the road with our now familiar and well-versed little vertical family: first and foremost, the extreme filmmakers from Timeline Production, Franz Hinterbrandner and Max Reichel.

You could almost say that Max and Franz have grown and grown up with us. It all started with the first modest climbing videos from back home. Friends filming friends! Just for fun—getting the camera rolling. But it didn't take long before things got more serious. Franz and Max went to work with us, first on smaller but then soon on more serous endeavors, from the Dolomites and Yosemite Valley to the big walls of this world, until they celebrated their cinematic breakthrough as the main cameramen for *Am Limit*. It is a synthesis in which we inspire and support each other: we provide the adventures, they the moving pictures. And, similar to Heinz Zak on a photographic level, the two guys have become irreplaceable partners for us in the alpine. While Max was responsible for the cinematic program in Antarctica, Franz will document our every move in the vertical realm on Nameless Tower.

Alexander met our fourth team member, the East Tyrolean Mario Walder, Alexander, by chance in Patagonia. After climbing a few routes together, we quickly realized that Mario is a machine in the mountains—an excellent alpinist, fast, persevering, one who doesn't talk much but prefers to do, and who is brave but not a daredevil. One who acts calmly and thoughtfully far above the last piece of protection, a high-level alpinist who shares our ethics and philosophy of mountaineering. While he'll be supporting Franz and the filming on one hand, he is also here to fulfill a life goal of climbing the Trango Tower.

Once again, we are lucky enough to be fair-weather mountaineers. After just one week, we establish Camp II high up on the Sun Terrace, a ledge on the south shoulder above which the wall proper rears up. We have managed to acclimatize well. In this crazy place at 5,500 meters, we pitch our two tents on a slab of granite: an eagle's nest above the abyss. Above it, the massive Nameless Tower rises into the sky. Our view is indescribable, simply gigantic. To our right, the massive, blank big wall of Trango Tower; in the distance, Broad Peak, the Gasherbrums, and finally Masherbrum.

One reason we're still in a good mood, although we have been stuck in basecamp for more than three days due to bad weather, whittling away time drinking green tea: We freed the pendulum traverse at the start of the route right from the get-go. We found an elegant solution to climb past the blank section on the right and traversed a little farther up into the crack systems of *Eternal Flame* at a maximum grade of 5.12+.

After a week of bad weather, we get a call from Charly Gabl, our weather god based in Innsbruck. He is speechless and cannot believe our luck. The weather should be perfect for the next seven days. More Inshallah is simply not possible, and so we climb up to the Sun Terrace, our eagle's nest, bringing the ropes up with us so that we can fix our progress on the granite tower each day, letting us go for a summit push at the end of our toils.

We are on it come daybreak, so that we can start free climbing on the same day. Mario leads out first, belayed by Franz. He climbs partly free, partly aid, moving efficiently and not taking any chances, fixing the ropes for Franz, who in turn climbs with the ascenders and records everything on film: every failure, every fall, every little victory, every inch of progress, all the doubts and the euphoria—everything shot live, without artificial posing for perfectly staged pictures. It doesn't get any more honest than this.

Before we brothers jump in, we play another round of "Rock, Paper, Scissors." Alexander wins and starts off on the first pitch. We try to climb as far as possible, swapping leads, climbing free and not taking any falls. Our goal, our firewood to fuel the eternal flame: team redpoint (in which each climber frees each pitch on lead), from bottom to top. The first pitch is a smooth, easy warm-up. After that, we fire on our first go our new pitch, with its twenty-meter slabby traverse to gain the central crack system. This flow guides us up three more awesome pitches until meltwater stops us in our tracks. A perfect first day. We fix the ropes and float back to our sunny terrace.

The next morning, the Pou Brothers' traverse lures us onward. Seen from below, it is unspectacularly short, slabby, and, as expected, starting with an iced-up crack, which we can deice with a hammer, if necessary. In any case, the weather ought to be on our side. But our luck does not last for long. Bristling with motivation and full of confidence, Alexander clips the piton and gives it a go—but he soon sees himself hanging on the rope, doubting any further progress.

"No chance, Thomas!" he shouts down, unleashing a torrent of Bavarian expletives in hot pursuit.

I try to motivate him with a, "Go for it, Alexander—you've got this!"

But he comes back at me immediately: "There's nothing I can do, nothing I can hold onto, Zefix! Maybe I'm missing Iker's beta. Damn—I only see one micro-crimp instead of two!"

A short, embarrassed silence from both of us.

"Hey, Alexander, do you want me to . . ."

Before I can finish my sentence, he reprimands me.

"Well, Thomas, you don't stand a chance here either! I actually think a hold has broken off—at least, that's what it looks like."

While Alexander is still desperately trying to find a solution, because this darn single meter of climbing could influence the outcome of our entire expedition, my gaze wanders a little farther to the right. There, I discover a series of small flakes that might provide access to the hand jams above.

"Hey, Alexander, I'll lower you now—I have an idea!"

This idea is the breakthrough we need. By crossing a shallow scoop via those flakes, we reach the beginning of the hand crack, this time traversing in from right to left. It is anything but easy, but still doable. Wolfgang and Kurt would have certainly been full of joy watching us struggle and get creative high up on their masterpiece . . .

By early afternoon, we are sitting on the big band running across in the middle of the wall. We're pretty tired, but happy to have deciphered the secret of the *Eternal Flame,* with two improbable pitches graded 5.12d. The most cryptic free climbing is done, and now comes the daily grind—which turns out to be more difficult than expected.

On the third day, we are back on the big ledge. On the left, an icy, dark gully; on the right, a huge golden-yellow pillar, the *Eternal Flame.* There could not be a more appropriate name, and in the middle of it a crack, as if Kurt and Wolfgang had buzz-sawed it in in person, practically a carbon copy of the *Salathé* headwall on El Capitan, only in the high alpine up in the sky. Twenty years ago, the two of them jammed these cracks and defined the state of the art of their era: free climbing on the world's highest mountains was possible.

According to the Pous' topo, the crux links into this dream crack fifty meters higher—and suddenly the tables are turned on us once again. From a comfortable ledge, a very thin crack track runs through a totally smooth, vertical pillar for fifteen meters. At first glance, it looks hard as nails. Actually, there should be two bolts here, per the topo. But there is nothing to be seen of them anymore. Alexander slowly works his way up the hairline crack, but with every meter his enthusiasm wanes: "Hey, Thomas, we can't do it, at least not at this altitude!"

We do know that Denis Burdet must have climbed somewhere up through this section. But did he really go up this very crack? Or perhaps somewhere else? Maybe the slightly overhanging dihedral on the left? After Alexander has grumpily mumbled his way up the crack, aiding, we share the investigative work. While he checks out the route farther up, I tinker with the climbing moves along the "We are too weak crack" on a fixed rope.

My brother can climb all the single moves, but without any bolts, these few fifteen meters are unprotectable. This may be possible a hundred times in a row on toprope, but a redpoint is simply not in the cards for today.

When we meet up again at the belay, I wink at Alexander, who looks desperate, and say: "Hey, Alexander, the 'We Are Too Weak Crack' is okay. Looks a lot harder than it really is—a doable 5.13."

"Thomas, good thing you're such a fighter. I think my courage would have left me too quickly!"

We now work together on the moves, meticulously rehearsing the sequences, marking the tiny footholds, pinches, and crimps with chalk and even fixing a few small, wired nuts for pro. After an hour or so, we are ready. I go for our first attempt and get through the most difficult passage, but just before the belay one of the tiny footholds snaps off and I fall. I almost made it. But almost is worth nothing in high-end climbing!

Under the watchful eye of Franz's camera, Alexander gives his attempt. He breathes in deeply, filtering all the oxygen out of this thin air and pumping it into his forearms. He literally claws, jams, and fights his way through to the top. After five minutes, the liberating rope command "Belay!" ricochets down to my stance. I follow, with the rope coming from above. A little later, I'm hanging next to him, this time without taking a fall. Just below us lies perhaps the highest-elevation 5.13a ever sent on our planet.

But the end is far from sight, which dampens our euphoria. Above us, yet another hairline crack rises into the heavens, scarred by previous nailing and according to our topo graded 5.12d. Mario works ahead, aiding using Bird Beaks, Stoppers, and Knifeblades. This will probably not be an easy ride, which is why the summit is moving into the "unattainable" category for today.

In addition, it suddenly becomes damn uncomfortable. The sun disappears behind the ridgeline, and it gets cold fast—very cold. Our drive is gone. Finally, Mario reaches the next belay. Going for it right there and then takes all our courage. I quickly check out the moves of this pitch, take a short break, tighten my shoes, and set off. I give it my all, because there's nothing left to lose. If it goes wrong, I'll get a nice, long fall and be able to take in some air at over 6,100 meters.

My efforts are finally rewarded on the twenty-third go, but the joy freezes instantly due to the frosty temperatures. Alexander follows suit, bearing down on every hold, because he wants to make it—today and not tomorrow morning. I guide him step by step through the crux sequences, and he makes it on his first attempt. While the summit remains out of reach today, if the weather plays ball tomorrow, the way to the top will remain free!

The following day, in the most beautiful morning light, we climb the last two harder pitches—two perfect 5.12 hand cracks—and then the climbing finally relents. Only one more 5.8 to the summit. We are on the top, all four of us, exactly at lunchtime. We have made it and fall into each other's arms. I pray silently and say thank you for this immense stroke of luck. We loose our gazes across the Karakoram Range. Our hearts are truly fired up by this *Eternal Flame.*

A little later, Kurt Albert reveals why they gave this route such an epic-sounding name. It wasn't for this orange granite pillar that hugs the Nameless Tower like a flame, but for the song "Eternal Flame" by The Bangles, an earworm on loop in their heads whilst climbing to the summit—rock 'n' roll in the middle of the wild Karakoram, a climb inspired by four hot, rocking girls from LA. Not long after this chat, Kurt has a tragic accident on a via ferrata close to his home in the Frankenjura. Still, the *Eternal Flame* will burn forever—for Kurt and Wolfgang, who shaped the world of climbing and ushered in a new generation!

CHAPTER TWELVE
Through Valleys and Up Mountains

Up From Below and Back Again

"Only from the valley floor can you really see the greatness of mountains"—no sentence could describe my life better than this. How many times have I stood on top, gazing into the horizon and beyond, celebrating life, rock 'n' rolling it, feeling that infinite freedom? But life follows an arc somewhat like that of a mountaineer on a big climb: You climb up and reach the top, but then, at some point, you need to descend back to the valley. Only then do you realize how high up you were.

This perspective humbles you, fosters in you a longing for more, trains your warrior's heart, until step by step you need to set out again—out of the shadows and into the light, because you never forget how beautiful it is up there. A mountain without a valley would be a boring, perpetual summit plateau. It's when the valleys become canyons and block your view of the summits above that you truly need faith in yourself for the climb back to the light and the summit.

In the Vacuum of Time

The media limelight set me up with the freedom to live mountaineering as I'd imagined it. A life that was in turn the basis for the limelight, each fueling the other. This went so far that I could no longer imagine one without the other. An expedition was not complete until it had passed through the choreographic filter and been presented on the public stage.

Although we were always rewarded with ego-flattering applause for our heroic stories, this was not the main reason Alexander and I so frequently took to the stage. Through our down-to-earth tales of the alpine world, we were able to touch audience's hearts by giving them classic heroes' tales that, in our fast-moving times, reaffirmed the basic values of everyday life. The talks and slideshows also helped us bring in money for our families, to make up for all that we demanded of them with our seemingly egocentric way of living driven by mountaineering. Far from being egocentric vertical artists and summit-baggers to whom only the mantra "faster, better, higher" might apply, I began to see us as motivational turbochargers of the vertical realm, encouraging people to seek out their own happiness in life. Even if we only reached a few people with each talk, it was still a contribution to making the world a slightly better place.

We enhanced our colorful, gripping photos and videos of derring-do with humility, a respect for life, and tolerance toward people, no matter their skin color or persuasion. We celebrated the power of community—to grow through it and to tackle the impossible with courage; and the magic of failure—to learn from it to never give up, even when it seems to be "too late."

When Alexander and I were little boys, we would sit in our living room in front of a small, ramshackle projector. Even Grandpa and Grandma, who could never relate to our father's mountaineering, were present. While he slid slide after slide into the projector and sorted the shown picture neatly back into the wooden box, he told us stories from the Dolomites all the way to Chamonix. That was it, our first slideshow together as brothers. We already knew then that we would eventually slide our own pictures into this machine.

After my baptism by fire on the *Rebitsch Cracks* in the Wilder Kaiser—climbing this historic VI (5.9+) and realizing just how much passion I had for climbing—I got my first small, sturdy pocket camera at the tender age of 16. I used it only to shoot slide film. After two years, we brothers had collected enough photos of our various climbs, and we got the first request from a local alpine club to put on a slideshow for its members. We'd had the idea of giving a lecture for some time, and we had already decided on the title: "The Steep World of the Huberbuam." Only those in charge were not enthusiastic about our title, "Huberbuam," most commonly associated in Bavaria with a local folk-pop band rather than extreme climbers.

In the end, our poster read: "A Steep World: Thomas and Alexander Huber." We were kitted out with a compact projector, and with our father's small roll-up screen we told our story in front of 100 curious alpine-club members in a village pub. For the first time, we received applause for what we had accomplished—and 200 Deutsche Marks to boot.

But the lectures had a limited reach. Only a few individuals were interested in the stories of *Rauhnachtstanz, Moderne Zeiten, Blaue Lagune,* or the *Weg durch den Fisch*. These climbs were simply too steep and too dangerous, and some even deemed such exploits reckless, putting our lives on the line at such a young age. Logistically, meanwhile, we could only capture our exploits from a few, limited photographic perspectives: camping in the car, a wall photo from below, a climbing photo from below (known as an "ass shot" in the business), a picture from above, some summit photos—that was it. And our narratives were often repetitive for the listeners: specific climbing sequences, ropelength by ropelength. My mentor, Godl Wallner, put it in a nutshell: "You both climb better than you talk!"

After Alexander established his first routes graded 9a and I followed with the *End of Silence,* we suddenly had the finest climbing photos by Heinz Zak from amazing perspectives to add to the mix, and our talks increased in quality. We each fashioned our own personal narrative,

Alexander with "The 11th Grade!" and me with a revised version of "A Steep World." We added music to some passages, and for the time it was excellent craftsmanship: narrate, crossfade, insert CD, play, change CD, continue narrating, crossfade. our shows were exhilarating, not only for the viewer because of Heinz's photos, but also for us presenters. Nevertheless, we stayed within the boundaries of our home area. Only when Alexander celebrated a true international success with the *Salathé* and the Zak photos were to be seen on all covers of the climbing magazines did he dare venture outside Bavaria, putting on his new lecture, "Granite."

Then came the expedition to Latok II in 1997. I lugged along my first SLR camera, inspired by Heinz's work. I managed to approach people with a smile and photographed them up close, getting a glimpse of day-to-day life in Pakistan. Later, high up on the wall, even at 7,000 meters, I always tried to take that special photo, capturing a specific moment from the small span of our existence and preserving it for eternity. We brought home seventy exposed rolls of film in addition to a brilliant mountaineering success. After weeks of work, our first professionally designed lecture was on tour: "Latok II: The Wall."

Two days before the premiere at the Nockherberg in Munich, we held a dress rehearsal for friends at a Berchtesgaden pub. Their criticism was a punch in the face. True, the visual story and the music with its fade-ins and fade-outs were unique, but as storytellers we were both, to put it bluntly, a disaster—even "an utter failure," as our friends concluded. It was clear we couldn't perform like this at the Nockherberg, so we locked ourselves in at home and started to rewrite our talk. Word for word, we learned everything by heart, even re-quoting things we'd said in our preliminary interviews with the press. We had the jitters for real, and if I'm completely honest, I would much rather have climbed Latok II again than have taken the stage at the Nockherberg.

In a nutshell, we had done this to ourselves. I would have preferred to finish my degree, but instead, I'd followed my passion to climb the west face of Latok II with my brother, and this decision had catapulted us into the limelight. With slightly shaky knees and nervous voices, we welcomed our audience. I kicked off our visual journey with images of the crowded streets of Rawalpindi, showing the chapati bakers and carpet vendors. After five minutes, we gave the audience a breather, and, accompanied by avant-garde background music, I showed off local, characteristic faces transforming from old to young.

Then Alexander introduced the next chapter of our story—trying to stick to our script, stuck to the lectern in front of us. We brought the audience along with us on the highway into the Karakoram, later hopping into a jeep up to Askole and basecamp. It wasn't until we showed photos of our climbing on the wall that we were really in our element, allowing our nervousness to finally dissipate. We traversed under the "Fat Lady of Fate"—as Conrad had named the upper reaches of the mountain that send snow and ice missiles down the approach gully—into the vertical granite and were able to captivate the audience. Using humor, charm, and excitement, we brought them to the summit at 7,108 meters, followed by a bit of drama on the descent.

The parting image of Latok II, set to the music of the countertenor Klaus Nomi, emphasized the peak's grandeur, bringing a hush over the audience followed by riotous applause. After the clapping died down, we instinctively knew that the last feet to our summit had been finally conquered. We might be able to make a living off mountaineering after all.

In the years that followed, we started to pack all our adventures into presentations. The goal was always to have each new presentation be better than the last. Two projectors became four, and we later added a beamer for projecting moving pictures. We used the technology at our disposal to turn our initially classical structured lectures into true multimedia shows. The titles and the corresponding posters became fixtures on billboards across Germany: "Latok II: The Wall" was followed by "Limitless," then

"X-Dreams 2000," and finally "Ogre: Myth, Dream, and Reality."

Soon came the days when digital photography replaced analog film, and our projectors disappeared back into the attic. Instead, there was now only a beamer flickering in the middle of the theatre, throwing a bright, color-intensive, razor-sharp image onto the screen, powered by a high-performance computer.

Digital made everything much easier, better, and higher resolution. Gone were the projected condensation streaks, dust specks, and blurs, as the projector's autofocus zoomed in and out to sharpen the image. But gone also was the nostalgic clattering of the projector when the next slide dropped in. "Between Heaven and Earth" was my first digital lecture. At the time, moving and still images were perceived as separate media, but by using digital tools to blend them—dissolving from a still picture into a moving picture—I was able to catapult the presentation into a new dimension.

When Dean Potter referred to what we were doing in the mountains as art, it opened my eyes. And when the stage started to consume me, I realized that the completion of my vertical art could be achieved within the performative dimension of presentation. I wanted to explore all the experiences and secrets that our planet has to offer, letting others partake in our happiness and our experiences, and making the intangible tangible. A vacuum in which space and time dissolve, offering a portal into a world that remains closed to so many. This thought captivated me to such an extent that I soon wrote down a dramaturgical concept focused on my exploits on the Drei Zinnen, in Antarctica, and on Nameless Tower. "In the Vacuum of Time" was born.

The title conveys the essence: all three stories—from the Dolomites to Antarctica to the Karakoram—are interdependent, but related. They all culminate in the blink of an eye at home in Berchtesgaden. Just five minutes from my front door, on the Priesterstein. A boulder—the overhanging highball problem *Priesterrat,* graded French 8A+ (V12)—is the dramaturgical highlight of the whole story. Normally this problem ends after ten feet on a good jug. My goal was to add the last twenty-three feet of 7c (5.12d), turning the boulder into a spicy little solo.

I had already pulled through the boulder in individual sections, and even climbed the upper part protected by a rope. But I still lacked the strength to complete the whole thing, whether on camera or off. For perfect friction on the small edges, cooler temperatures were of the essence.

It's October 9, 2009. In the wake of a cold front, cooler air is spilling into the valley. Today could be the day—I can feel it. I pack my crag pack and throw the bouldering mats into my VW van, and then drive the five minutes up to the Priesterstein. It's all dry, and the grip couldn't be better.

I immediately phone my bouldering partner, Peter Berthold: "Hey, Mono"—his nickname, since he's deaf in one ear—"the Priesterstein is dry, and the friction is second to none. Say, can you spot me today? I'd like to try it, the highball exit!"

"You're crazy, Thomas, but yes, I'm coming. I'll there in half an hour!"

I then call Max and Franz to tell them to arrive in an hour with the cameras, so that they can shoot everything as per my dramaturgical vision. I'm excited, because I know I'll never get better conditions for this problem. In the meantime, I want to rehearse the upper part on a fixed rope one last time, also using the time to effectively warm up. I have everything with me: chalk, brushes, carabiners, climbing shoes, rope—except the damn harness. So I jump in my van, race the five minutes back downhill, park the car in our yard, sprint into the garage, and grab my harness.

"Baaammcrashhhhh!" Whatever that sound was, it was loud. Wooden shards from the garage door fly into the garage with me, and I turn around to see the van wedged against the door frame, where it's rolled to a halt. I am shaking all over, full of adrenaline, have some blood on my thumb, a slight cut, not bad—I was too damned stupid and too damned rushed to put on the handbrake. So much for my plan!

I push the broken door aside, buckle myself back in, and slowly drive up to the boulder. Mono is there by now. I get out of the car white as a sheet, tell him about my stupidity, and add a disappointed, "That's it for sending today. I can forget about the problem!" Wrapped in a warm hoodie, I put on my climbing shoes, wanting to get rid of the excess adrenaline in my body, and traverse a little to the left, then to the right, feeling the holds on *Predigtstuhl* . . . Oh, it's a shame, because the grip today is just . . .

"Thomas, you're crazy!" Mono's screaming interrupts my daydreaming. "Look where you are! You just pulled through the crux!" It's only then that I realize I'm clutching the exit jugs on the 8A+ boulder in my hands without really knowing how I got there. I rest at the jug, then finish out the forty-foot climb, ropeless. Unbelievable for Mono, unbelievable for me.

Later, Max and Franz arrive. They set up the cameras, and I climb like never before. I must force myself to fail as described in the script, because on this day I've miraculously managed to turn off gravity. I pull through the intimidating highball three times in a row. I feel lighter than ever, and on this day, I literally experience the vacuum of time.

After this successful lecture tour with "In the Vacuum of Time," I almost believed that I had achieved all that I could as a climber. My story was authentic, and I managed to convey it with ample humor, entertaining and surprising my audience with creative staging. For example, I re-enacted the nighttime headlamp debacle on the Westliche Zinne on stage using interactive lighting. My follow-up lectures, "Sehnsucht Torre" and "Steinzeit," built further on my success. Was I simply using these lectures as stepping-stones to my own, personal summit? If that really was the case, I hoped not to reach my final summit for a long time to come.

The Abyss

I fell into a bottomless pit, shocked to plummet into a black void. It happened unexpectedly, yet I could have guessed I was inevitably heading for the abyss.

After 2009, we were surfing a wave of success. The Milchschnitte chocolate-bar commercial produced shortly before ran on all the TV channels and catapulted us into proper celebrity status throughout Germany. Alexander moved to my immediate neighborhood in Marktschellenberg and ran a small farm there as a hobby. We seemed to succeed in everything we set our minds to, and for some climbing magazines, we had sold out to the man. We were in demand as never before, were on stage nonstop, climbed in between, and started our multi-pitch project *Karma* at the Steinplatte in the Austrian part of the Chiemgau Alps, but without standing the slightest chance of success. (We are still trying this testy and runout climb, bolted in the "Huberstyle" and with two pitches of 8b+, one of 8a+, two of 7b, and one of 6c.)

We were overworked, maybe even fed up, heavy-hearted, annoyed by everything—sometimes even by each other. In the public perception, we were still one of the best climbing teams of our era, but we had lost our Stone Monkey lightness and rebelliousness. Instead, we did everything expected of us—lectures, interviews, and talk shows—out of a sense of obligation.

Then came the fall. I told my story of the "Vacuum of Time" every day in a different city; up on stage, I'd come to realize that I was only reporting on that which I longed for, but was no longer living it. Shortly before Christmas, totally burnt out, I realized something had to change. Moreover, I'd been having stomach pain—from stress, I thought. Together with Alexander, I booked a flight to Argentina, Patagonia, for the beginning of January. El Chaltén would fix it. The mountains, good food, and friends were probably the best therapy for both of us.

But despite the upcoming prospect of Patagonian freedom, there was no relief from my pain. I went to the doctor. Besides stress-related gastritis, they discovered an irregularity in my left kidney. A day later, they put me in the tube. After a brief evaluation of the MRI scans, the radiologist soberly informed me that the abnormality was a full-blown kidney carcinoma, four centimeters in diameter. He recommended removing the tumor immediately—the tissue around it still seemed free of metastasis. Time stood still, and I gasped. I had cancer.

I tried to keep my composure in front of the doctor, even though his statement had sent me to the very brink. When I pulled his office door shut, my knees went weak and I fell into darkness. Patagonia, everything, just rushed past me: the colorful images from my life, childhood, youth, my first love, all the peaks, the walls, all that I had experienced, my children, Marion, my entire life. Now I was utterly at the mercy of fate, unable to change anything through my actions alone.

In desperation, I pulled out a rescue parachute to slow this free fall into existential dread. I tried to think clearly and searched for a solution. One day later, I was examined by Dr. Manfred Stangl, the senior physician at the Großhadern Clinic in Munich. He told me, "That's right, it's probably a kidney carcinoma, but if you're fortunate, it could also be a benign tumor. I'll cut it out, and then we'll see. We'll take it one step at a time now, just like you climb your mountains!"

So, on the day I had planned to fly to Patagonia, I lay on the operating table and placed my fate in the skilled hands of Dr. Stangl. The tumor was successfully removed, but it was still unclear whether the tissue he'd excised was benign or malignant. The findings would not be back from the lab until a week later. Living with this uncertainty was difficult, a game of heads or tails whose outcome meant I'd either live for a long time yet or for some much shorter and indefinite duration.

I tried not to think about it so much, which wasn't so difficult because I had other, more pressing issues. The surgery had been a massacre, my belly filleted open from the breastbone to below the navel. I was now in enormous pain, and it took days until my digestion worked properly. In tiny steps, I learned to walk again, one step farther every day, until I could climb my first small "mountain": from my ground-floor hospital room via the stairwell to the top floor. There I even found a small balcony that let me look over the roofs of Munich and see my beloved Alps on the horizon.

Here, I had time for myself. My thoughts flew over the roofs, past the Frauenkirche cathedral and farther over the highway to the Wilder Kaiser. Again and again, the images came back of how I had climbed the crux pitch of the *Rebitsch Cracks* at the age of 16, cheeky and without fear, of the climbing vacation with Alexander during which we were left to our own devices and dreamed up an adventurous future as mountaineers. Back then, life was going to last forever. And now everything was reduced to a lab report: Would I be allowed to continue living, or did I face the prospect of having to leave this life within the next few years?

For the first time in my life, I feared for my future. No one could take this fear away, neither the competent Dr. Stangl nor my family, who would have done anything for me during these dark times. (I wanted to protect them even then and not drag them into my innermost fears.) The only thing that could pull me out of this dark spiral was the notion, just as in mountain climbing, of taking one step at a time. As Dr. Stangl had also said: "Think only as far as the next step and only then start planning the next one." That was precisely how I had been able to climb the *Rebitsch Cracks* back in the day. I took these thoughts with me and descended from my first mountain to my sick room, where I waited for the lab results.

Days later, Dr. Stangl came in. He held a note in his hand and, with a smile, said, "Hey, Thomas, the results from the lab just came in; it's an oncocytoma, a non-metastatic tissue. That translates to being healthy!"

Flutters that I had never experienced before—what unbelievable happiness! All this—the limitations, the pain, and the long road back to the mountains—were no longer relevant. I was allowed to live on, to be a father, a husband, a friend, a brother, a climber, a mountaineer, an alpinist, a Stone Monkey, everything again. And fate was—at least for now—aligned with me again. Finally, I could restart my life.

I hugged Dr. Stangl and cried joyfully for this immense gift. Since then, I always celebrate two birthdays: one on November 18, the day I was born; and my "rebirth birthday," on January 18.

Back to Life

Baffin Island: The locals call it Qikiqtaaluk. We came for a few climbing moves comprising maybe ten feet of rock. That's not much, especially when compared to the countless miles we'd covered on our way here to solve the riddle of these triflingly few feet of granite. It was a bit crazy, because if you stacked all the statistics side by side, you'd be better off staying home. But that's precisely what had attracted us in the first place—numbers alone don't show the infinite dimension hidden in these ten feet of climbing. This little patch of granite was the focal point of everything we love and burn for: adventure, cracks, solid rock, small crimps, adrenaline, uncertainty, deprivation, struggle, fight, and pain. This package read, "Mount Asgard, Turner Glacier, Baffin Island, Canada."

Asgard, the realm of the gods: The mountains on Baffin Island in Auyuittuq National Park suggest that Norse mythology might have originated here. Perhaps the explorers and eponyms were inspired by this rugged, pristine landscape, unlike any other in the world, with its fjords and monolithic granite walls and spires rising straight from the sea. A strange world, mystical, mysterious—the ethereal world of the gods. It does not take much imagination to conclude that the world of the Norse heroes and deities must have looked just like it.

But it is not Odin's, Thor's, Tyr's, and Loki's mystical stories that inspired us to seek out this place; instead, a Bavarian beer and Belgian-Spanish music got us to this little island, a place utterly devoid of civilization.

1996, Bavarians in the realm of the gods: The Bavarian climbers Christian Schlesener, Manni Reichelt, Luca Guscelli, Bernd Adler, Markus Bruckbauer, and Toni Grad had just returned from their expedition to the far north. In their luggage, they had the most valuable thing climbers can bring back from such a trip: a first ascent called *Bavarian Direttissima* (5.9 A3), which followed a bold line up the 2,789-foot south pillar of Mount Asgard.

Soon after their return, these climbers invited us to a slideshow, the ritual conclusion to every expedition. My brother was there that evening in Rosenheim, Germany. Over a few beers and the hum of the projector, everyone sat together in the semi-darkness, and those who hadn't been there on Baffin marveled at the images that flitted across the screen. Alexander's mouth dropped open, and his fingertips started to sweat. An awe-inspiring climbing world opened up to him; when he squinted and looked more closely, he was sure he spied potential for new climbs.

After that evening, he noted the following in his journal: "Baffin Island, Canada, Mount Asgard, South Tower, best granite, El Capitan quality, free probably badass, if possible, but want to try." He didn't even show this journal entry to his brother. But that's how it is in this business of dreams, ideas, and visions. Everyone has their own stories that they need to keep to themselves. If we see a chance and the time is right, we reveal a secret page and an adventure gets launched.

Alexander has forgotten these notes for now, and other goals have pushed themselves into pole position on his climbing agenda. There are just too many climbs, and by God, one climbing life is not enough to realize the dreams in both of our notebooks.

2009, *Asgard Jamming*, a Belgian-Spanish summer vacation: The Spanish big-wall master Silvia Vidal landed on Baffin Island with the Belgian dream team of Stéphane Hanssens, Sean Villanueva, big-wall shooting star Nicolas "Nico" Favresse, and his brother, Olivier. They had chosen Baffin for an excellent reason: a wide range of big walls with beautiful lines that had not been attempted, second to no other region on our planet. Despite the myriad possibilities, the goal of the ambitious group was clear from the outset: Mount Asgard (6,610 feet), a massive granite peak with two cylindrical spires ending in planed-off summit plateaus.

Dozens of alpine routes snaked their way up the walls of Mount Asgard. Still, the team considered only two of them: the techno route *Inukshuk* on the north tower and the *Bavarian Direttissima* on the South Tower.

The team decided to attempt the *Bavarian Direttissima* because they were convinced that it was free-climbable—and they were right: After eleven days on the wall, the team deviated slightly from the original route on the final pitches to reach the southern summit plateau of Mount Asgard via a new exit, giving it their all in the process. Nico and the others christened their near free-climbing version the *Belgarian* and rated the 2,800-foot route 7c A1. They were only a few feet short of freeing the whole climb.

The news of their almost success spread quickly throughout the media, although an "almost" in climbing lingo means quite a bit—namely, that they had tried hard but it was not enough. Still, their success, as with all such remote big-wall climbs, lay in the journey itself: five friends set out to experience their idea of adventure, putting on an awesome climbing performance with a lot of heart and soul, passion, outright madness, and humor. They filmed this amazing adventure themselves, using a small handheld camera, showcasing their fearless mentality, and spicing it all up with jam sessions on the wall. This smorgasbord of film snippets was then used to fashion the film *Asgard Jamming*, which was widely celebrated by the climbing world for showcasing the pure joy of life, as experienced by these authentic Stone Monkeys.

A few weeks after the Belgian-Spanish team had returned from Baffin Island and we had returned from Nameless Tower, the ever-hungry Alexander put it to me bluntly: "They did exactly what I've wanted to do for a long time, but only almost." After the *Eternal Flame*, it was clear to us brothers that we now had to tackle this page from Alexander's 1996 notebook. The *Belgarian* was destined to be another chapter of the Huber Brothers. There could hardly have been a better reason to go to Baffin.

The master plan: In 2010, we wanted to climb a lot at home, maybe put up a challenging first ascent, to be suitably fit for Baffin Island come 2011. That was our well-thought-out plan. However, reality turned out quite different. The stress around work was too much; my oncocytoma came on top of it all. I clawed myself back into the realm of rock step by step, willing myself to train, but it wasn't going to be enough for Baffin. It wasn't until 2012 that we could book our tickets. We had to spell out our destination airport at the travel agency. P-a-n-g-n-i-r-t-u-n-g, Baffin Island, Canada. Not exactly the most common destination. No wonder this island in the northernmost part of Canada, west of Greenland, is not exactly a happy-clappy tourist destination. However, Baffin is considered the fifth largest island on our planet. At the same time, it is one of the most deserted areas, with just 11,000 inhabitants spread over half a million square miles.

I couldn't wait to finally travel and give it my all again. I missed the feeling of pushing myself to the limit and was motivated like I'd rarely been before. Secretly, I dreamed of pulling myself back into real life on the fine granite in the middle of the wall, just as I had ever since I was a kid. It was exactly this ten feet of impossibility—the A1 on the *Belgarian*—that inspired us to embark on the long journey north. Alexander and I trained like mad people. Myself in my own way with my longtime friend and coach, Rudi Klausner, Alexander following his own dictum. Shortly before our "island holiday," we also wanted to gift ourselves a present with the climb *Karma,* our 5.14 project on the Steinplatte. But nothing was to come of this. Far from it, I went down with Achilles tendonitis in my left foot. Hence, I had no chance of squeezing into the tight climbing shoes—and once again, I saw myself more desperate than confident. Shitty karma! What have I done to always get slapped around like this?

In moments like this, Rudi is my most important ally, and has always made a virtue out of these sorts of dilemmas. His calm and forceful manner made me understand that I could train my body tension—the neuromuscular activation from one's toes all the way up to the fingertips—much better by climbing with only one leg. And if I added to that his advanced campus-board training, I would come out of this stronger than I would have without my injury. When this all finally dawned on me, Rudi laughed mischievously and took a pleasurable puff on his pipe; all my doubts disappeared in his sweet cloud of smoke.

During this time, Alexander redpointed his masterpiece *Nirvana,* a seven-pitch 8c on the Steinplatte next to *Karma,* so we were both back in top form. Shortly before our takeoff to the cold north, I phoned Nico again to get some last-minute beta on the *Belgarian.* In his mind, he climbed through the integral route, offering valuable insights. I listened intently and took notes. All the pitches they'd freed were doable, Nico says, none clocking in any harder than 5.12+. Only the tenth pitch clocked in at around 5.13b—a bouldery crux section, well protected with a piton but consisting of complex moves on small crimps and fine smears in a shallow fingertip crack, used to finally move out left to better holds. Basically, all the difficulty was compressed into ten feet—all climbable, but in the end, they'd run out of strength for the last move.

I sensed that Nico was bitter that he hadn't made it, but he still wished us good luck. He was sure that the Hubers would pull it off: "If not you, then who?"—"Thanks, Nico, and if we really do make it, you're invited to Berchtesgaden, and we'll celebrate an Asgard party with the first ascensionists."

"What a great idea. We will come, party with you guys, and bring all our instruments . . . !"

"Bavarian Direct" production: With the whole film crew from Timeline—Max, Franz, and our East Tyrolean friend Mario—we set off. First, we flew to Montreal, then to the Arctic Island of Iqaluit, the capital of the Canadian territory of Nunavut, including Baffin Island. We searched in vain for a cinematic highlight, a historic city center, something that would make for a romantic Arctic story. Instead, there were wide streets, prefabricated buildings, and shipping containers lined up on the left and right. Everything looked extremely dreary, overlaid on an even drearier coastline. The only ray of hope was the single pub in town, albeit with expensive prices that were second to none. In return, the beer was served by a gaunt islander who'd been licensed to open the canned beer, a strange measure the Canadian authorities had taken to get to grips with the alcoholism of the mostly Indigenous population.

We flew to Pangnirtung the next day, all a bit poorer. I would never have thought there was a next level of "dreary": lonely, empty streets, trailer homes, simple wooden huts, all equipped with a satellite dish. In addition, there was a supermarket and a fast-food restaurant, but not a single pub because Pangnirtung is dry—alcohol free. Only Inuit, resettled by the Canadian authorities, live here. And only a handful of whalebone carvers with their art recalled for us those times when the population roamed the island freely, as nomads. Today, Pangnirtung's people all have a permanent roof over their heads and a television set. But the sedentary life has taken away an essential part of their identity. It wasn't until the motorboat dropped us off at the mouth of the fjord, and we were on our own, that we finally found what we were looking for.

The clouds hung low as we set off, lugging heavy backpacks, walking into the Weasel Valley across lush tundra along the meandering Weasel River. To the left and right, the granite walls towered above us, and we kept a vigilant lookout for any polar bears watching us from behind the boulders. A strange world. At the same time incredibly mysterious, a gateway to our own imagination. No wonder these granite mountains have taken their names from the Edda, the poetry of Norse gods and heroes. This is "Wall-halla," heaven crowned by the best big walls on Earth.

After three days and five river crossings without a single polar-bear sighting, we arrived at what must be the most mystical mountain on the planet: a tower, cylindrical in form, rising steeply—surely over 3,000 feet in places—smoothly cut off at the top and enveloped by a white glacier, with clouds of Arctic mist spiraling above.

Asgard: there could not be a better name for this mountain. The dwelling place of the gods, with a summit plateau that reminds the onlooker of Odin's table. Except that Thor must have once split the table with his hammer in a fit of rage, creating distinctive North and South towers.

To the right of the Turner Glacier, we found a good place to set up camp on a gravel moraine, granting a dreamlike vista of our objective. Via satellite phone, we gave our coordinates, and twenty minutes later, a helicopter rattled over the Turner Glacier to drop off our kit: tents, fuel, food for a month—everything we needed to realize our goal of redpointing the *Belgarian*.

Admittedly, our approach was rather lame compared to that of the Belgians, who'd dragged everything to the mountain themselves, crossing thirty-eight miles of rugged terrain. In the beginning, we had also had the best of intentions. But then came the idea of a film produced for the series *Bergwelten* on Servus TV. Ferrying such loads was beyond our capabilities, and so purist ethics were subsequently stricken off the agenda.

Thor's hammer: Arctic fog obscures the mountains. Mount Asgard gives us a cool reception. We use the time to organize our camp and climbing gear, and then use stones to build an Inukshuk, the traditional stone man of the Inuit, which serves as a signpost here on the island. Our Inukshuk points logically toward the South Tower, because that's where we're supposed to go when the Valkyries finally remove their veils.

After a few days, the fog lifts. In this light, Mount Asgard stands out powerfully against the bright-blue Arctic sky. Full of energy and laden with heavy backpacks, we set off, crossing glacial streams, until we gaze up at the mighty South Tower, enthroned before us like a monolith on a rock pedestal. Our anticipation mixes with unease. A constant thunder comes from the mountain, as if Thor himself—the God of Thunder—were sitting up there somewhere, banging his hammer against the rocks out of sheer boredom.

We reach the base, at the foot of a steep snow gully. The fun ends here. Boulders the size of cars, freshly fallen off the mountain yesterday or just a few hours earlier, lie on the glacier below. Our eyes meet only briefly, and we all know that if we want to climb up there, we have to get through this gauntlet now or never. To grasp these incalculable dangers, we must climb while the mountain is still in the shadows. Without losing many words, we climb fast, pumping our legs up the slope until our thighs burn. Luck is on our side—the god of thunder has chilled out, and all remains quiet. Only our panting breaks the silence, and after two hours, we reach a ledge directly below the impressive South Tower.

What we encounter now exceeds all our expectations. It is overwhelming, breathtaking, an absolute jewel in our climbing world, so steep, so compact, so beautiful we could never imagine how good this wall would be in real life. Our Bavarian friends knew what they were doing in 1996.

We are satisfied for today and stretch a fixed rope straight over the rock base down to the glacier. This finally offers a safe approach to the wall, free and clear of Thor's deadly gully.

Trickster Loki: We think we've already solved the biggest problem, because now the climbing is only difficult, not dangerous—and after all, we've trained hard for the difficult. For the dangerous, on the other hand, you need a lot of luck, and you can't train for that.

We are also fortunate with the weather. We move our camp to the rock band directly below the base. Full of expectations and anticipation, Mario starts up the wall, aiding the first two pitches and fixing the ropes; we attempt to warm up on the clean stone of these initial pitches, but soon realize the Belgians have played a dirty trick on us with their grading—or maybe they were influenced by the prankster god Loki? Because everything we have between our fingers here has nothing to do with 7c (5.12+) but feels more like 8a+ (5.13c), i.e., a good two or three full grades harder! What does this mean for the upper pitches? How hard is the pitch that Nico, known as a notorious sandbagger, failed on? If you extrapolate from what they freed already, their "8a" might be 9a.

We are annoyed by their sandbagging. Nevertheless, we try not to let these initial setbacks throw us off track. In the end, it's only the numbers that irritate us, but not the climbing, which is indeed stellar. Given how hard the climb is, we rethink our plans, going for the redpoint as a team swapping leads—i.e., a team-free ascent, in which only one climber needs to lead a given pitch, while the others second it free—and forget about redpointing every pitch individually, as we did on Nameless Tower.

Asgard packs a punch straight from the get-go—no red carpet awaits us at the base. To get your feet off the ground, you have to gun it 100 percent. I haul my body up the first pitch, crimping down hard, and am more than glad when I reach the anchor and can get a loud "BEEEElay!" off my chest. "Alexander, it went well, but that was a solid 5.12d, not 5.11d!" I holler. Alexander, now up at the belay having seconded the pitch, can't share my joy because he's already looking up at the next pitch, another alleged 5.12d. The crux, far above the last piton, appears to throw everything at you that Asgard can muster—it's a left-trending, slabby traverse with bad feet and small crimps that lead to a distant finishing jug. Even Nico took a sixty-foot whipper at this point, surely one of the most spectacular, if not scary, moments in the movie *Asgard Jamming*.

Alexander laces up his climbing shoes, dips his hands into his chalk bag, and starts climbing.

"Hey, Alexander, if not you, then who? You can do it!"

He grumbles in response, "Yeah, Thomas, it's fine!" It's probably the images of Nico's fall that are buzzing around in Alexander's mind, or perhaps the confusing numbers game played by the Belgians, with which they perhaps wished to show all repeaters that they are the coolest and strongest climbers on the planet.

"Hey, Alexander, just think of how lucky you are now to climb a Belgian 7c in the middle of the Arctic in the sun and with pleasant temperatures!"

"Yeah, I know! *Passt scho,* keep an eye on me, Thomas!"

He climbs calmly and smoothly on wonderfully beautiful granite crimps for the first sixty feet and clips the last bolt. Here, the original *Bavarian Direttissima* continues straight up on via a bolt ladder, drilled up a section too blank and slippery for free climbing. The free variant, therefore, pushes out to the right a bit but without any protection for the next thirty feet. Once again, Alexander shakes his arms out, dips his hands into his chalk bag, and continues to climb, calmly and silently forging his own path.

Then comes the most difficult section, the traverse to the left, way above the last piton. Alexander hesitates. His climbing shoes press into the microscopic footholds, barely maintaining friction. This is exactly where Nico was spat off. As I hold the rope, I'm spring-loaded, feeling Alexander's heartbeat inside my own body and getting ready for the worst. Then Alexander dynos and flies through the sky . . . horizontally to his left, stretches, grabs, and locks off the thank-God handhold, letting off an irrepressible scream that even the gods of these mountains must have heard. A hell of a guy! His "Beeelay" has pushed us both so far mentally that, from then on, we are no longer interested in the Belgian topo with its crazy grades. That was it—sandbagged 5.12d (so, more like 5.13) on a climbing expedition at the world's end.

Fighting like Tyson, we get into the groove and come to terms with the fact that we'll have to pull out all the stops. Mario aids ahead. We follow; inspect the pitches; mark the smears, handholds, dishes, and jams with chalk; practice and refine the sequences; and then go for an attempt. Most of the time, it works from the outset. Sometimes, we need two goes. On any given day, we manage three or four pitches. Three days later, we're hanging at the belay station in front of the still unsolved ninth pitch, and somewhere out to the left lurks the ten feet that shut Nico down—the small section of unclimbed rock that spurred us to take this trip in the first place.

We tense up again and teem with questions: Is this really the climb's crux? And, if so, how hard will it be—as hard as expected, as hard as hoped, or as hard as feared? And what if this crux is not feasible for us after all? What comes then? From the professional point of view of performance-oriented big-wall climbers, we will indeed have failed, and the bottom line of this trip will be one underscored by failure.

If we fail here, this adventure will not get a place on our "Wall of Fame" but will instead gather dust in a shoebox in the attic of our memories—a pathetic notion. Again and again, we stumble over our own egos, are chased by our own expectations of performance, and forget that this climbing on the edge continually reveals a mysterious, invisible world. This is worth more than any redpoint.

Slowly, the sun enters the corner and drives the last shadows from the wall. The granite reflects the light golden-orange far out into the Arctic landscape. We hang out amidst it, laughing and basking in the warming sun. I get ready for the next pitch without looking for answers anymore. We are here because we want to be and we are here to give this wall everything we can—and that's all there is to it. Ready, steady, go!

A fine crack continues vertically from the belay, but after about thirty feet, it loses itself in a hairline seam. Unclimbable. However, exactly at this point, a rib of rock crosses left onto the blank wall and runs another thirty feet higher to join a tips crack. This is the pitch Nico explained to me in such detail on the phone, where he failed repeatedly. The entry crack and the traverse to the end of the curved rock rib are already tough 5.12d—two good reasons to shake out your arms for a moment. Then the fine crack loses itself after a few feet in the compact granite, which is where Nico was stymied. However, three feet to the left, we spot a series of holds leading into well-climbable terrain; here, the divine mountain architects had a heart for free climbing. Alexander and I work on the moves together, marking all the holds with ticks and quickly finding climbable beta. The crux sequence culminates with a crafty climbing move, one we've never encountered before: an on-the-fly changeover of a fingerlock. You pull your two fingerlocked left digits out of the crack, and, in that brief instant of weightlessness—the deadpoint—you dynamically stuff the two fingers of the right hand into the vacated lock. The difficulty here is the timing and the precise execution—only a few millimeters off, and you're spat off the wall.

Finally, there's a dyno—a jump out left to a slopey rail. Soon after, you are in easier terrain and ready to rumble. Much to our surprise, the whole pitch with its ominous ten feet is not much more difficult than the Belgian "7c" ropelengths we climbed down below. Poor Nico: maybe he was just too burnt out after ten solid days of climbing . . .

In the evening, I try to redpoint the entire pitch, going wholeheartedly into battle mode and climbing until my fingers split. But it is not enough. I slip at the point where everything must be perfectly orchestrated, at this damned finger-jam changeover. We rappel and return to basecamp. Once again, the Arctic weather forces us to take a break, finally bringing us much-longed-for rest after the last few days on the wall.

During our rest days in basecamp, I often stand in front of our Inukshuk, close my eyes, and climb the pitch over and over again in my mind—up the first crack, the jump left onto the rock rib, the descending traverse to the rest before the crux, the dynamic fingerlock switchover, and then the culminating jump to the slopey rail high above—a jump into freedom, back into life as a climber after my difficult post-surgery period.

Five days later, we are all back on the wall, Mario, Max, and Franz above me with cameras running, Alexander belaying, and me in the middle of the action, poised to attack the crux. Once again, I shake out thoroughly at two good holds before the meat of the pitch. I feel light, strong as if I could swing Thor's hammer with one hand. It can't get any better than this. My fingers coated in chalk, I crimp the first edge, position my weight delicately, and lock off to reach into the hairline crack. Before I can squeeze my fingers inside, however, I'm off, dangling on the rope. "Shiiiiit, whaaaat?!" I scream in utter desperation. I want it so much, but I can't get it to come together!

A short time later, I'm back at the belay. Alexander also seems visibly disheartened by my fall, because it can't have been due to a mere lack of strength. No, this crux has become mental, and I realize I need to stop pressuring myself to send but must instead navigate the labyrinth of hand- and footholds out of pure joy, out of my love for climbing. To be fair, after all I've been through in the last year, I should be happy just to be here on this wall, climbing 5.13 in the middle of the Arctic with my brother. Besides, we still have enough time, as well as provisions for at least ten more days down at basecamp.

Then and there, these thoughts free me from any pressure to succeed. I take a deep breath and go for another burn. I climb smoothly to the shake-out point, rest, and let gaze wander over to Midgard, the North Tower; I forget myself in this Arctic kingdom, humbled and grateful to be allowed to live such an extraordinary life! I breathe calmly, clasp my hands together, gather my thoughts, and launch into the moves above.

I jam my left ring and middle fingers into the infamous slot a moment later. I position my body, and with a little rocking motion, pull the fingers out of the jam; in the same breath, I drive the two fingers of my right hand into the vacant slot. Not perfect, but it does jam, albeit with some slipping. My inner eye already sees me falling. Struggling, I fight against gravity, stuffing my fingers deeper, using the last of my strength. Still, I slip farther and farther out of the jam. I instinctively exit this fight with gravity and push off the tiny footholds, making no compromises, flying out left to latch the rail. Once again, with a cry that no one in these mountains can help but overhear: "JJJJEEAAAHHH, Alexander, I've got it!" Alexander follows it up with a Bavarian yodel, which is doubled through its echoes off the surrounding walls.

Alexander, Max, Franz, and Mario celebrate my send, and I have to laugh out loud with joy. As I've learned—like so many times before—the line between humility and the will to perform is a very thin one indeed. Essentially, they depend on each other: humility needs ambition, while ambition, in turn, needs humility so that even if you're already at your limit, you can still push further. Finding this balance opens the door to that invisible world of joy and freedom.

Now, at least, the technical crux is behind us. Another 900 feet of climbing up to 5.12 are left. In the middle of our vertical push, a new problem arises for which even the best climbers have no solution: the deteriorating weather combined with our dwindling provisions. This mixture is explosive, and after a few days, our nerves are raw. It rains and snows at the top of the mountain, and slowly but surely, our food supplies run out. Ultimately, we are only 500 feet short of the summit, with nothing harder than 5.11 left to climb. But without food and fuel for our muscles, we have almost no chance in these icy conditions.

In this unfortunate situation, we put all our eggs in one basket. With a last ration of food and in fickle weather, we ascend the fixed ropes to our high point. We take the full brunt: iced-up cracks, light snowfall, muscle cramps, drenched to the bone, wind, and fog as if the very gods in Asgard wanted to test us. Nothing is handed to us on a platter; even on the last few feet, we must fight fearlessly like tigers, throwing ourselves against this mountain, using all our strength. But we persevere.

It is ten o'clock in the evening, the sun sets, and a pale moon is visible in the sky. Five of us stand on the summit plateau of the South Tower, as large and flat as half a soccer field. A crazy summit, one of a kind. This is exactly what Odin's table might have looked like in Valhalla: the dinner table of heroes.

From the *Bavarian Direttissima* to the *Belgarian* to the *Bavarian Direct*: A few weeks later, we celebrate a festival of Bavarian-Belgian friendship with the route's first ascensionists, getting together with the Belgians at our home. We play our instruments, sing songs, drink beer, and tell each other stories about that which unites us: Asgard.

Late that night, the Belgians spill the beans. They themselves must smile a little about their 7c grading. They were so busy with life on the wall—cooking, eating, singing, making music, filming, plus their cravings for Belgian fries—that they neglected many other things. They were always highly motivated when climbing, but after they had done the route, they thought it couldn't have been that hard, so they rated everything 7c. When Nico asks if that irritated us, we all laugh out loud.

Finally on Top

The evening sun was already a hand's breadth above the glaciated horizon when we rammed our ice axes into the snow-white ice near the summit of Cerro Torre, a place where many alpinists had cut their teeth before us. But this year, the wind had been on our side, kindly sawing an easy path into the rime, allowing us all to climb the last feet together without a rope. Twenty axe strokes later, we stood atop this giant granite tower in a mountainous world as unique as the summit. To the west opened up a substantial glacial plateau; if you turned south, you'd see a village, behind it a vast lake, and then a road vanishing into the desert; to the east, meanwhile, was a wildly jagged mountain massif with towers, ridges, spires, and gullies. Turning to the north, we spotted three ice-crowned golden-orange granite towers lined up in a row, dominating the vista. And if you dared to gaze down, 6,500-plus feet of void sucked you toward the yawning crevasses of the glacier far below.

All of us—the Swiss duo Dani Arnold and Stephan Siegrist, the Argentine Matias "Tibu" Villavicencio, and myself—screamed our joy into the cardinal directions. There could be no better summit for doing so. No other could rival Cerro Torre, this miracle of mountains—the focus of desire for generations of climbers, going back to the 1950s. The name alone sounds like a vibrating chime: the rolling "r" in Cerro, and Torre makes you literally vibrate inside. Cerro Torre is undoubtedly one of the craziest mountains on our planet. It was the reason I'd initially visited Patagonia eight years earlier. This visit had had such an impact that I'd returned every year since. Patagonia offered everything I longed for: steep walls, sharp ridges, aesthetic mountains, wild, raw nature, and the mysterious history surrounding Cerro Torre. It took me eight years to summit; I finally stood here. That's also why we celebrated this moment so enthusiastically, and partied up here with no wind at sunset.

It took so long because I never wanted to bag this mountain just in passing. I wanted it to be a remarkable adventure—the route or the season had to stand out. Like this time round, Patagonia in winter. It felt like I'd truly arrived, putting a coda on my time in Patagonia, a region that had changed so much since my first visit.

In 2005, there was only one dirt road through the Estepa to the village. But just two years later, it was paved. El Chaltén was fitted with a highway of progress, and buses brought hungry tourists to the little town. Hotels, bars, and restaurants sprang up like mushrooms from the damp forest floor. The village was hungry; everyone sensed a chance to make cash off this unique mountain landscape. A new metropolis of the international mountaineering scene was born, a new Chamonix at the end of the world: El Chaltén. The village was young, bold, and dynamic, offering the ultimate outdoor experience. For boulderers, endless blocks and problems; for climbers, mountains par excellence; and for hikers, well-maintained trails to photo hotspots where everyone could create the ultimate alpine image for the family album: man, lake, glacier, steepest mountains, and blue sky with UFO-like cloud formations hovering over the peaks.

El Chaltén became the Mecca of the global mountain world. As a treat, there was a newly designed climbing guidebook that advertised the endless possibilities in a user-friendly format, much like the menu of a five-star restaurant. In combination with the newly interpreted weather models, mountain climbing in this Puta-gonia became seemingly more calculable, but not safer. On the contrary, all these trappings masked the fact that these granite towers are still the most exposed mountains in the world: If something happens to you way up there, if you get seriously injured, then you're typically done for. Anywhere else, a helicopter would come and pluck you off the mountain, but not here. Here, the locals will do everything possible to prevent an accident in the mountains. But rescue is exclusively human-powered, and because of the long distances and approaches, the locals have limited options if things go sideways. Often, a compound fracture high on these peaks ends in death, a one might be reluctant to deal face. What remains is the incredible setting: the orange granite stands out majestically against the white glacier and has become the dream of most climbers.

Because it is so beautiful, more and more crowds have pushed into these mountains. The administration of Parque Nacional Los Glacieres reacted by regulating the onslaught with new rules, forbidding the previously customary transport of luggage by horses to the camps near the mountains and removing the historic hut in Campo Bridwell—and with it all my romantic memories of the early years.

Right then, an Argentine-American team climbed all four towers of the Torre Group, snatching from under my nose the traverse that I had been planning for years. My heart stopped momentarily when I learned that the *Torre Traverse,* which felt like it belonged to me alone, had been accomplished by others.

It took me some time to recover from this lashing and to realize that only my ambitious ego had taken a beating. Indeed, in these mountains, there can and must be no claims of ownership. Any climber is compelled to go if they see an opportunity or a weather window. I had not gone for reasons of my own, and now Rolando Garibotti and Colin Haley had been faster. They were at the base at the right time, and we weren't . . . and that was it.

On the other hand, over the years, I climbed Cerro Standhardt three times, Punta Herron four times, and Torre Egger twice in my failed attempts to get the traverse done. And, with a larger perspective, it becomes apparent that this traverse will always remain a first ascent—these mountains are constantly in flux, dynamically changing their form due to wind and weather. The traverse will never be the same route twice!

Yes, the weather has always been the biggest hurdle in Patagonia, even with the best forecast. But even in this terrain seemingly beyond human control, there has been a change: climate change, which has increasingly mellowed the stormy, sour weather such that there are longer periods of perfect weather, during which the temperatures have catapulted to heights never experienced before. The Austrian competition climber David Lama benefited from shift, becoming the first to redpoint Cerro Torre via the historic *Compressor Route* after Americans chopped several of Maestri's bolts. This mountain seems to always be a backdrop for records, superlatives, and controversial discussions, as if Cerro Torre itself were an extension of climbers' egos. But really, to the Torre, none of this matters. It merely adapts to the weather, and its summit mushroom is sometimes too steep to be climbable, but also sometimes gently inviting, as it was on our ascent. We captured this moment of the second winter ascent of Cerro Torre with a photo—or was it the third one, after all?

Stephan Siegrist and his team would have been the second to climb the Torre via the west face in winter. But at that time—July 1999—the summit ice mushroom was split in two, and in the end they found themselves standing on the lower of the two formations, as in lower by a mere two feet. The path to the slightly higher ice mushroom was no longer possible due to time constraints, so they left it at that. However, in mountaineering record-keeping, documenting the "first time," "second time," "third time," etc. is exact and meticulous. Thus, the only official winter ascent of the Torre was made in 1985 by the Italian Ermanno Salvaterra and his team. But this day, Stephan stood on top, and in the end, it doesn't matter whether you are second or third. More importantly, you're at the top—the very top.

The setting sun drops toward the horizon, and the light turns the surrounding towers into a blazing inferno of fiery orange; even the ice glows in a delicate rosé. We rig the first Abalakov V-thread anchor and start rappelling over the headwall, through the night onto Col della Esperanza, and then down to the glacier in the Circulo de los Altares arena. Here, at last, the sun will rise again. Then it's back in a seemingly endless march across the Viedma Glacier, over the Paso Marconi down into the valley, past Lago Eléctrico, Piedra del Fraile, and back to El Chaltén. Finally, as always, we will celebrate our successful winter ascent of Cerro Torre via the west face with an asado at Don Guerra's.

Even though everything has changed in and around El Chaltén, the world seems to have remained the same for Don Guerra. Progress rushes past him, and as a true original, he still authentically embodies Patagonian life. His hut stands at the back of the village, roughly cobbled together from the gnarled wood of the forest. A tug on a torn climbing rope opens his plank door into a spacious room.

A few old tables and chairs are neatly stacked in one corner on the trampled clay floor; shovels and tools lean against the wall, while a large fireplace—the heart of the hut—dominates the center. Above it hangs a colossal pot fashioned from an old metal sheet.

Don Guerra animates all this with his Patagonian serenity and has been doing so for over thirty years. He stokes the fire and adjusts the large logs with a shovel; in an instant, the room fills with the smoky aroma of burning lenga wood. As the fire crackles, an old tape recorder plays Don Guerra's tapes, folklore campéro, the music of the gauchos who work with horses and dogs in the cold winters and windy summers on the farms of the vast Estepa. When the sun sends light through the cracks in the wood to mix with the smoke, the result is mesmerizing. Patagonian magic does justice to the mystical atmosphere that surrounds Cerro Torre.

Don Guerra routinely skewers a lamb on an iron spit, letting it roast for hours above the fire—the original Cordero Patagónico, as the dish is known. After a while, the guests arrive, bringing beer, wine, and instruments. All likeminded people, friends, and Stone Monkeys. Among them are always the brothers Luis and Hector Soto, the doctor Carolina, Fidel, Celina, Melisa, Mariana, Giro, Iñaki, Tibu, Tehuelche, Mecha, Cabeson, and Anabel, as well as those who are just in El Chaltén for mountaineering like the Austrian Markus Pucher, the one and only Toni Ponholzer, Mario "Bastardo" Walder, Hansjörg Auer, Much Mayr, David Lama, the Belgian Sean Villanueva, the Americans Dean Potter, Winky, Josh, Ted, Cam, and Quinten, the Italian Matteo, and the two Luka's from Slovenia. Every year anew, we celebrate freedom, friendship, and the coming together of an insanely passionate community.

At some point, the lamb is cooked, and then Don Guerra enters. He lays the lamb on the wooden table, pulls the iron rod out of the softly cooked meat, and cuts off rough pieces with his long gaucho knife, ever tucked into his broadly wrapped belt. Coyly, with a smile, he beckons us over, saying, "*Buen provecho.*" One of the local "monkeys" replies, "*¡Un aplauso para el asador!*"

This is followed by a big round of applause for Don Guerra, and then everyone rushes to the table with a knife and a piece of white bread like hungry predators and eats, standing up, with their fingers. Very tasty and very original. Afterward, we drink beer and wine, play our instruments, primarily guitars and flutes, accompanied rhythmically by drums, singing songs about Patagonia, love, the mountains, and the longing that drives us on, makes us go, explains why we do what we do. But we also sing of those who can no longer be here today, like Bean Bowers, Kurt Albert, and Alberta Nuñes.

Late at night, I pick up the strings, close my eyes, and go on a journey way up into the icy heights: "I'm here to go, I'm here to flow, the wind will show, the way I'll go, there is a special love in my life, burns in my soul, it's cold, rocky, and icy, Cerro Torre." Rolling the "r" of Cerro and Torre like a never-ending love story. Every time, we party late into the night, and every time, Don Guerra ends up falling asleep on his wooden chair against the wall of his hut, a small table next to it, a half-empty glass of *vino tinto* resting on top. A still life for eternity that will never change.

The Wave

A fat year is usually followed by a lean one. But 2014 was a truly miserable one. We'd planned an expedition to Latok I in the Karakoram and were en route to Munich Airport, my brother and myself, accompanied by Dani Arnold and Mario Walder. But because of a terror warning for Pakistan, which was issued on the day of our departure, we had to cancel the expedition one hour before we were to leave. Our replacement trip to Patagonia in winter was smothered in snow, and in the end, we didn't have much to show apart from some high travel expenses.

In 2015, the situation in the Pakistani crisis region calmed down somewhat, and we tried again—the same team, going back to the same mountain. Preparations were in full swing, our equipment had already been sent to Islamabad, and we trained hard and hoped that after the bad year of 2014 there would now be a great year in its wake. Then came the infamous day that brutally ripped through our little Stone Monkey community.

Monte Brento, Italy, May 17, 2015, early morning: Ivo Ninov and his friend Walker Mackey stand on the precipice in their wingsuits. In front of them, 3,000-plus feet of air lead to the scree below. A perfect BASE, which I have also jumped umpteen times. The morning sun warms their faces, the air is calm, and birds fly about, singing. Ivo and Walter, too, are about to fly. A last mutual check, a last glance, a nod, then off they go. A short breath, and Ivo gives the command, "Three, two, one, see yaah!" They push off. After about three seconds they start to fly, past the yellow limestone walls of Monte Brento, over the "sun slabs" below, over the heads of the climbers and on to the landing meadow by the road. They open their canopies still far above ground and land safely. A broad grin stretches across their faces. For them, such a flight is the best start to a day. In the café across the road, they dip croissants into their lattes, and then quickly pack their parachutes for a second jump before the *viento*—wind—blows through the valley, making it impossible to safely BASE jump.

While the two are packing their parachutes on the lawn of the café under the olive trees, a call comes in from America. Dean Potter's girlfriend, Jen Rapp, is on the line, and what she has to report pulls the rug out from under Ivo's feet: Dean jumped from Taft Point in Yosemite an hour ago, in the evening local time on May 16, with his friend Graham Hunt. They flew a risky line, "The Notch." Since their exit, there has been no trace of either of them.

Ivo stares at the phone. He's dazed for a moment, because he knows immediately that a message like this almost always implies that the person in question is dead. But Ivo tries to suppress these dark thoughts and hopes for a miracle. He calls Winky immediately, but can't get through. The very next thing he knows, he's on the phone with a friend from Yosemite Search and Rescue, explaining that Dean and Graham are missing. Walker, also a good friend of Dean's, and Ivo pack their parachutes into the trunk and drive back to Bulgaria, both pale and silent.

Santa Cruz, California, May 17: It's 6:00 a.m. local time as Winky stares sleepily at his cell phone, which he always sets to silent mode when he goes to bed. There are umpteen incoming calls listed, plus a text message from Ivo. A cold shiver runs down Winky's spine as he reads that Dean is missing in Yosemite and that he should call back immediately. He slumps, holding back tears, knowing that BASE jumpers don't just go missing. The ringing of the phone snaps him out of his morbid reverie. It's a friend from the Yosemite Search and Rescue team; he yells into the phone to drown out the roar of the helicopter blades: "I'm so sorry, Dean . . . !" Before he can finish the sentence, everything fades into static. At that moment, Winky knows that his dark premonition has become a hard, painful truth: Dean Potter is dead.

Winky drives to Yosemite immediately. Low, heavy clouds hang over the walls. Meanwhile, the helicopter crew has recovered Dean's and his friend Graham Hunt's bodies. It begins to rain, as if everything in the Valley is crying—El Cap, Half Dome, the waterfalls, the trees, all together with the Stone Monkeys mourning silently together in the Center of the Universe.

When Ivo gets the sad confirmation of their deaths from Winky, he dials my phone.

Right then, when it rings, I'm training in my home gym finger boarding.

In a brittle voice, Ivo tells me what he needs to: "Hey, Thomas, Dean died last night in Yosemite. He jumped from Taft Point with his partner Graham, who also didn't survive the jump." I gasp, not even wanting to know what happened, because that won't bring them back in any case.

"Ivo, thanks for the news—what a crappy day. I can't say anything right now; please, let's speak tomorrow."

"Mucho love, brother!"

Dazed, I see Dean right in front of me, sitting on the precipice of Taft Point that long-ago day. In the background, El Capitan shimmers in the evening light, and with his deep, warm baritone, he gives an interview for our speed-climbing film, *Am Limit:* "We look for the answers here in the mountains, and that's also the reason why we keep returning there—to experience the higher meaning of life!" He later let me know that for him, wingsuit flying, climbing, and highlining were more of an art in dealing with the elements of Mother Nature than adventure sports. His was a metamorphic art, he said, in which man could transform himself through the elements into another level of consciousness. The highest level would be when everything happens only in the spirit: climbing, although one does not climb oneself; flying, although one does not fly. "Baaabooom!"

With tears in my eyes, I send a smile out to Dean, somewhere out there where he is right now, because I know he has found his answer, and now he is free and flying, climbing, and balancing on his highline forever.

CHAPTER THIRTEEN
Latok 1

The North Face

I cannot believe it. Finally, I'm back in Pakistan, and what I see in front of me is almost indescribable. A climbers' paradise, or simply the Choktoi. A range like no other. All the mountains—Latok IV; Latok III; the Ogre II; the pyramid of Ogre I, at 7,285 meters the highest of the group—are between 5,800 and 7,000-plus meters. But from the Choktoi Glacier, Latok I towers above everything with its 7,011 meters of altitude. Beside these giants are countless granite needles, all around 5,000 meters in height, whose names I don't know—a fantastic valley, so lonely, so beautiful. I am glad to be here now. To be able to switch off because Dean's death is still very much on my mind. I'm writing a song to deal with this immense pain, about finding the souls of our friends who have passed away, not at their graves, but in the mountains. Here, I can finally take a breath, and I instinctively know that this path is the only right one because, through our actions, the stories of our deceased brothers live on.

The most arduous part of my expedition is already behind me: the farewells back home, as always emotional. There was also the heat of Islamabad, the endless Karakoram Highway, the lovely Skardu with a cool Coke on the calmly flowing Indus River, the dusty rodeo Jeep ride to Askole, and the three-day march with horses and porters to our basecamp in Choktoi. The setting here is a dream: there is a stream, a large rock for bouldering, a little green meadow dotted with colorful alpine flowers, and a beautiful spot filled with fine sand for our tents—a beach holiday at 4,200 meters. On the moraine, a vast stone plate shaped like a petrified couch offers the best view of the mountains: the VIP lounge for observing this Latok symphony.

Our climbing team comprises four: Dani, Mario, Alexander, and me. A funny Austrian, Seppi, joins us as a photographer and cameraman. Ali and Ashraf staff our kitchen this time around. And Ismail is here, too, of course. Over the years, we've developed a brotherly relationship I would not want to miss when up in these mountains. Later, when climbing, he will pray for us as always. And that feels good to me.

During the acclimatization period, we hike through the Choktoi as if we were on an alpine sightseeing tour, and we bump into another expedition: the two US boys, Kyle and Scott. Kyle Dempster is undoubtedly one of the best American alpinists, having climbed the third ascent of the Ogre and also being awarded the Piolet d'Or. His climbing partner, Scott Adamson, is a top-notch ice climber from Montana. He has a wild persona, highlighted by his black, broadly curved mustache. They are likable and cool guys. Their project is the still-unclimbed north face of Ogre II. Their basecamp is not as nice as ours. Their tents stand on stone platforms, surrounded only by scree and rock. We chat, eat a snack, and wish each other the best for our plans.

After six days of harsh weather, the mountains are again visible and bright. Avalanches thunder into the valley, and Charly from Innsbruck forecasts perfect weather for the coming days—no precipitation, hardly any wind, and pleasant temperatures. We want immediately to acclimatize on our local mountain directly above our basecamp. It's a beautiful summit, about 6,000 meters in height, easy at the bottom, a little climbing at the top. Up to the final 200 meters we are cruising, and everything goes smoothly. But on the last pitch, we can't get any farther with our minimalist climbing gear due to the snowed-up granite slabs. The mountain has truly outmaneuvered our experienced team of four. At basecamp, we packed according to the motto "Light is cool," but now we curse our arrogance and start our descent.

Our next project is the southern flank of Latok III. I am sure that this near giant will play a key role in enabling us to tackle Latok I later. I'm the only member of the team who believes we can pull Latok I off—too difficult, dangerous, and strategically unfeasible, say the others, though I don't quite share their doubts. With the experience all four of us bring to the table, we can climb all walls. Dani is a machine and one of the best mixed climbers on planet earth. Mario is indestructible and never shows any weakness on the mountain. And we brothers have gained so much experience on this kind of terrain on past expeditions. In the end, I believe in the magic of flow. For now, we'll do Latok III, and that will give us all such confidence that we'll be able to see Latok I's north face through entirely different eyes.

At 2:00 a.m., we start up toward Latok III, loaded down with heavy backpacks. These moments are among the most beautiful for me, when we hike at night under a starry sky, trekking over the rugged, frozen glacier: everyone alone and a wanderer between worlds. Our thoughts soar to memories of home intermingling with this mountain world, while our breath synchs to a melody—sometimes it's rock 'n' roll songs, and sometimes it's folk music from the homeland.

Still in twilight, we reach the first corn-snow slope, and everything changes in a heartbeat. With every step, we break through the crumbly layer of snow to our knees. The going becomes brutal, our morning reverie interrupted by the harsh reality of mountaineering. We feel the far-too-heavy backpacks, torture ourselves, gasp, hyperventilate in the thin air, and fight against the inner hound holding us back. We slow with every step; it's dawn, and way too soon. The morning sun is scorching the 50-degree, 500-meter couloir, which ought to take us to the plateau where we'll set up our camp for today. We assess our current situation—the heat, the exposure, the gully—and quickly realize that our only option is to deposit our gear and descend right back to basecamp. Anything else would not only be reckless but deadly insanity. We find a rock spur where we can stash our gear and be protected. Then it's as if someone has flipped a switch: the mountains come to life, initially small snow slides turning into avalanches that thunder from the flanks and gullies surrounding us. We are in the middle of it all, protected only by this rock spur.

It's clear there will be no turning back today. We pitch our small tents in the tightest of spaces while wet snow slides rush down every minute and the avalanche field below us grows ever larger. Around 3:00 p.m., the sun disappears behind the mountain, and it is amazing how quickly everything around us calms down again. From now on, it is quiet, and the magic of shadow eliminates all the objective dangers.

In the safety of the night, we continue climbing, and Dani fixes the first 300 or so meters of the rock pillar together with Alexander. We spend the rest of the day in the sweltering heat of the tent on the snow plateau and descend to basecamp the following night.

One week later: the weather will be good for three consecutive days. We are lying in our high camp, wrapped in our sleeping bags. Mario is with Dani in the tent and me with Alexander when, suddenly, the nocturnal silence is shattered by an explosion above us: a thunder, an infernal roar. I tear open the tent as a white wall a few hundred feet to the left thunders over the rock face toward us. Quick as a flash, I zip up the tent and scream in panic: "Guys, shit, an avalanche—brace yourselves against the tent!" The next moment, the shock wave hits us with full force. We are shaken to the core and latch on with all our might to the tent's walls, hoping that no more than fine ice dust will hit our camp.

A moment later, everything is over. No one can believe what has just happened. Everything around us is dusted with the finest ice crystals. The air glistens in the light of our headlamps, and an eerie silence prevails. Pretty quickly, we realize how lucky we have been. Dani's backpack is gone, and Mario's ice-climbing gear, crampons, and two helmets have also disappeared. The ice storm swept everything into the abyss. It could have easily hit us, too, and this night traumatizes us.

At dawn, we descend and find both helmets and Dani's backpack far down on the last glacial plateau. We walk in silence, processing what happened. Back at basecamp, I sit next to Ismail, drink a good coffee, and tell him the story of the serac that collapsed not so far above us during the night and almost became our undoing. "Today is perfect because you had much luck, and Allah put a hand on you!" he says. He is right—it is a good day, because we got lucky and survived. But it is also a difficult day, because no one knows how things will continue from now on.

We have been sitting in basecamp with blue skies above for days. The avalanche has left deep traces in our minds, and as much as I would like to climb, none of us is willing to go toward Latok III again, let alone give Latok I any thought. The sun-drenched Choktoi feels oppressive, and this unexpected warm weather forces us to do nothing. Every day we get a new weather update from Charly. He forecasts brilliant weather with rising temperatures until further notice. We analyze all possibilities again but do not find a suitable plan to justify another attempt in these unstable conditions. Mario is satisfied with having survived once, and Alexander, Dani, and I see the risk as noncalculable. Seracs calve off at random—the ice avalanche does not necessarily have to be due to elevated temperatures—but we are nevertheless unwilling to continue. We don't feel it anymore, and these mountains that were the best, most beautiful, steepest, and most awesome a month ago now seem merely deadly. Together, we decide to prematurely end our expedition in the Choktoi.

After a dramatic experience on Ogre II, Kyle and Scott are also back at basecamp and preparing to leave. They were climbing through their chosen route when, just below the summit ridge, Scott took a 20-meter whipper and broke his leg. Their retreat from the wall was arduous, but they made it most of the way down. Then their ice anchor blew out, and they both tumbled across the final ice field, sliding 200 meters together into the shallow glacial basin. They survived the dramatic event without any permanent damage. They, too, must have had their guardian angels working overtime.

I bury my dream for now, knowing that I will be back. One last look back at my mountains, and then it's home again.

Months later, I'm sitting in the Kuckucksnest, our dark rock 'n' roll bar in Berchtesgaden. I'm back on stage with my band, Plastic Surgery Disaster. We play loud, deep, and heavy rock, and the atmosphere is close to boiling over. Every note, every riff, every cue, every break fits, and we are surfing the wild wave of rock 'n' roll. After an intense, loud booming hour comes our last song, "Mountain High." As my boys kick off the first riff, interweaving a melodic bass line, I close my eyes, and the stage becomes my metaphysical platform. The guitars erect giant walls of sound, and I'm standing right in the middle, surrounded by these walls. Hidden within, I visualize the perfect line. My line, an iced-up crack, the ramp leading out right, and a last section to the top-out. "[You] go so that I will go." Yes, because you go, I will go, too; because we trust each other, together we can break the limits of the impossible.

With this self-confidence, I hammer my tools into the brittle, vertical ice, set my crampons, and place ice screws as protection. All fears and concerns fall away, and we climb higher and higher. It is cold and icy; repeatedly, we are doused by spindrift. But we will certainly not give up. Poised above the abyss, we forget about time, even though we have been on the move for days. We climb over rugged mixed terrain out into the sun. The last few meters: a sharp ridge of corn snow. A cutting wind from the west hurls ice crystals in our faces. We feel them like little pinpricks. Then we can't go any farther. We are at the top. There is nothing above us anymore.

I fly, feel the hands on my sweaty body, carried through the Kuckucksnest as I crowd-surf with the mic. And I sing, "We are on mountains high . . . " The music becomes a gateway into another world. Into my world. The mood is exuberant, and the rock 'n' roll night doesn't want to end: "One more song, one more song, one more song . . . " chants the audience. Of course, we can't let our people down; we up our game and play "Desire" as an encore. I wrote the lyrics at the foot of Cerro Torre. A slow intro ends in a thunderstorm of drums, bass, and complex guitar riffs. Then comes my single sentence: oblique, hard, half-song, half-primal scream—"There is hope today; if you think higher, we have to go this way; it's our desire, come on. There is a place down here we'll get on fire. Can we follow our hearts? It's our desire! Believe in what you left behind; look inside and stay alive! There is a point of no return; go ahead to mountains high . . . desire."

For the finale, Wolfi whirls on the drums, Manni and Peter send a last riff into the amps, and Andi hammers a final stroke on his bass. What a night. Everything is intense; I feel every note and every word down to the last fiber of my body. I'm tired, like after climbing a big wall, and now it's time to drink some more—another never-ending night in Berchtesgaden.

After this night, I feel alive, having rekindled my passion—this insane yearning—for the mountains, especially Latok I. And when something means so much to me, I am much like a child and must have it. But it was not going to be so easy to find a team that shared this passion. Alexander, Dani, and Mario had signaled to me back at basecamp in 2015 that they did not want to come to these mountains ever again. But I was persistent and phoned all my contacts until I'd assembled Team Choktoi

2016: Toni Gutsch, with whom we had been successful on Latok II in 1997; and Sebastian "Sebi" Brutscher, a passionate climber, alpinist, and mountain guide from the Allgäu. Both of them shared my euphoria and determination, and I once again obtained the permits for Latok III and Latok I.

Lastly, three Americans—Tom Engelbach, Jim Donini, and George Lowe—wanted to share basecamp with us. Jim and George are true mountaineering legends and were part of the legendary team with Jeff Lowe and Michael Kennedy that nearly reached the summit via the north ridge in 1978. They were on the wall nonstop for 26 days, and in the end, they were only about 100 meters short of the summit when they had to turn around due to Jeff Lowe's having fallen ill. Nevertheless, their expedition was hailed internationally as "The most remarkable failure in alpine history." Since then, more than 30 expeditions had attempted this wall, but none made it as far as Jeff, Michael, Jim, and George on the ridge proper!

I was lucky enough to meet the heroes of the Latok I mission two months before our expedition got going. Jim, George, and Michael were still climbing, while Jeff, who suffered from an incurable neurodegenerative disease, had become wheelchair bound. Although he could only communicate via a speech computer, he radiated so much energy and joie de vivre that I sensed he was still the old warhorse at heart, full of humor and zest for action. He truly inspired me. I presented my vision of a central line up the north face, and Jeff immediately told me that it was the logical development of their initial idea. And since they were too old for that by now, I was the candidate to complete it. We all had a good laugh, and I finally knew where I was heading.

While training for the expedition, I received the sad news that my BASE instructor, Uli Wambach, had been killed in a wingsuit jump in Italy. He'd always said BASE jumping as we practiced it was safe. But now I felt there was no such thing as a calculated risk in this sport, and the only way to survive was to stop. That was the moment I hung up my BASE rig for good.

Simultaneously, filming was underway on a documentary for Servus TV. Alexander was 49 by then, and I was 51, a total of 100 years of living. To mark the anniversary, the film's title would be *100 Years of Huber Brothers: Blood Is Thicker Than Water*. The storyline was beautiful and simple: each brother climbs a route right on their doorstep, Alexander with *Stiller Ozean* on the single-pitch, knobby vertical face terrain of the Kleiner Barmstein, and me with *Watzmannflimmern* on the three-pitch, semi-alpine walls of the Brendlberg. Meanwhile, shots from the film archives of Timeline Productions—from home to Yosemite, from Pakistan's Ogre, Nameless Tower, and Latok II to Patagonia, and from Antarctica to the Arctic and Mount Asgard—would be interwoven, helping portray the breadth of our life in the mountains.

At the beginning of July 2016, Alexander had finished his segment of the film and left for Greenland. Now it was my turn for interviews and climbing. Michal Grassl, an excellent friend with whom I have climbed most of the routes on Brendlberg, belayed me on the three short pitches of *Watzmannflimmern*. Max and Franz filmed the long shots with a drone on our first run. Then I lowered Michal 200 feet to a small ledge at the base, fixing the route with an old climbing rope so the camera crew could film close-ups.

I rappelled down, and four feet above the small ledge, the rope slipped through my fingers, through the Grigri. Everything around me suddenly blurred and started spinning . . . then silence. I sat on the forest floor, the sun flashing through the trees; everything seemed peaceful but unreal. I was disoriented, with no idea where I was or what had happened. Then Michal was next to me. From far away, I heard his voice: "For God's sake, Thomas . . ." Everything sounded so dramatic. I took a deep breath and saw my middle finger, deformed—twisted like a corkscrew. This sight catapulted me back to reality at breakneck speed.

"Thomas, for God's sake, stay seated, don't move. We'll get help—you've fallen . . ." The next moment, I jumped up and said, "Michal, what a shit fight; look, my finger, we must get to the hospital immediately." I couldn't be stopped; I just wanted to get down as quickly as possible; I slipped on my sneakers and marched off, Michal following behind. Franz and Max rushed toward us. Panting, out of breath, they were simply happy to see me on my feet. They helped me with the exposed downclimb. All at once, Michal, constantly talking to me, sounded far away again, and I ran on as fast as I could, having as my only goal to keep running down, down, down. Then I heard the siren and saw the flashing lights through the trees.

Twenty-five miles and twenty minutes later, I was in the Traunstein trauma surgery emergency room. I assured everyone there that I was fine, that I only had slight headaches my finger was merely crooked. As a matter of routine, they pushed me into the MRI tube, where I was scanned from head to toe. "Is everything okay so far? Will the finger be okay? Because I'd like to go on an expedition to Pakistan in six weeks."—"The finger is the least of your problems. It's just a simple dislocation that can be quickly sorted. But your skull! We see clear fractures, partially reaching into your spine!" I was speechless and meek and only wanted to know how bad it was. As the medical staff told me, "The one on the skull will have to be operated on immediately. The fractures on the spine, on the other hand, look stable." After that, everything went very quickly, and the anesthesia put me into a deep sleep. Hours later, I woke up in intensive care and was gazing up into the relieved faces of my family. Marion, Elias, Amadeus, and Philo were there. Thank God!

I'd been on the operating table for over four hours, during which the surgeon had put the bone splinters back together with titanium plates and micro-screws. My great luck was that my meninges had withstood the bleeding pressure and no hemorrhage had reached the brain, which is the best prerequisite for avoiding brain damage.

During the initial visit, the surgeon told me how fortunate I must have been when I'd fallen, that the operation had gone without any hiccups, and that I would soon be back on my feet. He added that the spinal fractures affected none of the spinal processes and should heal by themselves; all that was needed was immobilization. Meanwhile, the finger had been set and would soon be ready for use again, and if everything went according to plan, I could return to the regular ward after four days and be home again after another ten days!

These were not bad prospects. Three days after the operation, I asked cautiously if it would be possible to consider climbing mountains in about six weeks. The doctor laughed and said that he did not know anything about mountaineering. All he could do was assure me that the skull is not responsible for mobility but only holds together that which steers mobility. According to the doctor, everything should be healed up simply fine in six weeks. But he could not answer whether mountain climbing at high altitudes would be justifiable. His non-answer was enough for me, because, with it, there was a spark of hope for Pakistan, the Choktoi, and Latok I.

Beyond my sickbed, rumors were spreading like wildfire. For some, I was already dead and buried while for others, I was parked in intensive care and beyond repair. "Extreme mountaineer Thomas Huber has a fatal accident" read many a lurid headline. To debunk all the rumors, I posted on my social media channel, "Contrary to all reports, I'm fine, had 1,000 guardian angels, see you soon, your Thomas."

After ten days, I finally came home and had time to process everything. Why had it even come to this? Usually, when I climb alone on the Brendlberg with a fixed rope, I use a standard sixty-meter cord. However, Michal's old rope had been trimmed to fifty meters, a fact I didn't know. It was precisely this ignorance that had led to disaster—the devil always hides in the details.

I slowly returned to everyday life and started training again, a little more each day, making perceptible progress. After a week, I did my first easy mountain run with Michal and felt good. A neurological examination after two weeks highlighted extensive recovery; in my eyes, nothing stood in the way of my trip to the Choktoi. Many people thought I was crazy; some doubted my sanity and even thought I might have been knocked a little bit harder on the head than I was letting on. I let them talk and went my way.

I told them not to worry, because I knew the Choktoi was the best rehabilitation center for someone like me. A good friend shouted at me that I should be careful, for God's sake, so that these know-it-alls wouldn't be proven right.

In mid-August, I was finally back at basecamp, my personal Stonehenge in the mountains. I had been through a lot in the last month, and was glad just to be there. Up on the Choktoi, I didn't have to answer any annoying questions, report on my health, or justify "why" I was going on another expedition right after my accident. The Americans Tom, Jim, and George were also with us, and had the goal of climbing a smaller Choktoi peak. Climbing with me would be Sebi and Toni. Max from Timeline Production would accompany us with the camera. As always, Ismail was our man on the ground, while Ali had taken over the reins in the kitchen tent. I inhaled and exhaled the air from this valley, and finally felt healthy again.

But as exuberant as our mood was at the outset, it soured dramatically after six weeks on the Choktoi.

It all started with Kyle and Scott. The two Americans were on the Choktoi Glacier, just like us. We had our plan; they had their mission. After acclimatizing, they took up their north-face project on Ogre II again, but in highly dubious weather. On their planned summit day, thick clouds rolled in and it began to snow. Days later, their cook, Gafour, came to us at basecamp and asked for our help because the two climbers should have been back long ago.

Sebi, Toni, and I left immediately for Ogre II. After five hours of marching over the flat glacier, we were at the icefall, a glacial break at the foot of the Ogre. We found their skis stuck in the snow. Otherwise, there were no traces of the two boys. We bivouacked in the tent in front of the icefall, waiting and hoping for any signs of life. Then it started snowing overnight, thirty inches of fresh snow, and we couldn't see anything; we were in a proper whiteout. We alternately yelled, "Kyyyyle!" and, "Hey, Scooooott!" and then stared into the white nothingness, waiting. But there was no response—only silence. Defeated, we returned to our basecamp.

Meanwhile, their relatives in the United States had raised funds, and a large-scale rescue effort was launched. Everyone was hoping for a miracle. On September 3, ten days after the boys' last sign of life, there was finally a turn in the weather. It was cloudless! The Pakistani military had two helicopters, so I flew with them because I knew the area. We circled the mountain for an hour, flying up to an altitude of 7,200 meters several times along their route up the north face and then along the northwest ridge over their planned descent, looking for them in the crevasses, valleys, and flanks. But we saw and found nothing, absolutely nothing, and in the end, we were left with the tragic realization that there would be no miracle in the Latok Group.

Once again, we tried to get an answer for the relatives about their fate and climbed toward the northwest ridge on Ogre II. But it turned out to be a hell of a trip. We reached a height about 400 meters below the summit, battling heat and rockslides. We were damned lucky to have survived ourselves. There was still no trace of Kyle and Scott.

After that, Max's health became a concern. He went back to civilization with the help of our porters, and back home, he immediately ended up in intensive care—heart failure due to an infected heart muscle. After this drama, Toni and Sebi no longer had much appetite for the mountains, and we all marched dejectedly back to Askole. What sad and dramatic times.

Back home, I still had a pilgrimage of my own I needed to make, back to where I had fallen three months earlier. I walked this path alone, traversing the narrow, exposed trail to the Brendlwand. Admittedly, my heart was pounding. I took a deep breath, turned the corner, and stood there. It was electrifying. I could feel the intense energy, and sat down in the very place where I had landed, a little flat spot beside a tree above steepening terrain and a huge drop-off below. Above me, the too-short fixed rope still hung from the wall, and, looking at it, I only now realized that my survival had been down to immeasurably good fortune. A guardian angel had stopped my fall on this tiny ledge, and I was incredibly grateful to be here now. The sun flashed through the trees as it had back then, and, in that moment, I understood that we should not be afraid of death. Death is a moody companion. He comes when it suits him, not when you think he should turn up. So let us live life richly now, filling it with the most beautiful and most loving moments. Because that's what life is for—to enjoy and share true happiness with others.

Still, I knew I could only find the true key to my happiness within. Stupidly, I always told myself that there was only one path to happiness now, and it had five letters: L. A. T. O. K.—my way, my line, my truth in which I choose to believe. But in the last few years, I had been beaten up by reality, and in the meantime, this Latok within had become an insurmountably smooth wall. Perhaps "Latok" was my silent master who wanted to teach me that one must be willing to free oneself from the shackles of compromised freedom to find absolute freedom. Jeff Lowe had set a benchmark example: he first had to get an incurable disease before recognizing where the boundaries dissolved and total freedom began.

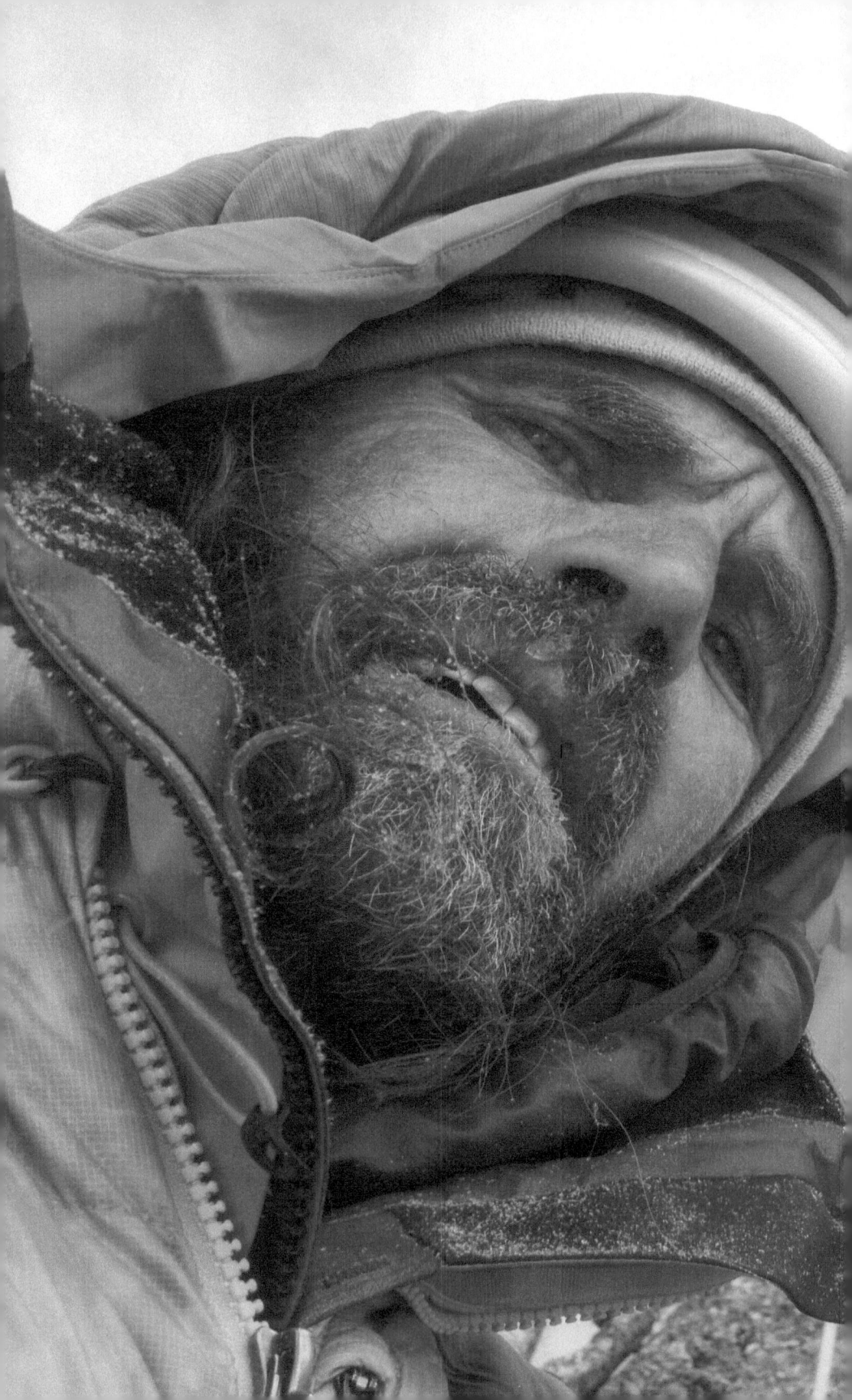

CHAPTER FOURTEEN
Cerro Kishtwar

Courage and Success

It's rare that you understand an issue and then get to perfectly implement your findings. For this reason, it was tough for me to finally banish the "never-ending Latok story" from my mountaineering heart. Nobody around me wanted to hear the word "Latok" from my mouth again. I faced a dilemma because, no matter what happened, it was always clear that I would plan another expedition to the Choktoi.

My salvation from this impasse came from Switzerland. Stephan Siegrist, with whom I had recently repeated Jeff Lowe's wild big wall *Metanoia* on the north face of the Eiger, gave me an excellent helping hand in getting Latok out of my life, even if only briefly. He showed me a picture of a crazy mountain. An orange granite tower, steep and compact, it bore some resemblance to Cerro Torre. "I'm going there, to Kashmir, with a good friend from Interlaken, and if you like, come along," said Stephan.

I began to think, and the longer I stared at this picture of Cerro Kishtwar, the more diffuse the Latok image became. Plus, Kashmir was a novum—a new world and a fresh start. I believed this wall would be easier to bag because it did not seem as dangerous and complex as my north face.

Finally, an expedition with a higher success rate, indeed over 50 percent, so a realistic goal and not a pipe dream. In addition, I thought it would do me good to summit something again so that people would realize I hadn't forgotten how to climb—I'd be creating something, with the added benefit of regaining my self-confidence. This is the key to success for future expeditions: to know, no matter what, that you can pull it off.

Even if I didn't say it, I knew deep in my heart that it was all about one thing alone, finding my way back to the light. Cerro Kishtwar was a means to an end—a way back to Latok. Because no matter how much I tried, I could not banish this latter mountain from my thoughts.

In the end, I also said yes to this expedition because the central, unclimbed line on Kishtwar's northwest face was simply a fantastic wall—awesome, vertical, and solid granite, as steep as Trango Tower, Cerro Torre, El Cap, or Mount Asgard. A perfect big wall, a dream line right to the summit, and together with Stephan to boot.

In the early 1990s, English climbers began to explore the untouched mountain region of Kashmir, and Cerro Kishtwar (6,155 meters) moved immediately onto their radar. This perfectly pyramidal needle stands out as an ultimate challenge and, as a climbing objective, is second to none in the region. In 1992, the Englishmen Andy Perkins and Brendan Murphy were on the northeast face for seventeen days, climbing icy cracks and dihedrals, dealing with harsh weather and spindrift, and ultimately failing 100 meters below the summit. Their food supplies were nearly depleted, and they had given it their all. The following year, Mick Fowler and Steve Sustad, also English, arrived and were the first to find a way to the summit of this extreme peak.

In the mid-nineties, Kashmir—a border region long contested between India and Pakistan—closed for political and military reasons, and no foreigners were allowed to visit the region. While mountaineering boomed in the rest of the Himalayas and the Karakoram, the mountains in Kashmir thus remained dormant. It was not until 2010 that the regulations relaxed. In 2011, Stephan Siegrist teamed up with Denis Burdet, Robert Frost, and David Lama and kissed the mountains of Kashmir awake once again. Their goal was Cerro Kishtwar, which they climbed alpine style via a bold ice line on the right side of the northwest face.

Stephan traveled to Kashmir four more times in the following years, putting up seven first ascents. Even though many beautiful, exciting mountains in this region were still awaiting a first ascent, the Cerro never left Stephan's mind, whether for its beauty, the wall, the immaculate granite—the entire line! Yes, a wall that is rarely found on the planet we call home. A unique alpine objective that got our team of four together. Our youngest, at 27, was Julian Zanker, a friend of Stephan's a good climber, alpinist, and BASE jumper, with his red hair resembling Prince Harry from the English royal family. The three of us were accompanied by Stephan Bühl, a photographer from Hamburg.

Kashmir, the northernmost province of India, is a politically unstable region. Many who live here fight for their independence; some feel they belong to Pakistan, others to India. The English left behind this chaos after they gave up their colonial claim to the Indian subcontinent. A provisional border was drawn through ancient India, and what originally was one became artificially separated. The predominantly Hindu section was added to what is now India, while the Islamic part became Pakistan. In the mountains of Kashmir, the English had left behind a Line of Control, i.e., no fixed border. Since then, the military superpowers of India and Pakistan have been in constant strife, shelling each other throughout the warmer summer months.

We passed through heavily armed military checkpoints several times as we rode the bus into the hinterlands of Kashmir. I had had a new passport issued for this trip, and that was a good thing because, with a stamped Pakistani visa in my old passport, I never would have seen the mountains in person.

But finally, I did find myself with Julian and the two Stephans directly beneath the northwest face of Cerro Kishtwar, and our mouths remained open. I was thrilled, not overwhelmed, because this far exceeded the picture Stephan had initially shown me. The first 400 meters presented a steep ice flank with some mixed climbing thrown in, followed by 600 to 700 meters of overhanging granite. For the layman, an utterly smooth wall. But we immediately recognized the distinctive and unique features! To the left of our prospective route, we could see the deeply incised ice-runnel system that Perkins and Murphy had attempted. Still farther left, we could even recognize Mick Fowler and Steve Sustad's ice route, used to make the first ascent of this granite monolith. On the far right was the ice line taken by Stephan Siegrist et al.'s route *Yoniverse*, from 2011. Our aim was to follow the central thin-crack lines right up the middle of the wall, clear to the summit! The route looked difficult and wild, but in recompense, no seracs threatened us overhead.

We fixed the first 300 or so meters of the ice field, stashed our portaledge, sleeping bags, and climbing gear, and then started planning our climbing tactics. A fine crack marked our desired line of ascent. This feature was visible even to the naked eye, so we were relatively relaxed about the challenges ahead. Whoever felt best on any given day climbed on, belayed by another, while the third lazed around in camp, recovering. This tactic was bound to be maximally efficient, and we estimated that we would need about four days for the vertical wall, maybe a maximum of five. If you consider that the *Nose* on El Cap runs for 3,280 feet (1,000 meters), and Alexander and I had done it in 2:45, we could easily rock up this 700-meter wall in five days.

The weather, your health, and team dynamics are essential for a successful climb, but the main limiting factor is always time, as determined by your provisions. Of course, we could have taken food and fuel with us for ten days, but then we would have been much too heavy, the backpacks would have been difficult to carry, and we would have been much too slow. Any success always starts with a perfect planning phase back at basecamp—you want to carry neither too much nor too little, quantities we could "measure" through experience alone. Therefore, there was always much discussion. In the beginning, the climbing gear and provisions weighed about 110 pounds. Then every single carabiner was discussed, and everything was optimized regarding weight. How many energy bars did we need per day? Did it have to be four, or were two enough?

The trick is to sift out all nonessential items until you're bringing only the bare minimum. Then you are light, and only then can you be fast and efficient in the mountains. Ultimately, we reduced the weight by forty-four pounds, giving us food rations for four days and fuel for six days. We could stretch the food to six days but not the fuel, because, at higher altitudes, that always limits your time on the mountain. Without gas, you can't boil snow or ice for water, and athletic pursuits at altitude become extremely dangerous if you get dehydrated, a condition that can become life-threatening sooner than you think. We were well prepared, fully motivated, and in good spirits to meet the challenges ahead. As a delicacy and small luxury for when we were in the thick of it, I smuggled a small piece of speck (cured ham) from home and a package of gummy bears in my sack.

On the last day of September, the high-elevation wind shifted to the north, and the residual moisture that kept bringing a little precipitation each afternoon disappeared completely. Azure sky, no clouds in sight, and a slight drop in temperature.

It was time to climb.

On October 1, we say goodbye to Surij, our cook; Happy, our liaison officer; and our basecamp. October 2 at 10:00 a.m., we are standing at the base of the wall. Everything suddenly seems different. The wall is shadowy and cold, and the rock color has turned an unfriendly gray. Only the afternoon sun finally colors the wall in the familiar warm orange of Cerro Torre. I chop a small platform out of the ice. In front of me, a hairline crack stretches 4 meters upward, losing itself in slabby, compact granite. This already looks impossible. Ten meters to the left, however, a prominent crack system kicks off that will hopefully take us up to the snow band 150 meters above. In any case, everything already looks much more complex than we imagined. But who will take the first lead: Julian, our youngest; Stephan, who had the idea; or me, as the oldest? Before I can ask, Julian clips the cams, nuts, pitons, and Bird Beaks in assorted sizes to his harness. The young savage wants to find out what he is made of. Climbing shoes and chalk bags will have to stay in our haulbag for now, primarily because it's about -15 degrees Celsius.

Stephan sets up camp, a portaledge for three people, pure luxury up here. I put the rope in the Grigri, while Julian places the first Bird Beak three meters above the belay. With this wondrous steel invention—a hybrid hook, or perhaps better, a mixture of a Cliffhanger and Knifeblade piton—you can master nearly-blank cruxes without having to drill a bolt hole in the rock. It is now the most essential tool in a modern aid climber's arsenal, but Julian takes his time despite it. After three hours, he finally has a proper stance thirty meters higher. It took a long time, and it was cold, too. But most importantly, we have set off.

In two hours, the sun will reach this northwest side of the mountain; then, the cards will be reshuffled. I'm too cold for climbing, while Julian is mentally burned out, so it's Stephan's turn. When he starts climbing, the sun is already coming around the corner. The rock begins to glow, and everything immediately seems more friendly and enticing—no longer so hostile and serious. I enjoy the warming sun and the time in the portaledge, snuggled up in my sleeping bag. I feel perfect now, but I have no illusions that we will reach our goal for the day, the snow band 150 meters above us. Swiss German epithets ricochet off the rock, Stephan laboring 30 meters above my belay.

All the cracks run out, says Stephan; this is all a *"hure Schissdreck"* ("fucking shit"), and we are stuck. I ignore these complaints because I cannot change anything anyway. I simply continue to enjoy being there.

Come sunset, Stephan has managed another 20 meters. If you add it all up, we've climbed a mere 50 meters out of 700. This is too few if we want to stick to our ambitious plan. If we continue like this, we will be far from the summit in five days! A bit exhausted, we return to our camp to eat, drink, and finally crawl into our portaledge. Julian and I share the space on top, while Stephan beds down in a hammock below. In this cramped space, it takes time for everyone to get into their sleeping bags. But once we're in there, it's perfect: you're entirely in the world of your warm sleeping bag, and whether the portaledge is hanging in an apple tree in your back garden or here at 5,400 meters, on the icy northwest face of Cerro Kishtwar no longer matters. The only thing that counts: it's cozy, warm, and blissfully comfy.

October 3. Today is my day to push the route ahead! I'm out into the cold with a few quick spoonfuls of muesli and a cup of coffee made with the dissolved leftovers of yesterday's noodle soup. I jumar the fixed ropes to yesterday's high point. Julian belays, and I place my first Bird Beak two meters above the belay. Making a reassuring "ZZZssssssiiiiinng, ZZZZssssiiinnng, ZZZZsssiiingg" noise, the steel wonder piton sinks into the seam with each hammer blow, by its tone letting me know the protection is solid. The seam looks to rise diagonally upward for all eternity. But I'm not intimidated—I'm just thinking from placement to placement, meter to meter, hook to hook. Many are good; some hold my body weight. Sometimes a cam gets wedged behind a hollow flake, making me hold my breath for a second. Then again, a Bird Beak whistles, singing into the crack to calm my nerves. I gradually work my way up, slowly but surely gaining ground, and around noon I reach the large snow band.

I am happy to be here, and the ledge immediately gets an appropriate name: "Happy Ledge."

Slowly, the sun creeps around the corner again, and the dreary wall transforms into a sea of orange granite, immediately shifting the mood. And it gets even better: If the previous climbing was complicated, tedious, and complex, the next 50 meters are pure pleasure. We jam perfect hand cracks in the evening light, forgetting the previous day's unforgiving start in a heartbeat.

October 4, around noon. Our camp hangs off the exposed Happy Ledge in the middle of the wall, and the Swiss team is climbing. I make myself comfortable and finally have time to do nothing. But my hours in this seclusion and isolation pass much too quickly. It is already evening, and the setting sun bathes the surrounding mountains and the wall in a peaceful, warm light. It's almost too cheesy for a photo, and if there weren't snow on every little ledge, you'd almost think we were hanging out on sunny Californian granite somewhere high on El Capitan. In a moment, Julian and Stephan will have to float down from above, back to camp, and will hopefully report on another stellar day of climbing. I fill the water bottles and boil water for dinner, so the boys will have something to eat immediately. Because when you work a lot, you get hungry! Julian gets the hunter's pot, Stephan the pasta napolitana, and I a nasi goreng. Everything out of a bag: tear it open, add hot water, let it hydrate for ten minutes, pack everything in a down jacket so as not to lose any heat, and our dream menu at 5,500 meters is ready.

Finally, the two heroes from above arrive. But their mood is subdued, and Julian says, "It doesn't look good, Thomas; it was tough, only hooks, and bloody complicated for a first ascent!"—"Yes, that's normal when it's hard," I try to encourage him, but I'm also curious. "What doesn't look good?"—"It took me seven hours to do forty meters; I tried but could not go any faster!" I'm preparing our instant packet menus, and my spoon almost falls out of my hand. "Only 40 meters? Yes, that's not good news, I must say!" Stephan adds: "Yes, and it's cold on top of that and endless. It goes on forever.

Then no one says anything. The only thing happy here is the ledge. Damn, 40 meters are clearly too few, and what gives me even more of a headache is Stephan's statement that the terrain does not change. This would imply only 60 meters or a maximum of 80 meters tomorrow. It will also be our fourth day on the wall, with only 250 meters out of 700 in the bag. Regarding provisions, we would only have fuel for two days, with significantly reduced food rations as a result: one main meal for three per day. While we could make this work, because we always climb any wall according to the motto "A good one can take it," the fuel could still become a limiting factor.

The facts are disheartening: 250 meters in four days compared with the roughly 500 meters we'd been hoping to climb in two days. Our backs are against the wall, and I know we can't possibly make it even though the weather is perfect, albeit very cold. Even if we conserve gas, the most we can do is hold out on the wall for one more day. But in the end, this would get us to only 250 meters shy of the summit before we'd have to give up. I'm all churned up inside. Everything has been perfect: the team's vibe, the weather, the objectively safe wall. But we underestimated the climbing.

Everyone quietly and greedily spoons up their bagged meal. Thanks to the spices, the noodles with barely perceptible meat pieces are just palatable. And as the saying goes: hunger is the best cook. Today there is no soup, no extra ration of gummy bears nor a slice of bacon. We do not have much food left, and what little we do have will need to suffice for the next few days. With growling stomachs, we lie in our sleeping bags, any sleep out of the question. There are too many question marks. Nobody knows how to proceed, and everybody is busy with himself and his problems. Today, Stephan's hand developed a painful swelling, which could stem from tendonitis, and he's not sure it will improve. And, since yesterday, Julian has had numb toes due to the extreme cold, while I am struggling with the fear of failing once again in the mountains.

What a bloody mess. It all started on such a positive note, and I want to scream, "Shit!" into the night. But nobody will hear except Stephan and Julian, who need their rest. I know we will go to the extreme, because turning back now makes no sense; the weather is too lovely for that. And that's the biggest problem: We will keep climbing until we've squeezed the last gas out of our cartridges, and then a little farther until dehydration kicks us in the gut. Then we'll probably burn out below the summit and have to turn around and get down fast before our situation becomes life-threatening. After that, there will be no more attempts; we will simply pack up and head home.

I toss and turn in my sleeping bag. I don't want to follow this path. Then those bastard memories of Latok come up again—I damn well don't want to fail here, too. I'm so tired of looking for reasons and explanations as to why Latok never worked out. I was convinced that the Kishtwar would finally get me back into the groove, fighting hard for a goal, going to the extreme to come out on top. I wanted to break the wave of failure so that I could once again pronounce: "It was hard, challenging, crazy, and wild! But up on top, I was so happy, so free, and had tears in my eyes!"

I distract myself with beautiful memories from home and try to sleep. One thought sticks with me: Philo presenting me with a small pebble as a good-luck charm shortly before I left for this expedition. This pebble has the word "courage" written on it, and she sincerely let me know, "Dad, take this with you; I think you'll need it!" I stashed the pebble in my jacket along with a family photo, to keep my loved ones closer. With them in my pocket, I wouldn't be lost alone on the precipice, and perhaps the photo and the pebble would bring that extra bit of luck you always need on an expedition.

From their snoring, which keeps me awake, Julian and Stephan are already in the land of dreams. Caught up in my own realm of endlessly looping thoughts, I keep hearing my daughter's phrase: "Dad, take this with you; I think you'll need it!" This stone with the word "courage" written on it. What was she trying to tell me? She was right. Courage is precisely what is needed now. Not to doubt, but to act. Finally, be courageous; get going! If not now, when? Quietly, I ask Philo, as if she were lying right next to me in the portaledge, "Philo, what did you want to tell me with 'courage'?" There must be some meaning to it all. In vain, I wait for an answer.

My thoughts fly back and forth, and four interlinked notions keep coming to the forefront: cowardice, courage, descent, and ascent. The logical thing to do in this weather would be to keep climbing, courageously and fearlessly, hoping for easier terrain farther up to speed our progress. Then my thoughts turn in a new direction: We could also sack it in, turn around, fix our ropes over the most challenging passages while we descend, and return to basecamp. After a short break, we would then return to the wall with renewed energy and restocked provisions. With the help of the fixed ropes, we could surely reach our current high point in a day. We would only have to accept the risk that the weather would not be as good as it is now—but at least we'd a real chance of reaching the summit.

The further I delve into this scenario, the more my daughter's answer rings true. We need to make a brave decision now, and not act foolishly. There is only one proper choice! We must be brave and descend in the best weather, setting ourselves up to summit at a future date!

October 5. I have not slept all night. Finally, morning arrives. It is icy cold, not a cloud in the sky, and the vista is gigantic. We boil water, everyone sips a hot cup of coffee, and then we're off. "Thomas, do you fancy the lead?" Stephan offers to belay me, letting Julian tend to his numb toes. "Yes, I'll give it a shot," is my hesitant answer, because now I have a different plan. I take another sip of this black brew and start: "Hey, guys, before we go, we must think everything through again. I almost think how we do it now will ultimately be decisive."—"Yes, okay, but what do you mean—are you going to present us with a new climbing style?" Julian asks me, while Stephan adds wittily: "Yes, maybe a Bavarian one; that would be super sexy; I'm excited!"—"Well, none of the above. I have thought of something completely different!"

I sketch out my plan: to descend, fixing our ropes to lay the groundwork for a future attempt. They are both momentarily speechless, and I can see they aren't thrilled to leave the mountain. Julian tells me he doesn't feel like starting all over again, while Stephan says, "Thomas, say, all kidding aside, what's the point? Just look at the weather; we'll never get another window like this. There's only this one chance—a second is rather unlikely!"

Stephan knows what he's talking about; he has already been on four expeditions in this region and has experienced awful weather one time too many. "Well, Steph, let's keep going like this!" I say.

I continue, "But you must agree we won't make it to the summit if things keep going as they are. We only have two cartridges of gas left—enough for three days at most, and for one day's food—and we can't feed ourselves on 'will and fighting spirit' alone!"—"Yes, you might be right." Our debate rages for another hour, at least, but in the end, I prevail, convincing them to descend right after our last sip of coffee. Then everything happens very quickly. We fix the most difficult passages with the climbing ropes, and by late afternoon, we are back at basecamp.

October 6, basecamp. The weather is perfect. I know we made the right decision, and I'm doing well.

October 7. Clouds come in, and temperatures are on the rise. The first spring clouds appear in the evening, and light snowfall sets in. Despite this somewhat unsettled weather situation, we decided to go up again—first thing very late tomorrow night!

October 8. At 3:00 a.m., Surij, our cook, rouses me from my sleeping bag with a military, "Wake up, sir." The clouds from the evening before have cleared, and the stars are out. After a short breakfast, we head back up toward the mountain. It's now or never—there will not be a third attempt. Everyone has his superstitious pre-climb: Stefan scans the sky for shooting stars, his omens of good luck, and I'm glad when he sees one; Julian always puts on his left mountaineering boot first; and I pray on an oversized, heart-shaped slab of rock just below basecamp whose top points toward the mountain. After Our Lord's Prayer, I quickly request that we recognize all dangers and make adequate decisions. Off we go, mentally ready for this endless wall.

We reach Happy Ledge after eight hours, laden with enough gas and provisions for our attempt. The camp lives up to its name again—all of us are happy! It is not as cold as a few days ago, and the wind has changed from north to west, bringing masses of humid air into the Kashmir mountains. After a clear morning, the clouds gather in the afternoon; in the evening, it snows just like before.

It will stay like this for the next few days. We will not see the sun again, knowing it will be a shady and miserable endeavor. These are not ideal conditions, but our attitude has fundamentally changed. No matter what, we will make the best of what Kishtwar has to offer. Iced-up cracks, spindrift, evening snowfall, snow inside the portaledge, snow in the sleeping bag, clammy clothes, ever-present damp—bring it all on!

We sleep well, and even though it is still snowing, we know there will be clear morning skies. We battle, motivate each other, climb in the most adverse conditions, and swap leads repeatedly. It feels like day after day, the wall is getting higher and higher, stretching endlessly above, and yet we keep climbing because there is only one way left for us, and that is up. I have tunnel vision and hardly need any food; I lack for nothing, my muscles don't cramp, and I live only to exist in this ascetic world of the Kishtwar!

It is already the fifth day on the wall, and in the afternoon, it snows like every day. Above us towers a feature we've named "Texas Flake" for its resemblance to the American state and the eponymous feature on the

Nose. It's a vertical granite slab, 110 meters tall; through its middle, an okay hairline fracture seemingly stretches into infinity. Again and again, a gust of wind hisses around the edge of the rock, swirling fresh snow through the air, pouring it over us like a waterfall. Textbook spindrift, a thing no one needs. It's time to crawl into our camp. But Stephan, who has already belayed me on one pitch today, says: "It doesn't look good right now, Thomas, but you're doing well today. Come on, lead another pitch. What we do today, we don't need to do tomorrow."

He's right, and I place my first nut in the shallow seam and carefully load it. It holds. From above comes the next load of snow. Head down, hood over the helmet, and wait until it's over. Then, onward again. The work feels infinite. One could despair now, but I have devised a good tactic for leads like this: Only the next few feet matter—not the end of the pitch, because that will come along eventually anyway. In any case, with each completed section, you get closer to the end. After some technical moves along the seam, a rock flake leads outright.. I grab the Cliffhanger hook off my harness, place it behind the feature, and load it. "Ahhhh, watch me, Steph!" It stays in place, and on we go again free climbing. Then some more hooking, then free again. I am henceforth quickly gaining height.

I like to call this form of climbing "murmuring"—gaining height as quickly as possible, with everything hanging off your harness. Aiding, freeing, doing whatever—only speed counts. You can only allow yourself to do this if a fall will be clean—into space—and not catastrophic. Then my most delicate piece of protection comes into play, the No. 0 X3 spring-loaded camming device, a miniature mechanical miracle. The cam is designed for the thinnest cracks and should hold falls; at least, one hopes so. I place it high above me and weight it; it expands into the minimalist feature. I breathe in deeply. It sticks. Higher up, the crack widens. I quickly find the right size, the No. 0.4 gray cam. In it goes, loaded, and I pull through. Further up, a placement for the No. 0.5, the beloved purple cam: "Rrrrraaaatsch."

Suddenly, I find myself five meters down, clasping the cam in my hand, the No. 0.4 dangling on the rope. But the tiny one held: the No. 0 X3. It's a miracle. I shake off the shock of the fall and get back to climbing. Another cursed ice shower from above—spindrift—hits me. I wait for a bit, then I'm off again, the same procedure; this time, though, the No. 0.4 cam holds. A shallow gully full of ice bars passage a meter or so higher. Impossible. I am, for a short moment, lost. Suddenly Stephan's voice rings clear: "Hey, Thomas, yes, mate, keep it up."—"I'm trying, but it's so hard."

I have no choice but to try; maybe something will work after all! I hit the ice with my hammer, looking for a way past the obstacle without placing a piton. I hammer away and find a placement for the No. 3 cam, the big blue one, with its lobes half-open between ice and rock. Now it gets exciting. It's hard to imagine that this dicey construct will take any weight. Carefully, I pull on the cam, watching closely for shifting. It's not a nice feeling to expect a gnarly fall at any moment. "Steph, now you have to pay close attention!" I say.

The cam lobes are eating into the ice on one side and resting on rock on the other. I take another deep breath. What's the point, anyway? The cam is currently fully loaded. "Ahhhhh"—it stays in place. I grab a Bird Beak off my harness, place it above me in a hairline crack, and drive it home with singing blows.

"Yeeeeaaahhhh!" I shout, while Stephan cheers in Swiss German, "Bitching—you are a machine!" Again the spindrift pours over us, but we don't care anymore. The day is saved. Thirty feet higher, I set up our belay and then rappel back to camp on the fixed rope. Julian has just cooked up some pasta Bolognese, but all I need is soup. I haven't been hungry for days, and all I really want is the peace and warmth of my sleeping bag. It doesn't take long, and I'm off to the land of dreams.

The next day is a carbon copy of the previous one, and although the climbing remains difficult, cold, and complicated, we reach a small ledge at about 6,100 meters, and above us, the wall leans back. Today we can laugh because we have left the endless granite desert behind.

October 14. Early in the morning, we ascend from our last high camp via the fixed ropes, back to our high point. As always, the morning sky is cloudless. The rising sun tickles the surrounding mountains with its first rays, and I am once again overwhelmed by the beauty and wildness of these Kashmir mountains. The last 100 meters to the summit are a true gift.

Easy mixed climbing brings us to a saddle; from here, it is only a few meters to the summit. The weather is perfect, and it will stay that way. We almost feel that we are not alone, and will be rewarded with some unique gift for all we have been through. We walk the last meters together, incredulous to be here—at this moment in time.

Five hundred meters higher, veils of clouds move in the jet stream, yet we stand warm in the sun, feeling no wind at all. The three of us embrace, silently. I have tears of happiness in my eyes, as do Stephan and Julian. After a while, I can finally say what's on my mind: "Hey, guys, I am so grateful to be here with you. I thought I had forgotten how to climb mountains. But now I know I still can, and I get to stand on top of such a crazy peak again with you two. Thanks, guys, for hanging in there with me!"

What a moment, what a story. All three of us know that we only made it because we acted courageously as a team. And the catalyst for our brave decision was my daughter's pebble. I stash a small stone from the summit in my backpack and send Philo a heartfelt "thank you" back home. That same day, we rappel the entire wall; around midnight, we reach advanced basecamp, then are back in basecamp the following day. *Har-Har Mahadev* will be the name of our route up the northwest face of Cerro Kishtwar. This comes from Hinduism and essentially means "Increase moral values so that you overcome fear, to master all dangers!" Or, as we would say in Bavaria, *"Scheiss da nix, dann feed da nix"*—"If you don't give a shit, then nothing can bother you."

October 15. Back at basecamp, I stand again on my heart-shaped stone slab and look back at the mountain. I start smiling because this Cerro has grown so much for us in these seven weeks. We almost lost because we underestimated the mountain and the wall. But when we recognized the Cerro's actual size, we were able to climb it. Our success is again proof that the impossible exists only in your mind. Impossibility, however, loses all meaning if you trust your experience, act with courage, and let yourself be guided by heart and intuition.

Home-Dahoam

I am finally back in my Dahoam—the Bavarian word, you'll recall, for "home." Here, everything is said with a *"Servus"* or *"Hawedere,"* and words are kept to a bare minimum. It's where my roots have grown into the soil—the source of my energy and my charging station for adventures to come. Here, I can be as I am and live out my traditional, sometimes quite conservative habits as I wish, and no one bats an eye. Dahoam is also where the beer tastes best—and it tastes best in Berchtesgaden, of all places. The light Helles with the green label, cooled in our wooden trough in the garden, drunk directly from the glass bottle as I sit around the campfire with my family. That's Dahoam.

CHAPTER FIFTEEN

The Line of My Heart

Choktoi Again and Again

The mountains etch considerable shadows against the night, a luminous, starry sky stretching high above them. I have rarely seen something so beautiful. This time, my tent is pitched on the stone moraine with a view into the Upper Choktoi. Next to me stand the tents of Yannick Boissenot from France, Simon Gietl from South Tyrol, and Rainer Treppte from Allgäu. It took a while to assemble, but I'm glad to have found this team, who enthusiastically celebrate this newest iteration of my Latok obsession. When they're not playing cards, Ali, Ali, Shokur, and Ismail are cooking and chatting away down at the beach, where our kitchen tent is pitched.

It's autumn in the Karakoram. We have deliberately scheduled our expedition for late in the year because I am convinced these mountains are too dangerous in full-blown summer. It is incredible how mountaineering has changed due to climate change since our expedition to Latok II in 1997, twenty-one years ago. Everything is crazy, at least this year.

Events in Choktoi have been tumultuous, and I'm no longer sure our tactics are optimal. Two Russians, Sergey Glazunov and Alexander Gukov, climbed Latok I's legendary North Ridge to the end but had to turn around due to exhaustion at the summit ridge. Sergey took a fatal fall in the process, while Alexander was spectacularly rescued by the Pakistani military's longline helicopter at 6,400 meters. Subsequently, Britain's Tom Livingstone and the Slovenians Aleš Česen and Luka Stražar found the path of least resistance up the north side of Latok and reached the summit. The media was all over the place; Latok I's North Face had been climbed and the curse of failed efforts lifted, at least for the time being.

My heart skipped a beat when I heard this news, and only when I learned where the North Face route actually went did I relax again. The trio had climbed the North Ridge to 6,500 meters, and then traversed horizontally to the right across snow slopes to the saddle between Latok I and Latok II at 6,700 meters. They climbed over steep corn snow on the mountain's south side, finally reaching the summit. Admittedly, a brilliant idea, but far from the ideal of my north-face line.

Now we are alone in the valley, and the local "hill"—Panmah Kangri—makes an ideal mountain for our initial acclimatization. After making camp at 5,000 meters, we climb to the summit on the second day, over the ridge where we were forced to turn back in 2015. It is almost windless, with not a single cloud dotting the unreal cyan-blue Karakoram sky. Yannick lets the drone rise and conjures up breathtaking images stored on his memory card. Our mouths are agape at this beautiful, powerful, silent, and lonely spectacle. In the glistening morning light, we see the monstrous pyramid of K2, next to Broad Peak, and on the other side of the vista, the most beautiful and rugged mountains in the world: the Latoks. It's a steep paradise where only a few climbers have been lucky enough to summit—behind this beauty, there also stands a brutal reality of tears and suffering.

Hours later, we celebrate our small success at basecamp, enjoying an ice-cold cola. Ali whips up a perfect pizza on his Kero sink stove. It truly has been an ideal day. The sun disappears behind the Ogre, and we drift into well-deserved sleep. I am first awakened by the whirring of the kerosene stove and Simon's, "Good morning, Thomas, shall we have coffee?" Simon is not only a super climber; he is also an enormously charming chap, with a smile always on his face. We are kindred spirits and can handle any situation, no matter how difficult.

Yannick is also an ultra-cool guy who speaks good English in addition to his native tongue. Everyone speaks English except Simon. He only knows the South Tyrolean dialect. Although they can't communicate linguistically, Yannick and Simon understand each other perfectly. They laugh and discuss with hands and feet, using this basic nonverbal vocabulary—it's a language that first has to be invented, but when the chemistry is right, it works. Rainer, on the other hand, finds it rather difficult to integrate into our little community. Somehow, I sense that these dark walls in the Choktoi are getting to him. But I remain calm. First, we have a good coffee, and when a little time has passed, we will get used to many things. Then we can move forward step by step and see what works.

Once again, we have breakfast at midnight. The coffee we brought turns night into day, a few spoonfuls of muesli are thrown in afterward, and then we set off. It is moonlit, and we can do without our headlamps. We hike through the nocturnal world of the Choktoi toward Latok III. Our senses are on high alert, and the silence mixes with the crunch of our footsteps on the glacial ice. Our breath sets the rhythm, and the mountains merge with the starry night.

Again, I feel like a wanderer between worlds, and any doubt about why I am here falls away. Everything feels good and right. The mountains lose their malevolence.

Yannick stays behind on the glacier, to try to capture us on film using his unique drone. At dawn, we climb the couloir on a firm layer of hardpacked snow. It feels like only a short moment later before we're standing on the ice plateau where, in 2015, the shock wave of a gigantic avalanche affected us so much that we aborted the entire expedition. At a safe distance from this death zone, we traverse right, up toward the actual climbing.

By now, we are fully exposed to the morning sun, it is pleasantly warm, and above us, the rock pillar glows orange-red. The conditions couldn't be better; Rainer, however, feels under the weather. In terms of timing, it is still justifiable to be out on the glacier alone—the snow is still frozen, so Rainer decides to go down. "Take good care, Rainer, and please call me on the radio when you get to basecamp. Rest so you are strong again when the going gets tough!"—"I will and have fun climbing!"

Yes, we can hardly wait to climb up here. We have been gifted the best conditions imaginable, and the climbing is enjoyable and easy. Yannick's drone, which he is controlling from 1,000 meters below, right from the glacier, buzzes next to us. As the Gietl-Huber rope team, we harmonize perfectly and always have something to laugh about, and in less than three hours, we are back at my high point from 2015. The rucksack that we left behind is still hanging from two pitons. For three summers and winters, the two sets of cams, pitons, a hammer, gas, a stove, gloves, a chalk bag, and Alexander's climbing shoes have endured, now frozen into a block of ice. After a quick de-icing, everything except the chalk is back in working order. We fix our ropes and abseil.

In the meantime, Rainer has also reported back to us. He has arrived safe and sound at basecamp. With this news, everything is now genuinely close to perfection. My heart sings because Simon is laughing and by my side. He is young, calm, forthright with his beliefs, thinks like me with a South Tyrolean cheerfulness, and is strong. He fills me with confidence, and often takes some of the burden of the decision-making off my shoulders while up on the mountain. I have grown too old to bear the stress of organizing an expedition solo, as I did in 2001 on the Ogre. Yannick also fits our ropeteam perfectly, with his French sense of humor; he is always watchful, motivating, and an actual film and photography artist—a real Frenchman.

Only Rainer becomes more isolated as the days go by. His poor health is also an excuse to distract from the real problem. It's crazy how the Choktoi affects all of us, including me. I am also self-aware enough to realize that it's often my persona—my unbending will, obsession, desire, and almost convulsively positive attitude toward this wall and toward my line—that is causing issues. This place is intense, and so am I.

I sleep poorly and dream crazy stuff. About Latok, the avalanches, Jeff Lowe, and then suddenly I'm standing alone in the middle of the glacier, lost. I also dream of Berchtesgaden, images of home wildly thrown into the mix without any context. When I open my eyes, I'm exhausted. I crawl out of the tent; the clouds hang low and dark in the mountains, just as dark as the coffee Ismail is brewing for me on the kerosene stove with our Italian coffee maker. "Weather looks terrible today! Better sitting tight in basecamp and playing cards!" There is nothing to add to that.

We finally have a relaxing day ahead of us, because there's nothing outside for us today. We shift the day's activities into our tents. The weather is perfect for finishing the book I started, catching up on missing entries in my diary, and later drinking umpteen rounds of tea with Ismail, Shokur, and Yannick. Then, finally, given the time difference, we can talk to our families on the phone. All is well in Yannick's, Simon's, and my homes, but I still receive a message that shakes me: last night, Jeff Lowe passed away from his chronic illness. It comes as a shock, although it was also a kind of liberation for him after his longtime suffering. Was it a coincidence that he came to see me in a dream today? I wanted to bring him a stone from the top of Latok and tell him that I'd been up there.

In the meantime, it has started to rain, and as cold as it is, it will likely snow soon. My thoughts at this moment belong only to Jeff. I thank him for his inspiration and for showing us how a positive attitude and human strength can overcome all obstacles. I pray for him and feel that, in a very special way, he is still in this valley.

Since the news of Jeff's death, it snows almost daily, and even climbing Latok III is becoming less and less likely, not to mention our plan on Latok

I. Ismail, my soulmate, convinces me that winter is knocking on the door, that the mountains are too snowed up and therefore too dangerous. He also senses the problematic situation with Rainer and advises me that it would be better to abandon the expedition entirely. He also says, with a mischievous grin, "One thing, Thomas, is sure: the mountains are not running away; they will always sit here, and Inshallah, you come back next year with Simon and Yannick. I think this is the best!" Ismail has given me the answer that's been simmering inside me for days, but that I had yet to speak aloud.

We quickly agree that the mountains are unclimbable under these wintry conditions, and everyone agrees to end the expedition prematurely.

During the walk back, Yannick, Simon, and I make each other a promise to try again together the very next year. I might also be able to convince Julian Zanker to join. After our climb of Cerro Kishtwar, I became convinced he would be a perfect addition to our Latok team. With this anticipation, I experience a beautiful autumn in Berchtesgaden, with a bit of climbing and hiking with the family. That November, I take the stage with my new lecture, "Stone Age."

At the end of February 2019, it was a beautiful Sunday in Berchtesgaden; I got a call from Switzerland: "Hey, Thomas, Stephan here. Hey, something bad happened: Julian fell yesterday afternoon on the Eiger, on the classic route, on the ramp leading to the waterfall chimney!"—"What, how bad is it?" At that moment, I didn't want to accept what Stephan was leaving unsaid. "Hey, Thomas, Julian is dead! They recovered his body by helicopter, and he's now lying in the Funeral Hall in Grindelwald. Tomorrow, his closest friends will get together to say their goodbyes.

Please see that you come!" My voice failed me, and I only managed a quiet, "I'm coming, Steph" before hanging up. The news hit me with full force. I cried, and with me, my whole family.

I drove to Switzerland, lost in thought, and was pulled over for speeding three times, so I had to give up my driver's license a month later. Toward evening, I reached Grindelwald, at the foot of the Eiger. Twenty of Julian's friends were there. We drank beer and told each other stories. In a side room, Julian lay in an open coffin. Next to him was his backpack with a rope. It looked like he had just come from the mountain and was taking a short nap. At that moment, death seemed far from ominous; Julian looked so peaceful, freed from all earthly things, and it almost seemed as if he was going to wake up any moment, open his eyes, and say, "Did I oversleep? Hey, the Eiger was great, and the conditions for our climb were second to none. When do we get after it, Thomas?"

I had to smile softly in my immense sadness. At that moment, I was so grateful to have experienced those six intense weeks with him on Cerro Kishtwar. Julian was cremated the next day, and his ashes were scattered in his mountains.

As Simon, Yannick, and I planned our comeback trip to Choktoi this year, another deadly avalanche rolled over the alpine world. David Lama, Hansjörg Auer, and Jess Roskelley were caught in an avalanche in the Canadian Rockies. For days they were missing, and all still had the hope that, somehow, somewhere, they would emerge from behind a ridge and tell of their good fortune in surviving this white inferno. It was almost like it had been with Kyle and Scott on Ogre II. In times of uncertainty, hope for a miracle was always front and center, because the apparent truth was so unbearable.

But the longer the search went on, the more hope dissolved until the cruel reality became a certainty. All three were found in an avalanche. Dead. I immediately had images of David standing alone at Lunag Ri's summit and Hansjörg climbing free solo through the "fish" on the

Marmolada. Both were bold, seemingly invulnerable, sublime climbers, apparently liberated from restraints. The exhilaration at the top of a peak miraculously conceals the deadly abyss below, and one feels immortal.

But even expert climbers are fallible, and the list of names of our friends who went to the mountains and didn't come back alive grows longer and longer: Uli, Dean, Kyle, Scott, Julian, and now David, Hansjörg, and Jess. It was unbelievable.

In the middle of May, I drove to the Ötztal. The mountains, white with spring snow, shone against the blue sky, and it would have been a perfect day to climb, go on a ski tour, or paraglide on the spring thermals. But today, we all stood united in silent mourning at the church in Hansjörg's home village. Each wearing their traditional costume—the mountain guides, the climbers, the alpine club members. His coffin was carried through the village, past blooming spring meadows, old farms, and narrow streets. The silence was moving. Only birdsong and the constant prayers to the Virgin and Mother of God, Mary, along with the quiet footsteps of the crowd, accompanied Hansjörg on his last journey.

After many farewell speeches by friends, club members, and mountaineers, Hansjörg was carried to his grave, and again I stood by the coffin of a friend whose voice I could still hear ringing clear. What crazy hours we had experienced in Patagonia, that "Jhhheeeeeaaaa" to freedom at the summit of Cerro Standhardt. *Even if you can no longer be with us on the rope, you are always with us in what we do. Rest in peace, Hansjörg.* Afterward, we met in a restaurant, eating a traditional pork roast and washing down the sadness with a few beers.

David was given a Nepalese funeral ceremony. His ashes were buried in Nepal, and I was already in Pakistan by the time his funeral service was held in Innsbruck.

This time we were in the Choktoi not too early and not too late, but simply in the middle. It had been less than a year since we had been here last—a strange feeling. Every stone was still in the same place; every tent was in the same place. Simon and Yannick were there, only Rainer was not. Ali and Nasim cooked in the kitchen tent, and Ismail played cards with Shokur. It was almost as if time had stopped ten months earlier.

It was a cloudless day in high summer, the sun scorching the ground below from a blue sky. Simon described it aptly: "*Putana,* a monkey heat, and that at 4,200 meters!" It felt simply too warm and dangerous for these mountains, and we were again at a loss. We didn't know how to take advantage of the brilliant weather for climbing. Indeed, everyone had thoughts about the sense and nonsense of what we were doing and whether we had gambled wrongly in July, the hottest month of the year. But we were inspired by the British-Slovenian success on Latok I, which had gone down in July. I no longer knew what was right and what was wrong.

The only progress these days was made by the temperatures. The zero-degree line was already climbing to over 6,400 meters, and it would get even warmer in the next few days. We felt like chess pieces in a risky game, defeated by climatic circumstances. We were blocked, and only the hope that it would eventually cool down again kept us here, waiting.

The sun sapped our mental fortitude—dream weather, but not for us climbers. According to the forecast, the zero-degree mark would now climb to over 6,500 meters. So the only option would be to climb at night, because it would be safer. Suddenly, a rumble of thunder tore us out of the discussion, and we rushed out of the kitchen tent. Above us on Panmah Kangri, gray clouds were billowing into the air: a landslide. We all ran to our moraine, and shortly after that, room-sized boulders slid across the remnants of snow into camp. Behind them, a brown avalanche of mud, debris, ice, and water spilt out and almost grazed our kitchen tent. We had been more than lucky once again. But the mud was now clogging the "drain" of our torrent, and the whole camp was in danger of flooding. We had to act immediately and work like berserkers against the sinking ship. With the strength of desperation, we rerouted the torrent. Once again, we were more lucky than wise, and now we knew once and for all that it was time to pack our bags. Mission abort.

To say our goodbyes, I walked once more with Ismail across the glacier to Latok I, and when we had a perfect view of the wall, I stopped. "Let's wait a little here, Ismail!"—"Okay, so I smoke a cigarette, you look!" Once again, I looked for my line up the north wall. Those contours so burned into my heart. The ice pillar, the bivouac niche, the ice fields, the headwall, the ramp that leads right, and the dihedral that ends right at the summit. I again explained my line to Ismail and asked, "Ismail, do you like this?"—"Yes, this line looks very nice but difficult. Inshallah, you will climb this, but not with me!" He laughed mischievously and took another drag on his cigarette. Then he added: "When you climb, I will wait in basecamp and pray to Allah for your health. I think this is better because you have no time to pray, you have to climb, and somebody must pray because this is very dangerous, and with prayer, inshallah, all is good, and you have no problem!" I laughed and cried at the same time.

As we were getting ready to leave, he casually said: "Look, Thomas, everything here is great, but the most important thing . . ." he paused for a moment, looked at all the surrounding mountains, and then back at me, " . . . is life, because with no more life, there is no more mountain, but with life and happiness, you can do whatever you like." At that moment, I knew I had made all the right decisions.

Grasping for Freedom

A conscious step over the wooden threshold, a whispered thank you, and then Dahoam rolled over me and took over all my senses.

The smell of our house, the cats that curled around my legs and meowing a welcome, and the incredible joy of my loved ones, Philo, Amadeus, Elias, and Marion. In addition, there was a fresh pretzel from the baker and a cold beer. It felt so good; I didn't want any more curry, rice, Coke, or mountains of snow and ice for quite some time. I needed my family, friends, Bavarian food, beer, the Bavarian countryside, our local mountains, and sport climbing.

My local mountain, the Untersberg, actually ticks quite a few boxes. After a week, I went up to my project, which I had first bolted two years earlier with my friend Michal Grassl. Admittedly, it was lofty goal after an expedition, when you're not in top shape for cutting-edge rock climbing. This project was a tough nut to crack—at least solid 8b+.

In any case, a perfect line. The first 330 feet climb overhanging yellow rock that requires athletic power, but what follows is absolute madness: A blue-gray overhanging water runnel 330 feet long leads to the exit. Hidden within is the best climbing you could wish for: difficult, tricky sections on small crimps, pockets, sloping traverses, jumps, crucifixes, and lockoffs—simply everything a climber's heart desires.

But I must admit, as an aging climber, such routes are a real challenge. A younger top climber like Megos or Ondra would laugh their way up the route. A cakewalk—just a relaxing climbing day on the Untersberg. On the other hand, I have to train for weeks to climb this route, eating a special diet to reduce my body weight so that my relative strength is maximized. Only then do I stand a chance—while the guys and gals of the new generation are probably able to send my project, *Stoneage,* on their first "go," i.e., onsight. This is frustrating, even more so because many expect that a real Huber Brother should be able to do the same. But both of us, Alexander and I, are far from the current level. Even if we still seem to be in full, hairy shape, age has also taken its toll on us.

It's a fact that climbing into the upper grades when you're 50 is a different story than when you're 20 because it feels like the crimps and pockets you're holding on to get smaller yearly. And so, it's a real challenge to squeeze out an 8c or an 8c+ when you're over 50. In contrast, getting older has a more beneficial effect on expedition mountaineering. On a big, mixed wall, you must persevere, dig in, and fight, and often iron will and years of experience are the keys to success. But here on the rock, in addition to an iron will, you need brute strength, which, in turn, depends on the biochemical processes in the body, which become increasingly sluggish with age. Only when I came to terms with this reality did I find my recipe for success as a senior climber: have fun, be relaxed, train hard, regenerate well, and accept your age.

It was a beautiful autumn in Berchtesgaden. I would head out to the Untersberg every other day, and with eleven less pounds on my ribs, I could get through the complicated moves and cruxes more smoothly than a few weeks earlier. Meanwhile, I had long forgotten my experiences in Choktoi and was fully immersed in my project, *Stoneage*.

My first attempt: "Hey, Thomas, you can do it today. I have a good feeling!" With these words, Michal sends me up the first pitches in the dim morning light. It all goes quickly—and well. After two hours, I'm already hanging below the last two pitches, which also happen to be the most difficult, graded 8b and 8b+.

Once again, I dip both hands into my chalk bag, blow the excess chalk off my fingers, slap my thighs hard, clip the first bolt, and get going. With each move, the climbing becomes ever more complicated. Without a real point to shake out, my forearms get considerably pumped.

I pinch, tear through dynos, pull on pockets and slopers, and eventually, it's done. "Beeeeelayyy!" Now the next one. A dream of an 8b+. But I lack the fuel for it right at the end. At the final crux, I fly onto the rope. Michal, however, tells me he will come back with me next time.

It is the beginning of November, the golden autumn says goodbye, and winter is indeed coming. A Genoa low pushes dark snow clouds over the Alps, and above us, the mountain pines rustle in the Föhn wind. For the fourth time, I'm standing at the base with Michal, and today is the last chance this season to pull off my *Stoneage*.

Temperatures are borderline—it's almost too cold for perfect grip—and I surprise myself that everything has gone smoothly so far, and that now I'm at the last pitch. I pull on a down jacket and gloves, sip warm tea, and eat a chocolate bar to warm up. Again and again, the Föhn whips gusts of wind against the wall. It's downright Patagonian. I close my eyes. In my mind's eye, I climb through the most challenging moves and coach myself, "You can do it, you can do it," conjuring up my inner courage. Then I open my eyes and get ready to set off. I lace up my climbing shoes and remove my jacket and gloves. And finally, the T-shirt. Michal is freezing at the sight of my naked torso amidst the storm. I, on the other hand, no longer sense the cold. I want to feel as light as possible, and am already in the middle of the vertical mosaic of the fifth pitch. I know these moves so well: I'll need to lock off with the right, set up the sidepull neatly on the left, stand on a small, sloping foothold on the right, shift my center of gravity and dynamically stab into a two-finger pocket, extend to a sloping ledge with a small, dynamic kip, bring the left foot up, and then jump to the jug out left.

Again, gusts of wind hiss up the wall; Michal shivers and clenches his teeth. I sense none of this; I'm in my own world, which is just perfect. At the last rest before the crux, I shake my arms out one last time, clearing away the lactic acid. Nine feet above lies the finishing jug—paradise, almost the summit, because the climbing eases off afterwards. Only one more delicate 7b section to the exit. But even this final bit of the pitch still demands balance, dynamic movement, finger strength, and will.

Slowly the snow clouds press over the Watzmann, but here on the Untersberg, the Föhn rips apart the clouds. Sunshine at last. "Michi, I'll do it!" It's now or never. I dip my hands into my chalk bag and, without second-guessing, I pull off the series of complex moves: left toe hook, left small flake here, extend into the pocket, fully lock off, follow up with the right, catch the momentum on a small rock rib out right, climb, grab, deadpoint, stick it, now dynamically latch the jug. "Jjjaaahhhhh! Michi, I haavee it!" I'm hanging off the infamous finishing jug. The remaining sixty-five feet of 5.12 pose no further difficulties. "Michi, beeelay, rope fiiiiiiiix." With this last rope command, everything falls off my shoulders. The pointless waiting for better weather in Choktoi, the hard training for this redpoint. Now everything is good. I look at the mountains. Everything is so lonely and beautiful. The mountain pines dance with joy amidst the storm. At the top, Michal pats me on the shoulder: "Hey, Thomas, you did a great job today in this cold. We've earned ourselves a beer." Michal fetches two bottles of our local beer, Berchtesgadener Helles, from the winter room of the Stöhrhaus summit hut—bottles he has stashed for this very purpose. "Cheers, Thomas, to you and your *Stoneage!*"—"Thank you, Michi, for everything!" It was intoxicating!

A Stone Creates Ripples

I consider myself fortunate, even if I didn't get what I had been looking for, for quite some time: Latok I. The line in which I invested all my faith. Latok, I had convinced myself, would bring salvation to my wretched soul, but only through a successful ascent. What I got instead was *Stoneage* on the Untersberg. No ice fields, ramps, or iced-up cracks, but rough, gray rock with sidepulls, crimps, pockets, slopers, underclings, *gottes d'eau* (water pockets), and runnels. Although the one is not comparable with the other, and the alpine skills needed for each endeavor are entirely different, I felt I had reached my inner summit with *Stoneage*. I was immediately overwhelmed by an indescribable sensation of inner happiness. I had finally and truly found that which I had been searching for.

Even if the path there was littered with boulders, often tricky, and full of hardship—an approach that was in obvious from the outset—ultimately, *Stone Age* still got me to everything I had longed for: namely, freedom. As a climber, all too often, you fall back into your old, familiar habits as the fire of all-encompassing freedom slowly dies. Then, suddenly, it reappears. This line and the question of whether you might, just one more time, go all in . . . ? But whether I will eat again from this paradisical sweet but sour apple, I leave to my future self. Looking back, what had passed had been most often wild, chaotic, unpredictable, and, above all, usually the complete opposite of what I had envisioned. In the meantime, I learned to enjoy surprises.

When I was unsure of what to do during the dark days of my obsession with Latok, I would play with a stone for hours at the lake of Königsee in my hometown. Lost in thought and frustrated, I'd then throw the rock into the waters. I wanted to throw away my *Schicksal*, my fate, and watch it sink into the cold lake. But this deed had the opposite effect: it opened my eyes. The whole secret of life was revealed! The stone was gone, never to be seen again, forgotten at the bottom of the lake. However, it left behind circular ripples that spread in all directions. This throwing away, like letting go, is irrevocable, but it leaves behind an unstoppable, seemingly infinite energy that spreads in all directions.

Thus, every moment is unique and also unrepeatable. The great art of it is to accept everything, to filter it, to get intoxicated from adventure, to learn from the bad, to strengthen oneself from the difficult, and in the end, to have the confidence and courage to do the right thing at the right moment. If you know how to practice this art, you are an artist of life, like our father. If arrogance had made him continue his climb on the Hörndlwand, he might have fallen. Maybe today there would be a memorial with his name somewhere at the entrance of the Redwitz chimney, but with his story otherwise lost to the ages. But he did the only right thing at that moment in time. Turning back was the beginning of his wild story as a climber and, simultaneously, the foundation of our—his, mine, and Alexander's—life in the vertical.

CHAPTER SIXTEEN
Toward Freedom

Why We Do What We Do

They have been shooting for twenty minutes straight, the Christmas cannoneers with their handheld fireworks at the poinsettia above our village. "Wrumms," short pause, "Wrumms," brief respite, mostly at even intervals. Cannon firing around Christmas time is a great tradition in the Berchtesgaden Valley. Shots are fired using gunpowder, which is compressed in a handmade firework fitted with a wooden pin and ignited with a detonator. Although it should seem easy to load the firecracker, compress it, and pull the trigger, it takes a sense of proper rhythm. When the neighboring shooter releases the shot, you wait for that "whoosh" to echo back from the opposite hill, and the trick is to let your shot blend with the other's echo: "Whoosh!"—"Whoosh!" So, it sounds like a wave, from left to right. When everyone is done, the first cannon fires back up again.

To the left of this artistic star shines a "20," and to the right is the "19." Between Christmas and New Year's Eve, each township in the valley fashions these stars at an exposed location from wooden slats and light bulbs, sometimes more artistic, sometimes less, but always highly visible and shining bright. Our star from the "Au" is, of course, the most beautiful, and we, as a family, stand as one.

On the snowy Kloiberbichl, a meadow near our house, the Watzmann mountain stands out against the clear, starry sky; shooting stars draw their paths, and a few rash people who can't wait ignite their rockets prematurely. Then another shot is fired every three seconds, and slowly but surely, the old year moves on.

It has been a turbulent year, with the death of friends, then repeatedly Choktoi—again and again, failing to make the summit. Is it my fate that I held on to this dream for so long until everything took care of itself through the passage of time?

Five minutes before the turn of the year, silence sets in. Now the holiday revelers shoot the last three firecrackers, this time in unison—the salvos. The last one synchronizes exactly with the turn of the year. The nocturnal silence is broken by the master of ceremonies—*"Schüüützeeen, aaaauuuuuf . . ."*—while his subsequent "Fire!" gets immediately drowned out by the immense torrent of sound. Fifty fireworks fire at the same time. The first salvo thunders mightily, echoing off the mountain opposite. The shots fade into the winter night, and then silence reigns again.

I concluded one story this year with a perfect moment: *Stoneage*. Then, finally, a feeling returns that I have been missing for a long time: being on top and not having to go any farther. The path to freedom is an inner, mysterious one, decoupled from a specific mountain, route, or destination. There is no need for a line like on Latok, no need to cross some real or imaginary border. There is only the path that one treads with passion, devotion, and love.

The second salvo thunders, and we all stand together as a family, looking forward to the new beginning. After a short wait, Philo again sees a shooting star flying across the horizon. No matter what might have happened this year, the most important thing is that we have each other, and everyone is healthy; everything else should take a back seat.

"Wwwwrrrrruuuummmms." Hard on the echoes of the fireworks comes the seamless transition to our village church's ringing bells. Then the 19 on the star is replaced with a 20. All the best for the new year.

The new year kicks off at full speed. I'm on tour with my multi-media performance "Stone Age," on stage several times throughout January, with a sold-out venue on each occasion. Each time I relive the story anew in front of an audience illuminated by the screen, it is fun. As a Stone Monkey under El Cap, as an alpinist under the clear, starry sky of the Choktoi, and while cranking hard on *Stoneage* on the Untersberg. I make the audience roar with laughter but also think. I serve them all the emotions on a platter, and see mostly content faces at the end of each show. After my lecture, many individuals seem inspired to start down their own paths toward freedom.

Eleven months later, I again stood on the Kloiberbichl with my family. And again, it was a starry night. Above our village, the Christmas star with the year 2020 was shining brightly, but today the year was not shot out by the Christmas cannoneers, because it had been forbidden. We technically weren't allowed to stand here either, because, from 9:00 p.m. onward, a general curfew had been imposed. It had been a year that no one would forget too quickly.

The coronavirus had our planet firmly in its grip, and we were soon facing the most extensive global challenge in decades. Instead of our usual freedom, our lives were marked by closures, cancellations, postponements, and prohibitions. The force of this pandemic paralyzed everything, and non-essential institutions shut down completely. This soon included all cultural life. For Alexander and me, this meant that all our lectures were canceled indefinitely.

Despite all this economic and social horror, the pandemic was an opportunity for us brothers to get back after it as a team. Since Latok 2015, our project preferences had grown apart; we were still brothers, but no longer a climbing partnership. We no longer had the opportunity to go on expeditions, so together we took the bull by the horns and made the best of the situation, bringing our expeditionary attitude to the table. He who complains loses. We accepted our limitations and shrank our world down to the Berchtesgaden Valley, rediscovering lines that we had long forgotten while off chasing international objectives.

We were on the Untersberg, this time on the "Yellow Wall," on a perfect gray water streak that seemed almost as smooth as marble. A section of rock defined by the best climbing imaginable. A climber's feast for us brothers, a ropeteam working just as well as it always had.

We trained for and worked the route on the Untersberg, and toward the end of the summer, succeeded in climbing our route together, naming it the *Sonnen König:* the *Sun King.* Because our experience had been so beautiful, we went ahead and cranked through another old project on the Göll massif, which we named after the Patagonian band Siete Venas from Del Monte. Both routes were graded 8b+, and the climbing was second to none! The *Sun King* stood out for its beauty, and *Siete Venas* for the craziness of the climbing. Nearly 500 feet above the base, a 30-foot roof jutted into space. I'd bolted the route right out the middle of the feature with Michal Grassl a few years back.

The climbing moves through this overhanging terrain resembled the famous opening jump move of *Action Directe,* only it was completely inverted and you were leaping to a proper jug instead of a tiny pocket—very much unlike Güllich's milestone. So, in a sense, *Siete Venas* was an *Action Directe* for older gentlemen, but with a butt-clenching 500 feet of air underneath. It was a hell of a climbing summer for us, after all. We were in the mountains often, leaving the pandemic, debating, bickering, and societal problems down in the valley. We climbed until our fingers were sore, laughed a lot, and motivated each other.

Come fall, we climbed with our father up the 6,562 feet of the Watzmann's East Face, renowned as the tallest rock face in the Eastern Alps. At 81, he cruised through the vertical Salzburg Pillar, the most challenging route on the wall, topping out on the south pillar. On the summit, there was a traditional handshake with a joyful *"Berg Heil."* Our father's hands were bruised from the climb, but his eyes were alive as he said, *"Schee was's, Buam,* and thanks for taking me with you!" He scanned the east face back down to St. Bartholomä and over to the Königssee.

He had stood in this very spot a small eternity ago as a young rebel and slung his Sunday hat down the east face. It was the moment when he freed himself from the shackles of tradition, and the mountains became his life's focus. He taught us the way of living your freedom, which he was able to find in the mountains. The mountain offers freedom on a silver platter if you know how to look for it. All we had to do was go for it, which is what we did.

There is a little bell on the cross atop the South Summit. I nudged it, and with the ringing, our father snapped out of his thoughts. To this day, he remains our greatest role model. To still be so fit and full of energy at age 81, to still have plans in his head to go for objectives in the mountains. He gave us a little life lesson in his self-deprecating manner: "You want to be good mountaineers, but a really good mountaineer is an old mountaineer!" He laughed at that and nudged the little bell. It was a touching moment, and yes, according to this, our father is a pretty good climber. Still, to grow as old as he is, he also needed some luck.

Because the pandemic continued to complicate world travel, the following year we decided to go with old, outstanding projects dotted around our home country. These included *Karma* on the Steinplatte and an ancient project on the Untersberg that I had started with a friend twenty years earlier, just left of my masterpiece *Stoneage*.

It soon became too warm for *Karma*. So we concentrated on our project on the Untersberg, a three-pitch route that couldn't get any better. Right at the start, a monster roof, 8c for sure, led to a few feet of easy scrambling, and then the finale defined by a full pitch as hard as 8c+ or 9a along a gray water runnel. Our masterpiece: *Moasterstückl.* The name said it all: just like with *Karma,* we wanted to make one last statement before we began to approach climbing with a more laid-back attitude.

Sadly, summer did not make it easy for us. It was humid, hot, stormy, wet, and all too often, we took two steps back instead of one step forward. But we didn't give in, and as autumn approached, conditions were finally better, and a successful redpoint was back on the agenda.

Then, once again, out of the blue, disaster struck, and once again, I was the victim. Just as I was clipping the rope into a quickdraw, my climbing shoe popped off a minuscule smear. I lost body tension and fell, but I got caught up on the carabiner and peeled the skin entirely off my finger.

Everything was finished. All had been for nothing—just all of it, including the training sessions over this whole pretty shitty year. The hand surgeons were put to the test, patching up all the scraps of skin. As is often the case in my life, however, I was also fortunate. None of the tendons were damaged, and I soon regained my full range of motion. In such a situation, many things came into perspective, and the most important was that I could climb again. How often had I not understood that there is real magic in every moment, even if it's hard to feel it in that instant? After such a bust year, being aware of these magic moments became even harder!

January 18 is one of my two birthdays. On that day in 2022, my friend Anderl from Berchtesgaden and I were at the airport in Munich, drinking a cold beer to celebrate our trip to Patagonia.

It was not a trip but rather an escape from our ordinary madness. All the pandemic restrictions of the last two years, this daily tug-of-war, and the search for the truth. Everyone claimed to have the absolute truth; it all drove me crazy.

FREIHEIT

Even though I had everything my heart desired in Berchtesgaden—mountains, friends, and family—I still longed to travel as I had in the past. But these days, international travel required a vaccination card, COVID tests, and a health affidavit in addition to a ticket, baggage, motivation, and a destination. It was all quite the hassle until we were finally on the plane. We flew endlessly to the other end of the world, and now we were speeding down the arrow-straight road toward the mountains that have become my second home. On the skyline, the slender Cerro Torre was silhouetted against the clear evening sky, with the Fitz Roy Massif dominating the vista. My heart laughed, bringing a grin to my face, and El Chaltén sucked me in as if this village had held its breath awaiting my return.

"Hey, Thomas, good to see you. How's life?"—"So far, so good; glad to be back with you!" It wasn't until a young Argentine asked me what my latest adventures in these mountains were that I realized I was now an elder statesman, at least when it came to mountaineering. And yes, it was true. At 55 years of age, with my graying temples and beard, I was no longer one of the young guns in this Patagonia. Nevertheless, the little rascal was still raging inside me, dreaming, rebelling, and stubbornly pursuing the goals that had accumulated over the last few years. The clock was ticking, the traverses were getting longer every year, the crimps smaller and smaller, and the walls steeper and steeper. It was now or never to realize my mountain dreams. My goal was to always remain a passionate climber, becoming old and wise like my father, with the gratitude of having survived it all.

After a week of village life, I was excited to see the weather models finally flick back to green. Everyone packed their backpacks and invaded the valleys around Fitz Roy and Cerro Torre. We decided to use this window for a romp up Fitz Roy, across the *Moonwalk*—the crossing of the Fitz Roy Range from south to north. At these temperatures, the Torres were just too hot and dangerous, in our opinion. The *Moonwalk* had first been done solo by the Belgian Sean Villanueva: seven summits, five days, all unsupported. A crazy guy with a flute, always laughing and defined by an enormous capacity for suffering. A real Stone Monkey through and through.

We got on, but it didn't go as I'd hoped. I was drained, tired, felt rusty, and that was already after the first summit, Aguja de l'S. I felt like I could no longer rely on my intuition and skills. I went off-route a few times, climbed timidly and fearfully, and after two days, I was so mentally exhausted that we ended our ride across the towers after the second of seven summits. Perhaps I'd put myself under too much pressure and wanted too much. Or maybe it just wasn't my day!

Disappointed, we descended to the Torre Valley and bivouacked for another night in Niponino, the climbers' camp. But this night was strange. Weird-looking cloud formations appeared in the sky, and I couldn't get any rest, tossing and turning in my sleeping bag, plagued by horrible dreams—perhaps because I was so physically and mentally exhausted and just wanted to return to the village, to just get out of these mountains.

Despite the extremely warm temperatures, there were incredible successes in Patagonia during this period of clear weather. Quentin Roberts solo climbed Torre Egger. Corrado "Korra" Pesce and Tomás "Tommy" Aguilo fulfilled their lifelong dream by sending their line up the north face of Cerro Torre. And Matteo Della Bordella, Matteo De Zaiacomo, and David Bacci from Italy succeeded in climbing the Torre's east face via the Burke-Proctor attempt from the late 1970s and early 1980s—aka the English Dihedral—naming their new route *Brothers in Arms*. These were awesome days. However, they became a nightmare when the dark clouds of tragedy crept over the Torres.

Polacos, another camp in the Torre Valley, in the Fitz Roy Range: Around 4:00 a.m., the Slovenians Lukas Lindič and Lukas Krajnc see SOS light signals on Cerro Torre. Far above, just below the north face. This news spreads like wildfire through the valley via our walkie-talkies. At 7:00 a.m., I inform the Parque de Los Glaciares via my satellite phone: "SOS emergency signal at Cerro Torre under the north face. Climbers in distress unknown." All the climbers camped in Niponino ascend toward Noruegos, the last camp under the Torre. The two Lukas's stay in Polacos, because from there one has the best view of the Torre and can see the accident site with binoculars. Two climbers are recognizable at the Mausefalle, the transition from the east to the north face. For the time being, no movement is discernible.

The main group remains in the Noruegos for the time being. Then four of us—two Americans, Anderl, and me—push up into the range. We are looking for a quick path across the wildly cracked glacier to the base of the wall. Around noon, the two Lukas's send us a radio message. A different, three-man team—the Italians, we'll later learn—is rappelling the *Compressor Route,* while out right there is now some movement from the climbers in distress: one of them is rappelling. Very slowly. Probably only with a short piece of rope toward the Triangular Snowfield. The other of the two climbers remains motionless, in the same place above.

Toward afternoon, events come to a head. A messenger's dispatch from the Parque about the those in distress provides more details: avalanche on the Torre. Korra Pesce is seriously injured, and it's Tommy Aguilo who is rapping, slowly, with the short piece of rope. They are asking for help. Further information from the Parque: fortunately, a helicopter can drop a rescue team on the glacier thanks to the clear weather. Then a radio message from Team Lukas, with a request directed to all of us: "Do not climb; the risk is not calculable. It is still much too warm. If only later, when the sun is off the wall. Please make decisions using your head and not your heart!"—"Thanks, Lukas. We don't have a good feeling either.

We'll just ascend to the base of the wall for now and wait at a safe distance. Please let us know if anything new comes up. Over."

When we reach Cerro Torre, we realize the extent of the tragedy. A massive field of avalanche debris welcomes us, interspersed with backpacks, sleeping bags, and the gear of the two climbers still up on the wall. Presumably, due to the warm temperatures of the past few days, a part of Cerro Torre's overhanging summit mushroom has collapsed. And in these mountains, it is typical that it cracks even more at night than during the day. Around 5:00 p.m., the three climbers rappelling the *Compressor Route* join us. They are Matteo Della Bordella, Matteo De Zaiacomo, and David Bacci. They are exhausted, briefly recounting their ascent of *Brothers in Arms,* saying they climbed the last part of the wall together with Tommy and Korra to the summit, standing on the Torre at sunset and celebrating their greatest triumph. While the Italians bivouacked at the top of the peak, Tommy and Korra rappelled at night down the north face, which they had just climbed for the first time.

Sometime during the night, the accident must have happened—the ice mushroom collapsed and crashed into the depths. Then comes a new message from Lukas: Tommy is now at the right end of the Triangular Snowfield. He is entangled somehow and can descend no farther.

Meanwhile, the first climbers are being flown in. The German Laura Tiefenthaler, the Austrian Babsi Vigl, and the Swiss Roger Schäli hurry toward the base, working together with El Chaltén rescue-team members. There is a new forecast: the weather might hold until tomorrow morning, then a storm front will bring snow. The only chance to save them is to climb immediately to Tommy and continue up to Korra. There is a risk of a secondary avalanche, but according to Matteo, who knows the route, the first part of the wall up to the snowfield is reasonably well protected. Everything else will have to be decided on the go.

Shortly thereafter, each rescuer's role is clarified. We put together a fast, efficient team. Even though Matteo is burnt out from the past few days, he must lead. He knows the 1,000 feet to the Triangular Snowfield like the back of his hand. Roger will clean the pitches afterward, while I will take care of wall logistics, haul the gear, and fix the ropes, supported by Indio from the local rescue team. Laura, Babsi, and Anderl will coordinate everything else at the base of the wall as well as the subsequent transport down the glacier. It's go time; we all need to work together perfectly and must not mess up, for the sake of our own safety and in order to rescue Tommy and, hopefully, also Korra, stuck near the top of the Torre.

Matteo climbs quickly, Roger follows, I fix and haul, and Indio comes last. That's speed. In three hours, we reach the Triangular Snowfield. Now we are crossing its 50-degree ice horizontally to the right. After a full ropelength, we find Tommy crouching in a rock gully tied to the end of his rope. When Tommy sees me, a brief smile comes over his drawn face. "Hey, Thomas, you are here."—"Yes, Tommy, so glad to see you. We will bring you back home now."

We give Tommy a strong painkiller. When we ask him if we should continue climbing up to Korra, Tommy gives a short nod of defeat. I send a new radio message to the Parque and the ground team: "Tommy is okay so far; he is in shock, hypothermic, responsive, and lucid. He has visible breathing problems, almost certainly multiple broken ribs. Also, severe pain in his left shoulder—he is immobile in this area. However, he can move well on both legs. Indio and I will rappel with Tommy via the fixed ropes; our estimated arrival time at the bottom of the glacier will be in about three hours. Matteo and Roger will continue to climb up. Korra's condition is unclear. We need food, drinks, and at least 1,000 feet of ropes. The end!"

By now, it's pitch dark. Above us, the wall of the Torre looms menacingly, while the starry sky sparkles beyond. Everything suddenly seems so quiet and peaceful. That's precisely how it must have been last night before the mountain exploded above them, the sky darkening in a heartbeat and a frozen inferno hitting them full force. I take a deep breath, try to focus my thoughts, assess the here and now, and look for solutions.

Unfortunately, we have few options to get Tommy safely across the nearly 200 feet of ice to the start of the fixed rappels down the rock face. We only have one chance: a rope rail fixed to a feeble belay—a Knifeblade, a small TCU (three-cam unit), and a slung, crumbly flake all equalized with a sling. This will have to do. Indio fixes the rope at the far end, and we tension it with all our strength, using a Micro Traxion to ratchet the line down as taut as a guitar string. "Please let it hold," I pray.

Once again, I take a deep breath. Then I hang my body weight on the rope and slowly guide Tommy across, trying not to do the math in my head of how much weight our anchor truly can hold. But luck is on my side—the belay holds strong. We reach the fixed ropes, and everything else goes exactly as we have strategically planned. Three hours later, Tommy is down on the glacier, and we hand him over to the ground team, which now numbers over fifty people. After a short break, I want to climb to Matteo and Roger again. A brief time later, at 2:00 a.m., they radio me that they've reached the top of the Triangular Snowfield but will abort because the risk of climbing further is too high. They will descend but fix everything for another rescue attempt later.

The ground team carries Tommy across the glacier through the night, having administered him some powerful painkillers. By sunrise, clouds roll over the Torres, and the weather gives us the answer that there is no longer an option to ascend safely. Having to give up Korra is a difficult and painful moment; for some who were very close to him, it is devastating. At that moment, the Torre is gray; there is only sorrow, anger, and sadness, and nothing beautiful or desirable about the mountain.

Slowly, the air starts to move again—it is now a race against time and the wind. The helicopter waits down on the glacier. The rescue team gives it their all, and finally, they make it. At the last possible second, the helicopter takes off with Tommy, carried out of the mountains by the wind. Everyone cheers euphorically; some cry. Somewhat dazed, we all sit on the glacier, indeed about seventy men, women, girls, and boys by now. Everyone who could help has, an incredible effort by climbers both Argentine and international alike.

In the end, Tommy survives. Our effort brought this father back to his little boy—that was all that mattered, and it's a far greater success than any traverse or Magic Line up one of those peaks. Still, that pain remains that we couldn't help Korra.

Now I can let go; I no longer have to function at this intense level, and slowly walk the sixteen miles back to the village. The wind pushes us across the glacier, out of the mountains. It begins to drizzle, blurring the tears running down my face. A rainbow stretches across the sky behind the Torre as if Korra is still trying to tell us that all is well. Days later, we'll have learned that he wouldn't have stood a chance; he could barely move. After Tommy and he went through all their options, he told Tommy to rappel, and said he would jump off. It is a statement that touches my heart. There is so much love, life, boundless trust, and devotion. Weeks later, they are still trying to find Korra's body, but without success.

Back in El Chaltén, it was not easy to return to alpinism as usual—to study the weather models, pack the backpacks, and start up into the mountains again. We could not pretend that nothing had happened, that there were only mountains, lines, and peaks. For a moment, to understand what had happened, we stopped seeing dreams and sought out the closeness of our community.

We talked and debated, drank beer, philosophized about life, death, love, and our shared pain, and tried to understand why we kept accepting mortal danger to chase our goals, dreams, and visions. And it was true: I'd been entirely focused on the *Torre Traverse*, Fitz Roy, steep ice, walls, and my dream line on Latok I, just as Tommy and Korra obsessed about their north face and *Brothers in Arms* haunted Matteo. But aren't these objectives just the mirror of one's ego? Is elevating them to our supreme goals and thus our personal Holy Grail solely to find personal happiness and catch a fleeting glimpse of freedom really worth it? If so, you only see yourself, not the mountains; you are blind to everything else, and live exceptionally dangerously. But if you can muster the strength to shatter this mirror of your ego, you suddenly see the true face of the mountain, the beauty, the danger—and, in the end, you become the hunter. You free yourself of all baggage and act on instinct, making the right decisions.

Even if the weather would have allowed us to climb a minor summit, we did not go up into the mountains but instead stayed down in the woods, bouldering. Together with the community, we pulled on crimps, enjoyed movement, connected with nature, and felt that we are all part of the universe, and that life is a great, temporary gift. Ultimately, it's up to us to enrich it with the best moments we can muster. This wisdom from the forests of Patagonia led us back to a familiar path.

The wait was too long for my climbing partner from Berchtesgaden, and he decided to leave the Patagonian storms behind and return home. However, I had a feeling that I should stay a little longer.

One day, I chanced across another climber, Pedro—we ran into each other on one of Chaltén's dusty roads. Pedro Odell. Young, talented, hungry, and easily the best young climber from the village. I asked him in passing if he could imagine climbing with me, up in the mountains, in the Fitz Roy Range, if the weather turned in our favor. His beaming face immediately gave me the answer: he would love to. What a team, Pedro only 18, myself 55, the wild and the wise, the brave and the crazy. In any case, he could easily be my son.

The window: everyone believes in this mystical Patagonian rule of thumb concerning the weather. The full moon toward the end of February always brings the best weather window. And that's exactly what happened

FREIHEIT

for at least three, if not five, days. All the Stone Monkeys packed their backpacks, and Pedro and I joined them in a heartbeat. We were planning to cross the *Moonwalk* on Fitz Roy.

The first day: We started early in the morning. It was foggy and drizzling, but we didn't let ourselves be distracted. We climbed up through the clouds and beyond, reaching the first summit, the Aguja de I'S, around evening, bivouacking on a large ledge above the sea of clouds. There it was again, that magic moment, in the middle of it, in my mountains. Everything suddenly felt so light and real; I had that sense again, that instinct of being in perfect synchronicity with my environment, able to sniff out danger. Now I was no longer hunted in the mountains, but the hunter. Everything was now in our hands. That's why we would survive this "moonwalk"—because we weren't looking in a mirror but seeing the real world.

The second day: We climbed quickly over the steep cracks of the *Austriaca* to the Aguja Saint-Exupéry, celebrated the summit with a Bavarian Jodler that echoed off the walls several times, crossed the knife-edge ridge over to the granite tower of the Aguja Rafael Juarez, traversed the summit, and rappelled down toward Col Sustad. It truly felt like Pedro and I had been climbing together for years. We were fast, smooth, and connected by the rope. I immediately felt years younger.

The third day: The tallest pillar lay ahead of us—the 3,000-foot south face of Aguja Poincenot via the classic *Fonrouge*. It was not a difficult climb, yet long and defined by complicated route-finding. The final 1,000 feet slowed us down, because all the cracks were iced up from the last round of storms. Toward evening, we finally reached the summit. Even though we were exhausted and had bruised fingers and aching feet, we still managed to send a satisfied smile out into this Patagonian Mountain Kingdom. We then rappelled down to a small notch at the foot of Aguja Kakito, a small, rocky spur between the giants Fitz Roy and Poincenot, and spent our third night amidst the awe-inspiring solitude of the *Moonwalk* traverse.

The fourth day: Via the messenger service inReach, we received a communication from our weatherman, Charly: the weather window would close the next night. So it was not difficult for us to decide to finish at the col of the Brecha de los Italianos, the notch in front of Fitz Roy halfway along the *Moonwalk*. We were happy about what we had achieved, and had gotten everything we wished for: silence, beauty, thrills, exhaustion, freedom, and, last but not least, the best time ever.

The asado: Everyone was back from the mountains. We celebrated an asado at Don Guerra's as usual, and it seemed like nothing had changed nor ever would in this place: the hut, the fire, Don Guerra, his Cordero Patagonicus, and even the guests. Late that night, Don Guerra was once again sitting on his chair, next to him on the table a half-full glass of vino tinto. His eyelids were drooping as we all sang songs about mountains, our lives, and why we do what we do.

BROTHERS AND SISTERS

Scan the code above to view the
Brothers and Sisters music video.

BROTHERS AND SISTERS

Brothers go out into the world
Sisters are full of rock 'n' roll
They do just what they love to do
Free minded, wild
They go together
Through fire and stone
Between heaven and earth
And fight against
The stupid rules . . . of society
Their lives are free, it's just insane Same blood runs through their veins
Their rule is that there is no rule
They follow the fiery path of their roots The inner voice will show them the way Free spirits, wild
They go together
Through fire and stone
Between heaven and earth
And fight against
The stupid rules . . . of society
Their lives are free, it's just insane Same blood runs through their veins
Splitting their heart sounds like Shallowness of mind . . . Never
Feel the beats of gravity
Respect humanity ever . . . forever!!!!!
All of us are here to show How we could save the world With love
No matter who you are
We will just go ahead Freedom

Music: Plastic Surgery Disaster; Lyrics: Thomas Huber

EPILOGUE

The Complex World of the Huberbuam

Dean Potter: "The one thing I can say about these brothers is they don´t give up. A lot of climbers have all the talent, but they never use it. These brothers, though, keep pushing and pushing. They are so connected with life in the vertical world because they have known each other their entire lives."

"Cheeky, curious, always wanting to discover something new" are the characteristics that have defined us Huber Brothers; today, we remain an inseparable climbing partnership, though we have kept our unique personalities. One brother—Alexander—is structured, focused, and always has a plan. The other—me—is brimming with childlike enthusiasm for the world, a dreamer, sometimes lost in fantasy. We could easily have become circumnavigators, desert explorers, paragliders, cavers, or long-distance runners. Still, our father was a passionate mountaineer who channeled our prodigious energy into the rugged mountains right on our doorstep. It was in this world where we found what we were looking for and cemented our brotherly bond.

As inseparable as this bond may be, we have also remained individuals, driven—some may say haunted—by an inner fire and the mantra "faster-farther-higher." Always perceived as a unit by the public—and at times even confused, one brother for the other—we, in private, were also each other's biggest rivals. And just like in climbing, there has never been a straight path to any lofty summit; ups and downs have marked our brotherly bond. It never felt right when one brother was better, stronger, or more successful than the other—perhaps this was our "most cutting edge in life," which could easily have severed our bond. However, we managed to turn this seemingly dark, competitive reality into a net positive: one brother's success became the other's greatest motivation to never give up, and we have always offset each other's weaknesses with our own, unique strengths. This has let the name Huberbuam became synonymous with success in the vertical realm, be it freeing aid routes on El Cap, bold multi-pitch first ascents across the globe, expeditions, 9a redpoints, and difficult free solos, all to the backdrop of long, wild hair, driving rock 'n' roll, tight black-leather pants, and the anarchic Stone Monkey lifestyle.

To tell our stories, we Huber Brothers took to the limelight, climbed up on stage, and communicated our adventures, inspiring people worldwide to get after their dreams! Thus, we became ambassadors of living free. Everything mingled, merged, as if preordained. Although our success was surreal, we have always stayed humble, close to home and our Bavarian roots and culture, and each started his own little family. Our strongest magic lies in this model of life, combining these two disparate worlds: the life of a Stone Monkey and that of a husband and father. As deep as we traveled into the mountains, we always returned home to ground and reset, and then when the time was right, packed our bags and set off again for a new adventure. Because our families allowed us to set off anew, we remained hungry and kept our longing for freedom, rather than having to live permanently on the move as so many Stone Monkeys did.

Our time in the mountains has shown us that the meaning of what we do is not found in some ticklist of new, hard climbs, but rather that climbing is the most wonderful way to understand our world. Or, as Dean Potter put it: "Climbing is art, and I think it's an important thing why we do what we do, to make the world a better place, and encourage everybody around us to live their life with passion and love."

I write these lines from El Chaltén, Patagonia, my home away from home in South America, where I have returned now—the austral summer of 2024—to this place where I've written so much of my story in stone. Alexander is not with me on this trip, but of course he is with me in spirit and in psyche, and we'll surely climb and train together when I return home, always with the next big goal in mind. We Huber Brothers are artists in our own unique way—definitely not better, faster, or crazier than anyone else . . . or even each other. We are simply different because we have always passionately followed our individual, nonconformist path and learned to live—and savor—a life both defined and sculpted by the mountains.

APPENDIX

Climbing Grades

YDS	UIAA	French
5.2	II	1
5.3	III	2
5.4	IV-	3
5.5	IV	4
5.5	IV+	4
5.6	V-	
5.7	V	5a
5.8	V+	5b
5.9	VI-	5c
5.10a	VI	6a
5.10b	VI+	6a+
5.10c	VII-	6b
5.10d	VII	6b+
5.11a	VII+	6c
5.11b	VIII-	6c+
5.11c		
5.11d	VIII+	7a
5.12a	IX-	7a+
5.12b		7b
5.12c	IX	7b+
5.12d		7c
5.13a	IX+	7c+
5.13b	X-	8a
5.13c		8a+
5.13d	X	8b
5.14a	X+	8b+
5.14b	XI-	8c
5.14c	XI	8c+
5.14d	XI+	9a
5.15a	XII-	9a+
5.15b	XII	9b
5.15c		9b+

PHOTO CAPTIONS

Chapter 1: The Huber brothers, Thomas (left) and Alex.

Chapter 2: We brothers pushed our skills in our home crag "Karlstein", in Italy- Arco and South France - - Buoux and Verdon, Spain- Siurana. Credit: Uli Wiesmeier

Chapter 3: The Watzmann, the landmark of our hometown Berchtesgaden. Credit: Georg Grainer

Chapter 4: Best crimpy climbing in the golden granite of "El Nino" on El Capitan. Credit: Heinz Zak

Chapter 5: Together with my family in the mountains of my Hometown: Philomea, Marion, Amadeus, Elias, me.

Chapter 6: Monolithic, steep and the best granite in the middle of the Karakorum: We climb to the first camp at 6000 Meter on the south pillar on the Ogre, one of the most difficult peaks in the world. Credit: Huberbuam

Chapter 7: The Shivling is one of the most iconic peaks in the Garhwal Himalaya. The early morning light draws a mystical line to the summit, the "Shiva´s Line." Credit: Huberbuam

Chapter 8: Firstascent of the Ogre III. I celebrate this amazing moment the Summit with Iwan Wolf and Urs Stöcker, in the background the iconic

"American Line", The Northridge of Latok 1. Credit: Huberbuam

Chapter 9: (1) At the end you will never reach the top. This picture tells even more then the 6th ascent of Torre Egger with Andi Schnarf. Credit: Huberbuam (2) The Brothers"of El Chaltén: Me, Tito Soto, Tehuelche Acuná and Joachim Arias. Credit:Fidel MGuirado (3) Moments of Freedom in Patagonia. On the summit of La Silla after our firstascent " El Bastardo" Credit: Huberbuam

Chapter 10: Dean Potter vibe'n at Camp Bridwell.

Chapter 11: Steep, cold with full of beauty: Right in the Middle in the vertical world of Holtanna West Face, Drygalskyrange, Queen Maud Land, Antarktis. Credit: Timelineproduction

Chapter 12: Best granite and poor weather on „Bavarian Direttissima", Mount Asgard; Baffin Island. We brothers had to exceed our physical and mental limits in this steep world. Credit: Timelineproduction

Chapter 13: Brothers in Arms in the middle of the Choktoi, Karakorum, Pakistan. Credit: Huberbuam

Chapter 14: Cerro Kishtwar Northwestface. It was cold, icy and it took us 11 days through this wall. Here I was belaying Julian Zanker and I took with my camara a selfie, that tells the whole story how does it feels to be on the edge! Credit: Huberbuam

Chapter 15: "The Masterpiece" on Untersberg; Berchtesgaden. The name is the program. At this moment this route is still my project, one of the best routes I ever tried. It is not easy around 8c, beautiful, amazing moves, perfect crux in the best environment I can Imagine. It is for sure my Masterpiece! Credit: Klaus Fengler

Chapter 16: There is a magic in every moment. Credit: Luis Soto

ABOUT THE AUTHOR

Thomas Huber is an extreme climber, mountaineer, and mountain guide. He is one half of the successful German climbing duo "Huberbuam." Huber has achieved spectacular first ascents, including ones in the Karakoram, Patagonia, and Antarctica. For his achievements he was awarded the Piolet d'Or and the Bavarian Sports Prize. In July 2016, while filming on a rock face near Berchtesgaden, Huber fell sixteen meters and suffered a skull fracture, but the injury didn't stop his adventurous spirit. The month following his injury, he set off on another expedition, and he has kept up with his travels and experiences since then.